THE CIA FILE

W9-BYU-953

THE CIA FILE

EDITED BY
ROBERT L. BOROSAGE
AND
JOHN MARKS

GROSSMAN PUBLISHERS
A DIVISION OF THE VIKING PRESS
NEW YORK 1976

ACKNOWLEDGMENTS: *The Observer*: From an April 9, 1944, editorial. *Parade*: From "William Colby, New Director of the CIA: He's Changing the Agency's Image" by Lloyd Shearer. Transaction, Inc.: The articles by David Wise, Richard A. Falk, Morton H. Halperin, Richard J. Barnet, Herbert Scoville, Jr., Thomas B. Ross, Robert Borosage, and Roger Morris are from *Society*, Volume 12, No. 3. Copyright © 1975 by Transaction, Inc. Reprinted by permission.

Library of Congress Cataloging in Publication Data
Main entry under title:
The CIA file.
  Proceedings and papers presented at a conference "The CIA and covert action" held in Washington, Sept., 1974, sponsored by the Center for National Security Studies.
  Includes bibliographical references.
  1. United States. Central Intelligence Agency—Congresses. I. Borosage, Robert. II. Marks, John D. III. Center for National Security Studies.
JK468.I6C3   327'.12'06173   75-33961
ISBN 0-670-22247-x

To Connie and Barbara
for good support in difficult times

PREFACE

In September 1974 a two day conference, "The CIA and Covert Action," brought together in Washington a group of scholars, legislators, former CIA employees, and experts on intelligence and defense. Their purpose was to explore, in a wide-ranging series of reports and discussions, the purpose, tactics, and implications of the clandestine operations of the Central Intelligence Agency. The conference was sponsored by the Center for National Security Studies, an arm of the Fund for Peace, and was hosted by Senators Philip A. Hart (Democrat, Michigan) and Edward W. Brooke (Republican, Massachusetts) in a hearing room of the new Senate Office Building. The dignity of the setting and the bipartisanship of the hosts, as well as the recognized expertise of the participants, lent weight to the proceedings and papers.

The participants were generally critical of the CIA's covert actions at home and abroad and voiced serious questions as to their legality, propriety, and justification. William E. Colby, Director of the Central Intelligence Agency, presented a paper in defense of the Agency's activities and participated in an extended question-and-answer period with a skeptical, well-informed panel and audience. The result was an extraordinary interchange that generated wide press coverage and discussion, even though the conference took place prior to the later revelations of the CIA involvement in domestic surveillance.

In view of the interest generated, it became desirable to make the substance of the meetings available to a broader audience. This book is composed in large part of reports presented at the conference—with some modifications to suit book form and to minimize repetition. Some later complementary pieces are also included. Neither Mr. Colby's address nor his unrehearsed responses in the colloquy have been edited, although some questions have been shortened in the interest of clarity and brevity.

Serious investigation of the CIA and its clandestine activities has been all too rare in this country. Peacetime covert actions abroad were initiated in 1948 without public or congressional discussion of their need or wisdom. The CIA cloaks its activities in secrecy and its agents in anonymity. The few books published by retired CIA employees are generally cleared by the Agency prior to publication and constitute public-relations puffery rather than serious analysis. In place of critical thought, the public has been treated to a lurid fantasy world of international espionage in television, films, and inexpensive paperbacks. The deadly and exciting games played by heroes and villains in popular spy stories are far removed from the purposes and methods of the CIA abroad.

We believe that a serious investigation of the CIA is long overdue. Covert action violates some of the basic principles of our constitutional order, of international law, and of values generally shared by American citizens. The only justification for these activities would be if our nation's security were dependent upon them. Yet, as many reports in this book suggest, the CIA's activities abroad seem to have little to do with the defense of the United States or the security of the American people, and its activities at home infringe upon our freedoms rather than protect them.

It is the hope of the editors that the following papers will illuminate some of the issues posed by secret intervention abroad. We believe it imperative to place limits on the ability of our government to undertake such activities without congressional approval or public awareness. Two hundred years ago, when asked what the founders had wrought in Philadelphia, Benjamin Franklin was said to reply, "A republic, if you can keep it." It is the hope of the editors that this book may play a some small part in the "keeping."

Robert L. Borosage
John Marks

CONTENTS

IV SUMMATION

10. The View from Langley / WILLIAM E. COLBY
   The Address   181
   Question and Answer Session, Senator James Abourezk,
      Chairman   187
11. The "Dirty-Tricks" Gap / RICHARD J. BARNET   214

Reference Notes   229
Notes on the Contributors   235

AN INTRODUCTORY OVERVIEW*

VICTOR MARCHETTI

Because of the legal action which the CIA has taken against me, I am forbidden to write out a speech and deliver it without prior approval of the Agency. However, the CIA still does not have an injunction against my right to talk extemporaneously—which I will do today—but my remarks will be brief. I shall try to describe what the intelligence community is, how it is organized, and how it functions.

To appreciate the true role and significance of the CIA and its covert actions, as well as the dangers this secret organization poses both abroad and at home, one should first have an understanding of the nature and purpose of the little known, but costly, conglomeration of agencies, bureaus, services, and other government components called the U.S. intelligence community. The community consists of roughly a dozen major components: the CIA, the National Security Agency, the Defense Intelligence Agency, Army, Air Force, and Navy Intelligence, the National Reconnaissance Office, the State Department's Bureau of Intelligence and Research, the FBI's Internal Security Division, and the intelligence units in the Atomic Energy Commission, the Treasury, and other departments. Together these agencies spend well over six billion dollars a year and employ, either directly or on contract, about two hundred thousand people. The big spender and the big employer is not the CIA but the Pentagon—with its NSA, DIA, NRO, and service intelligence commands. The Pentagon physically and financially dominates the U.S. intelligence community today. The CIA, with an annual budget of about $750,000,000 and a career force of some sixteen thousand people, is not, comparatively speaking, a bureaucratic giant. In fact, it accounts for only about fifteen percent of the overall size and cost of U.S. intelligence. While the CIA is primarily concerned with espionage and "dirty tricks," most of the military agencies' people and money are allocated for the collection, processing, and analysis of information; that is, the classical production of intelligence. Much is of a "national" na-

* Excerpted from an oral presentation at the conference on "The CIA and Covert Activity," Washington, D.C., September 1974.

ture, the production of studies and reports of value to White House policymakers and planners. A good part of the intelligence, however, is "departmental," for the benefit of the department—such as the Army or the Air Force—in which the intelligence service operates, and this type of data is aimed at satisfying internal bureaucratic needs.

Despite a lot of waste, redundancy, and excessive secrecy, the collection of information in an unprovocative fashion is a necessary and legitimate governmental function. Open sources, diplomatic contacts, and, of course, the extremely sophisticated spy satellites provide reams of data. Nevertheless, the military agencies also engage, to some extent, in clandestine operations. The Army, Navy, and Air Force all have operatives out in the field recruiting agents and even, on occasion, interfering in another country's internal affairs—largely under the command of, or in cooperation with, the CIA. It is with these activities that the CIA comes into the picture. While it also collects some information and does some analysis of information, it is basically designed as a clandestine or secret service—a service that is focused on espionage, counterespionage, and covert-action programs, including everything from spreading false propaganda through raising "secret" armies, to the overthrow of governments.

If one examines the CIA's organization and budget—which is very difficult to do—one finds that roughly two-thirds of the CIA's people and funds are directed toward clandestine operations and their support. The remaining third of the Agency—the clean, visible tip of the iceberg which CIA Directors have tried to convince the public and the Congress is the principal part—consists of the Directorates of Intelligence and Science and Technology. These analytical and technical directorates perform valuable work in trying to give top policymakers the best possible idea of what is happening in the world, and their work is much closer to academic research than espionage.

But the real CIA is a clandestine organization, as it has been from its very beginning. If one looks back at the CIA's predecessor, the wartime Office of Strategic Services, one finds that its primary activities were covert action and counterespionage. Espionage, or spying, was relatively unimportant as the OSS concentrated on trying to create guerrilla movements in occupied territory. When the CIA was formed in 1947, the operatives—most of whom had served in OSS—quickly got control of the Agency, and they have held on ever since.

Over the years, the CIA has, of course, greatly advanced the arts of espionage, counterespionage, and covert action. But it has been covert action—interference in another country's internal affairs—which has become the most highly developed: partly because it was almost impossible to place spies in the closed societies of the two countries that really mattered, the Soviet Union and China; partly because technical intelligence advances made human espionage significantly less important; partly because the CIA could not compete with the Pentagon in the fantastically expensive technical field and, bureautically, needed to find its own area of specialty; and partly because the operatives who ran the Agency really were not very interested in espionage. These men preferred causing events to happen in foreign countries, whether "destabilizing" leftist governments in Chile, Guatemala, and Iran or secretly strengthening repressive regimes in Vietnam, Brazil, and the Dominican Republic. They penetrated and subsidized labor unions, newspapers, cultural groups, and our own National Student Association. They created organizations like Radio Free Europe, Radio Liberty, and the Asia Foundation to spread propaganda around the world. They put their own "secret" armies into action in Laos, the Congo, and—disastrously—Cuba.

What the CIA's operatives really like to do is to play "the game of nations," and appropriately this is the title a former CIA officer named Miles Copeland gave to one of his books. As much as I disagree with Copeland and doubt his veracity, his title accurately describes CIA operations. The Agency has worked hard to penetrate political parties abroad and to put foreign political leaders on the CIA payroll—up to, and including in many cases, chiefs of state. In one country, the Christian Democrats may be the target. In another, it may be the Social Democrats because they are preferable to a more leftist government. In still another, the CIA may be trying to get inside a ruling oligarchy or a military junta. Always, however, the CIA is working to recruit foreign leaders in order to manipulate what happens in a country.

One can travel around the world and see example after example of the CIA's handiwork. The Agency's support is always justified on the grounds of protecting our "national security," even in a place like Vietnam, where U.S. government and CIA support for the Thieu regime only staved off the inevitable fall of a corrupt dictator who could not have stayed in power thirty days without us. Look at Greece. After years of our being lied to by the CIA and the rest of our government, we now know that the Agency was deeply involved with the junta and that some of its top leaders, including two of its former chiefs, Papadopoulos and Ioannides, had been on the CIA payroll. Yet the minute the CIA pulled its support away from the junta in 1974, it fell—literally overnight, without a shot being fired. Look at Cuba, where nothing worked but where for over ten years the CIA kept trying to overthrow the government. Look at Zaire, where General Mobutu is in power, where he would not be if it were not for the CIA's secret operations.

Go around the world until you finally end up in Chile. Here is an example, fresh in all our minds, of a government that was legally elected in the face of CIA covert-action programs specifically aimed to prevent Salvador Allende from taking power. Twice before, in 1958 and 1964, the CIA had intervened successfully to stop Allende's election, but in 1970 the Agency's dirty tricks were not sufficient to keep Allende out of office. Thus, the CIA, under the direction of President Nixon and especially Henry Kissinger, felt compelled to "destabilize" the Allende government.

The term "destabilization" comes from CIA Director Colby's secret congressional testimony, and I was particularly pleased he used it because in the last years I was with the Agency this had become one of the catchwords. The phrases "to keep the world safe for democracy" and "fighting the Communist menace" had by that time become rather threadbare, and it had become difficult to sell operations on these grounds. So the operatives started to talk about "stability"—maintaining it in places like Brazil, where the lid was tightly on, or creating our own kind in countries where we did not like the form of government.

The CIA's rationale is that it helps to support stability in the Third World, so developing countries can evolve gradually and properly toward democracy. The fact is that to the CIA promoting stability most often means supporting a junta or a dictatorship; otherwise, as in Chile, the Agency will destabilize the area.

The CIA has gotten us into wars in the past in places like Vietnam and Laos, and it is going to get us into future wars if there are not drastic changes. The Agency has caused a lot of trouble at home, and it is going to cause us more trouble. The men who run the Agency are powerful figures. They do not want to be reviewed. They do not want to be controlled, and they are going to resist reform in every possible way. These men are clandestine operatives who like their work. They believe they have the right to lie; indeed, they feel that lying is part of protecting the "national security," part of protecting their operations. And they will lie, as former Director Richard Helms did several times before congressional committees in 1973, when they are called to explain and defend their operations.

Therefore, it is going to be a very difficult effort to reform the CIA and the rest of the intelligence community. The push is going to have to come from outside and above. It is going to have to come from the public, from the media, and from the Congress. Only in that way will enough pressure be put on our Presidents, who have always looked to the CIA as their private army, to do things more openly and less arbitrarily.

I

Covert Operations Abroad

DAVID WISE

Covert Operations Abroad

AN OVERVIEW

1

Citizens who telephone the Central Intelligence Agency at Langley, Virginia, asking for a description of the Agency's activities receive a handsome blue-covered booklet bearing the CIA seal—a baleful eagle atop a shield emblazoned with a sixteen-point star.

The booklet, however, is less than a sixteenth of an inch thick and contains only eleven pages. The citizen reading it is told that the CIA produces estimates and "intelligence reports" to insure that the President receives information on foreign policy and national defense that is "complete, accurate, and timely." The booklet also gives the CIA's address with zip code, which is Washington, D.C. 20505. Nowhere in the booklet is it mentioned that the CIA conducts secret political operations around the globe, ranging from payments to foreign political figures, to efforts to influence elections abroad, to overthrowing governments—in which the target national leaders are sometimes killed —and to full-scale paramilitary invasions. Nowhere does the booklet mention that the CIA operates its own air force, and, at times, its own army and navy.

It is these covert political operations that have got the CIA in trouble, focused public attention upon its activities, and led to demands for reform. It is these activities, as well, that have raised fundamental questions about the role of a secret intelligence agency in a democracy, and, specifically, whether the requirements of American national security justify clandestine intervention in the internal affairs of other countries.

More recently, the Watergate scandal has dramatically demonstrated the dangers posed by secret intelligence agencies, when their personnel, resources, and methods are employed in the American political process.

For many years the Central Intelligence Agency has been operating domestically in ways never contemplated by the Congress. That fact may not have been understood by the public at large until it was revealed that the CIA had provided E. Howard Hunt, Jr., its former clandestine operative, with equipment used in the break-in of the office of Daniel Ellsberg's psychiatrist, and that the CIA had prepared two psychiatric profiles of Ellsberg. In addition, the burglars who broke into Democratic National Headquarters at Watergate had CIA backgrounds, and one, Eugenio Rolando Martinez, was at the time of the break-in still on the CIA payroll at a retainer of a hundred dollars a month. Thus, Watergate, to an extent, represented the application of covert intelligence techniques to American politics: President Nixon created his own secret police force—the "Plumbers" and their apprentices—to conduct covert operations against domestic "enemies," real and imagined. He resigned; the problem remains.

I. THE LEGAL BASIS

Some definitions are necessary before discussing the legal basis of covert operations. Intelligence is information, gathered either secretly or openly. Clearly, information about military, strategic, political, and economic conditions in other countries, and about the background and intentions of the leaders of those countries, may be of great value to the President and other leaders in making decisions and formulating policy. Intelligence is collected from electronic ears stationed around the globe, from reconnaissance satellites overhead, from newspapers, journals, and other open sources, and by traditional espionage. Some of the means of acquisition of intelligence are highly sophisticated and themselves secret. From CIA stations abroad, by cable and courier, tons of information flow into CIA headquarters at Langley every day. Once in house, it is sifted and analyzed, or it would be of little use to policymakers. In addition to analyzing, summarizing, and evaluating the information collected, the CIA also has an estimating function. On the basis of what it knows, the CIA attempts to predict to the President the likely course of future events in other countries. The intelligence process, then, consists essentially of collecting, evaluating, and estimating. It is basically passive, in that it is a process designed to *reflect* events and conditions and to draw conclusions and logical deductions on the basis of the information collected.

Covert political action, on the other hand, seeks to manipulate events, to *cause* them to happen. The clandestine operators of the CIA are engaged not merely in reporting events, but in attempting to shape them.

The organization of the Central Intelligence Agency reflects this basic split. Beneath the Director of Central Intelligence (DCI) and the Deputy Director of Central Intelligence are two principal divisions: the Directorate of Intelligence, headed by a Deputy Director (DDI), and a Directorate of Operations, headed by a Deputy Director (DDO).

The Directorate of Intelligence engages in overt collection, analysis, and estimating. The Directorate of Operations, or Clandestine Services, engages in covert collection and secret political operations. This is the so-called dirty tricks branch of the CIA.

The Central Intelligence Agency was in a very real sense a result of the Japanese attack on Pearl Harbor. Until World War II, the United States had no centralized intelligence machinery. During the war, on June 13, 1942, President Roosevelt established the Office of Strategic Services (OSS) under General William J. Donovan. The OSS gathered intelligence, but it also engaged in political operations and paramilitary operations, dropping agents by parachute behind enemy lines in Europe and Asia. Thus, the pattern was established under OSS of an intelligence agency that both collected information and engaged in covert operations. Many well-known Americans worked for the OSS, including Julia Child, Allen W. Dulles, Arthur Goldberg, and Arthur M. Schlesinger, Jr. In the autumn of 1944, at Roosevelt's request, Donovan submitted a secret memo to the White House urging the creation of a permanent U.S. intelligence agency.

The plan was put aside; and on September 20, 1945, President Truman issued an order disbanding the OSS. But the wartime experience had created momentum for a centralized intelligence agency. In January 1946, Truman established a National Intelligence Authority under a Central Intelligence Group, the forerunner of the CIA. Then Congress created the CIA, in the National Security Act of 1947. The same legislation established the National Security Council (NSC).

The duties of the CIA are set forth in the Act in Section 102 (d) which states:

> For the purpose of coordinating the intelligence activities of the several Government departments and agencies in the interest of national security, it shall be the duty of the Agency, under the direction of the National Security Council—
> (1) to advise the National Security Council in matters concern-

ing such intelligence activities of the Government departments and agencies as relate to national security;

(2) to make recommendations to the National Security Council for the coordination of such intelligence activities of the departments and agencies of the Government as relate to the national security;

(3) to correlate and evaluate intelligence relating to the national security, and provide for the appropriate dissemination of such intelligence within the Government using where appropriate existing agencies and facilities: *Provided*, That the Agency shall have no police, subpoena, law-enforcement powers, or internal-security functions: *Provided further*, That the departments and other agencies of the Government shall continue to collect, evaluate, correlate and disseminate departmental intelligence: *And provided further*, That the Director of Central Intelligence shall be responsible for protecting intelligence sources and methods from unauthorized disclosure;

(4) to perform, for the benefit of the existing intelligence agencies, such additional services of common concern as the National Security Council determines can be more efficiently accomplished centrally;

(5) to perform such other functions and duties related to intelligence affecting the national security as the National Security Council may from time to time direct.

There is no specific mention in the law of overthrowing governments or other cloak-and-dagger operations, but the CIA has carried out these activities under the "other functions" clause contained in subparagraph five. Richard M. Helms, while Director of Central Intelligence, confirmed this interpretation in a speech on April 14, 1971. Referring to the "other functions" clause, he said:

This latter language was designed to enable us to conduct such foreign activities as the national government may find it convenient to assign to a "secret service." These activities have always been secondary to the production of intelligence, and under direct control by the Executive Branch. Obviously, I cannot go into any detail with you on such matters, and I do not intend to.[1]*

William E. Colby, one of Mr. Helms' successors as Director of the CIA, also confirmed that the "other functions" clause is the justification for covert political operations. Appearing before the Senate Armed Services Committee at a hearing on his nomination, Colby told Senator Stuart Symington:

* Reference notes begin on page 229.

Mr. Chairman, the National Security Act of 1947 says that the Agency will do various things, and then in the last subparagraph it says that the Agency will conduct, perform such other functions and duties related to intelligence affecting the national security as the National Security Council may from time to time direct.

Now, that particular provision of law is the authority under which a lot of the Agency's activities are conducted.[2]

It is not apparent from the legislative history of the 1947 act establishing the CIA that Congress expected that the CIA would engage in covert political operations. Congress did express concern that the CIA might engage in domestic operations, and subsequent experience has proved these fears justified. James Forrestal, while Secretary of the Navy, testified in April 1947 that the CIA would be "limited definitely to purposes outside of this country."[3] Congressman Henderson Lanham, a Georgia Democrat, asked Dr. Vannevar Bush, a witness before a House Committee, whether there was not a danger of the CIA "becoming a Gestapo or anything of that sort?"[4] The report of the House Committee that handled the CIA legislation states: "Provision prohibiting the agency from having the power of subpoena and from exercising internal police powers, provisions not included in the original bill nor in S.758, were added by your Committee."[5] This language, an unsuccessful attempt to keep the CIA out of the domestic arena, was apparently added at the behest of J. Edgar Hoover, Director of the FBI, who did not want any competition with the bureau in the domestic-intelligence field.

But there is no indication that Congress expected the CIA to engage in covert activities, intervene in the internal affairs of other nations, overthrow governments, and launch paramilitary operations. The House report on the legislation simply states that the CIA was created in order that the NSC "in its deliberations and advice to the President, may have available adequate information." The CIA, the report added, "will furnish such information."[6] Certainly, the executive-branch officials testifying about the proposed legislation did not talk about overthrowing governments. For example, Lieutenant General Hoyt S. Vandenberg, Director of Central Intelligence,* stressed the collection and evaluation functions of CIA when he testified to the Senate Armed Services Committee about the proposed legislation to establish the CIA. "The oceans have shrunk . . . ," Vandenberg testified, "the interests, intentions, and

---

* Vandenberg held this title as head of the Central Intelligence Group, even though the CIA itself had not yet been created.

capabilities of the various nations . . . must be fully known to our national policymakers. We must have this intelligence if we are to be forewarned against possible acts of aggression, and if we are to be armed against disaster in an era of atomic warfare." Wartime intelligence sources are "drastically reduced as our forces return home," Vandenberg added. " Such information, which can be collected during actual combat, is largely denied us in peacetime. In times of peace we must rely on the painstaking study of . . . available overt material." The CIA, Vandenberg said, would engage in "research and analysis" and avoid "wasteful duplication."[7]

One small hint of what was to come was contained in a memo submitted to Congress by Dulles in 1947. He said the CIA should have "exclusive jurisdiction to carry out secret intelligence operations."[8] And, although some individual members of Congress may have realized that covert political operations would continue in peacetime, certainly the majority of the members of Congress reading the House report on the legislation or the Senate *Hearings* would not have reached this conclusion. Almost from the start, however, the CIA was in fact involved in covert political operations, which the "black," or clandestine, operators of the CIA prefer to call "special operations."

In 1948 the Truman administration was alarmed by the Communist takeover in Czechoslovakia and nervous over the possibility of a Communist victory in the Italian elections. Secretary of Defense James Forrestal wished to move to counter Communist strength in Italy. It was felt this would require a massive infusion of money. But the wealthy industrialists around Milan feared reprisals if the Communists won, and were reluctant to contribute funds. So members of the Eastern establishment literally passed the hat at the Brook Club in New York.

There was no CIA mechanism to deal with the problem—the Plans Directorate was not created until January 4, 1951. As a result, in the summer of 1948, the NSC issued a secret document, NSC 10/2 (pronounced "ten slash two"), authorizing special operations, providing they were secret and small enough to be plausibly deniable by the government. The same document created an operating agency under the euphemistic title of Office of Policy Coordination (OPC). Former OSS agent Frank G. Wisner was brought in to direct this office, which operated within the CIA but under the joint authority as well of the Department of State and the Department of Defense. In 1950 General Walter Bedell Smith, then director of the CIA, managed to eliminate control by these outside agencies and placed Wisner's group entirely under the CIA. Meanwhile, a separate Office of Special Operations (OSO) handled covert intelligence-gathering for the CIA. The OSO and the OPC were merged in January 1951 (while Smith was still Director of the CIA) into the new Directorate of Plans. The "other functions" clause became the eye of the needle through which the CIA has conducted special operations around the globe.

In 1949 the Central Intelligence Agency Act was passed, exempting the CIA from all statutes requiring the disclosure of the "functions, names, official titles, salaries, or numbers of personnel employed by the Agency." It gave the Director of Central Intelligence unprecedented power to spend money "without regard to the provisions of law and regulations relating to the expenditure of government funds." The 1949 Act permitted "such expenditures to be accounted for solely on the certificate of the director."

Once these provisions were law, the way was open for the CIA to engage in special operations on a large scale. In a discussion with graduate students at the Johns Hopkins School for Advanced International studies, on February 24, 1966, Robert Amory, former CIA Deputy Director for Intelligence, declared: "We went in through the NSC-CIA act because that was the only way we could get unvouched funds. OPC then went into Greece in 1949–50."

A series of highly classified National Security Council Intelligence directives have been issued since 1948, permitting the CIA to carry out special operations. The directives are known as NSCIDs; within the intelligence community they are called "Nonskids." In addition, the Director of Central Intelligence issues DCIDs. Under the authority of the NSCIDs, these apparently can be issued by the Director of Central Intelligence without further clearance by the NSC. These directives and other Presidential and CIA documents together form what is sometimes referred to as the "secret charter" of the CIA.

Thus, a secret agency engages in secret operations that carry the risk of war, under secret directives unavailable to the press, the public, or most members of the Congress. Indeed, until the Watergate revelations of 1973, Congress was not curious about this "secret charter." In July 1973, however, Senator Stuart Symington did ask some questions at hearings of the Senate Armed Services Committee on the nomination of William Colby to be Director of the CIA. Symington said: "We understand some . . . directives to the intelligence community are included in classified documents called National Security Council Intelligence Directives, NSCIDs. Would you describe in general the subject matter of these Directives; and, if you believe they should remain classified, would you tell the committee why you think so?"

Colby replied: "These Directives are the application of the [other functions] provision of the law that I cited, Mr. Chairman. . . . They include some general directives which describe the functions of the different members of the intelligence community and there is certain sensitive information in those. Those are National Security Council documents, Mr. Chairman, and I do not have the authority for the declassification since they originate with the National Security Council."

Senator William Proxmire had slightly better luck with Colby. In a series of written questions submitted to the CIA Director in 1973, Proxmire asked:

> QUESTION: What reason does the National Security Council give for not making public the secret "Charter" of the CIA, the NSCIDs?
> ANSWER: I respectfully suggest that this matter be raised with the National Security Council.

Next, Proxmire wanted to know whether National Security Action Memorandum #57 set out guidelines for restraining covert operations to a small size "and only then with adequate deniability." Colby would not discuss NSAM 57. What other NSC documents describing CIA operations would be available, Proxmire asked.

Colby replied: "Operations of the CIA and other intelligence components are conducted under the authority of the NSCIDs and a variety of other Executive Orders and directives. I have been authorized to brief the Committee on the basic ones, the NSCIDs, on a classified basis."

In 1963 former President Truman wrote:

> I never had any thought . . . when I set up the CIA that it would be injected into peacetime cloak and dagger operations. Some of the complications and embarrassment that I think we have experienced are in part attributable to the fact that this quiet intelligence arm of the President has been so removed from its intended role. . . . I would like to see the CIA be restored to its original assignment as the intelligence arm of the President and whatever else it can properly perform in that special field and that its operational duties be terminated or properly used elsewhere.
> We have grown up as a nation respected for our free institutions

and for our ability to maintain a free and open society. There is something about the way the CIA has been functioning that is casting a shadow over our historic position, and I feel that we need to correct it.[9]

Truman's quote is puzzling in the light of the NSCIDs issued during his Presidency permitting covert operations. It is possible, however, that Truman was appalled by the *scope* of these operations. By 1963, when Truman wrote these words, the CIA had received adverse publicity from the shooting down of the U-2 spy plane over the Soviet Union in 1960 and the ill-fated invasion of Cuba at the Bay of Pigs in 1961.

Symington questioned Richard Helms about Truman's statement during hearings on Helms' nomination to be ambassador to Iran in 1973. This exchange occurred:

> MR. HELMS: And as far as President Truman's comment is concerned I recall vividly when that was made in 1963 and we were all stunned, because the document signed off by the National Security Council which put the Agency in some of the matters was done during President Truman's administration.
>
> SENATOR SYMINGTON: It is incredible to me, has been for many years, that this committee does not know of your activities in foreign countries with which we are not at war. It not only doesn't make any sense, but it has resulted in heavy loss of both money and respect.

II. MECHANISMS OF CONTROL

Before discussing the machinery for the control of covert operations, the nature of those operations should be more precisely defined. Perhaps the best definition was provided by Richard M. Bissell, the CIA's Deputy Director for Plans between 1958 and February 1962, in which capacity he ran covert operations for the agency. Bissell was one of the fathers of the U-2 reconnaissance aircraft and the principal planner of the Bay of Pigs invasion. The minutes of a private discussion on intelligence sponsored by the Council on Foreign Relations in 1968 summarizes Bissell's view:

> Covert operations should, for some purposes, be divided into two classifications: (1) *intelligence collection*, primarily espionage, or the obtaining of intelligence by covert means; and (2) *covert action*, attempting to influence the internal affairs of other nations—sometimes called "intervention"—by covert means.[10]

It is with Bissell's second category, covert action—attempting to influence the internal affairs of other nations—that this essay is primarily concerned.

In the Council on Foreign Relations meeting, Bissell went on to list the dimensions of covert action.

> The scope of covert action could include: (1) political advice or counsel; (2) subsidies to an individual; (3) financial support and "technical assistance" to political parties; (4) support of private organizations, including labor unions, business firms, cooperatives, etc.; (5) covert propaganda; (6) "private" training of individuals and exchange of persons; (7) economic operations; and (8) paramilitary or political action operations designed to overthrow or to support a regime (like the Bay of Pigs and the programs in Laos). These operations can be classified in various ways: by the degree and type of secrecy required by their legality, and, perhaps, by their benign or hostile character."[11]

Bissell's categories pretty well cover the waterfront, although of course under each heading one could list many variations. To take one example, covert propaganda could include clandestine radio stations, either in or outside the target countries; disinformation, that is, deliberately false, or at least partly false material circulated within a target country but designed to appear authentic—a forged official document allegedly from the files of a foreign ministry but actually prepared at CIA headquarters in Virginia, for example. The distinction contained in Bissell's point eight is important. Special operations may be designed either to place pressure upon, or overthrow, a government or to maintain it in power. In *The Invisible Government*, published in 1964, Thomas B. Ross and I disclosed for the first time the existence of the "Special Group," the interagency government committee customarily cited by intelligence officials as the principal mechanism for the control of covert operations.[12]

The Special Group was also known during the Eisenhower years as the 54/12 Group and has been periodically renamed; during the Johnson years it was known as the 303 Committee—after a room number in the Executive Office Building—and during the Nixon administration, it acquired the name "Forty Committee." The Forty Committee is reportedly a designation taken from the serial number of the NSC document defining its membership and responsibilities. It was this committee (under its earlier name) to which Allen Dulles was referring when he wrote in a now famous statement, "The facts are that the CIA has never carried out any action of a political nature, given any support of any nature to any persons, potentates or movements, political or otherwise, without appropriate approval at high political level in our government *outside the CIA.*"[13]

In 1974 the members of the Forty Committee were the President's assistant for national security, the Deputy Secretary of Defense, the Under Secretary of State for Political Affairs, the Director of the Central Intelligence Agency, and the Chairman of the Joint Chiefs of Staff.

Since we are told that we must rely on the wisdom and judgment of these high officials and that every covert operation undertaken by the CIA anywhere around the globe is approved at this high level, it is not entirely comforting to note that during the period that John N. Mitchell served as Attorney General he was added to the ranks of the Forty Committee. As a member of the committee, Mitchell listened to CIA plans for cloak-and-dagger operations designed to influence the political affairs of other nations. Possibly he became so accustomed to this atmosphere that he was willing to listen to G. Gordon Liddy's plans for domestic political espionage. For it was while Mitchell was Attorney General and a member of the Forty Committee that he permitted discussions in his office of bugging the opposition political party, of financing floating bordellos to suborn Democratic politicians, and of planning to kidnap domestic dissidents and spirit them to Mexico in order to avoid any problems during the Republican National Convention.

It is perhaps tiresome to point out that we are a government of laws not men, but in citing the Forty Committee as proof of control over covert operations we are really relying on a group of men who operate entirely in secret and can, in the final analysis, approve almost anything. Mitchell's presence on the Forty committee is hardly reassuring in this respect. During a hearing of the Senate Foreign Relations Committee, Hubert Humphrey expressed some alarm about Mitchell's membership on the Forty Committee and asked Richard Helms about it. Helms confirmed that Mitchell had been a member of the committee while Attorney General, but added, "I know that after Mr. Mitchell left office, the succeeding Attorney General never attended any meetings."

Celebrations over that fact could be premature, as the dialogue that followed might suggest:

SENATOR HUMPHREY: Was Mr. Ehrlichman or Mr. Haldeman a member of the Forty Committee or did they sit with the committee?

MR. HELMS: No, sir, they were not members of the committee but that is not to say that they never sat. I believe in one crisis meeting, one of them came down one day . . . but they were not regular members, and I do not think that they were actually—well, they certainly were not participants.*

No more mysterious group exists within the government than the Forty Committee. Its operations are so secret that in an appearance before the Senate Armed Services Committee, CIA Director Colby was even reluctant to identify the chairman. The following exchange took place during a hearing on Colby's nomination:

SENATOR SYMINGTON: Very well. What is the name of the latest committee of this character?

MR. COLBY: Forty Committee.

SENATOR SYMINGTON: Who is the chairman?

MR. COLBY: Well again, I would prefer to go into executive session on the description of the Forty Committee, Mr. Chairman.

SENATOR SYMINGTON: [Incredulous] As to who is the chairman, you would prefer an executive session?

MR. COLBY: The chairman, all right, Mr. Chairman, Dr. Kissinger is the chairman as the Assistant to the President for national security affairs.[14]

Because of the cocoon of secrecy enveloping the operations of the Forty Committee it is very difficult to assess the extent to which the Committee exercises effective control over special operations. For example, executive-branch officials consistently refused to explain the actions of the Forty Committee to a Senate subcommittee investigating the role of the CIA and the International Telephone and Telegraph Company in Chile during the period 1970–1971. The Subcommittee on Multinational Corporations, headed by Senator Frank Church, Democrat, of Idaho, conducted the 1972 investigation of charges that ITT and the CIA were involved in a plot to prevent the 1970 election of

---

* Now truly alarmed, Humphrey pressed: "How many times did Mr. Ehrlichman and Mr. Haldeman come, to the best of your knowledge?"

MR. HELMS: Now, I am rethinking this and this may have been a Washington Special Action Group Committee meeting rather than a Forty Committee meeting; I regret my misstatement, but it tended to be the same membership for both committees.[15]

leftist President Salvador Allende of Chile. The record of this tangled story of CIA intervention in Chile is replete with contradictions. In 1973 Mr. Helms was questioned about the CIA role by Senator Symington.

> SENATOR SYMINGTON: Did you try in the Central Intelligence Agency to overthrow the Government of Chile?
> MR. HELMS: No, sir.
> SENATOR SYMINGTON: Did you have any money passed to the opponents of Allende?
> MR. HELMS: No, sir.[16]

However, John A. McCone, former Director of the CIA and a director of ITT, testified to the Church subcommittee that Helms had told him that, while the Forty Committee had decided against any major action designed to prevent Allende's election, some "minimal effort" would be mounted which "could be managed within the flexibility of their own [CIA] budget," without seeking additional appropriated funds.[17]

The ITT-CIA story is a complex one, but it is clear from the record of the Senate subcommittee that the intelligence agency's clandestine directorate was in constant touch with ITT, which had substantial investments in Chile, about ways to block Allende from becoming President. McCone suggested to Helms that the CIA originate discussions with ITT, and Helms had William V. Broe, chief of the Western Hemisphere Division of the Clandestine Services, contact Harold S. Geneen, the chairman of ITT. Later, McCone testified, Geneen told McCone "that he was prepared to put up as much as one million dollars in support of any plan" to oppose Allende. McCone testified that Helms had informed him that the Forty Committee had discussed the situation in Chile in June 1970 and decided that the CIA would do nothing of consequence to intervene in the September fourth election. On that date Allende received the most votes, but no candidate had a majority; as a result, the election was thrown into the Chilean Congress, which was to decide the outcome on October 24, 1970.

During this critical six-week period Washington apparently became much more receptive to plans to block Allende's election in the Congress. Charles Meyer, Assistant Secretary of State for Inter-American Affairs, testified that soon after the September fourth election, the Forty Committee met again to discuss U.S. policy toward Chile. Meyer declined to tell the Church subcommittee what took place at this meeting of the Forty Committee or what instructions were given to the U.S. ambassador to Chile. It is known, however, that on September 29, at the direction of Helms, Broe met Edward Gerrity, a top ITT executive, in New York and proposed a plan to accelerate economic chaos in Chile in order to weaken Allende's position. As the Senate subcommittee report states: "Mr. Meyer was unwilling to inform the subcommittee of the substance of the Forty Committee meeting. The subcommittee is, accordingly, unable to say whether Mr. Helms' instructions to Mr. Broe to contact Mr. Gerrity and make proposals to Mr. Gerrity for creating economic dislocation in Chile were a direct outcome of the Forty Committee meeting which took place shortly after Allende won a plurality in the September 4th election."

While the role of the Forty Committee in the Chilean affair remains obscure, it is clear that the committee could not possibly have exercised control over everything that occurred. For example, the initial discussion between Broe and Geneen was not the result of any instruction by the Forty Committee but of McCone's direct approach to Helms. Patently, the "old-boy" network was involved here. A former director of the CIA, the man who had appointed Helms as the agency's top covert operator, simply telephoned his old colleague. Since McCone was also a director of ITT, the interests of the CIA and the multinational corporation neatly dovetailed.

If the Forty Committee did approve intensified contact between the CIA and ITT just prior to the runoff election in the Chilean Congress, then the Forty Committee was merely seizing upon a channel of communication that it never opened in the first place. One may ask whether the Forty Committee, in this instance, was in the position of the tail wagging the dog. In any event, the administration was unwilling to describe the role of the Forty Committee to a duly constituted subcommittee of the Senate of the United States. Thus, we are asked to take on faith the assurance that secret operations conducted under secret directives are adequately controlled by a secret committee that makes its decisions in secret. Moreover, in the manner of the fox placed in charge of the chicken coop, the Director of Central Intelligence is a member of the Forty Committee. Although it is difficult to arrive at final conclusions about a body that operates in complete secrecy, it seems most unlikely that a committee of five men, one of whom is the head of the CIA and whose other members are busy men with important responsibilities in other agencies of the government, can exercise effective control over special operations.

Covert operations are a tempting shortcut to the achievement of policy goals. The covert operators can naturally be expected to make the best possible case to the Forty Committee. One official familiar with the operations of the committee has been quoted as saying: "They were like a bunch of schoolboys. They would listen and their eyes would bug out. I always used to say that I could get five million dollars out of the Forty Committee for a covert operation faster than I could get money for a typewriter out of the ordinary bureaucracy."[18]

Senator Proxmire, who has studied the intelligence community, has stated: "In practice, it appears that the 40 Committee mainly approves activities coordinated at lower levels. If a promising operation can be coordinated at a working level where the concept originates, it often rises through the intelligence community with little critical challenge until it arrives at the 40 Committee. There, because it has been reviewed by the 'experts,' it is frequently approved."[19]

"As compared to alternatives, the necessary approval for covert operations is easier to obtain," Morton H. Halperin and Jeremy J. Stone have suggested. "The President himself can often usually authorize them without having to go to Congress for funds or to make a public justification. But they also seem cheap and easy because they can usually be disavowed, if necessary."[20]

Since the President is not a member of the Forty Committee, its existence permits the claim that covert operations are controlled at a high level in government. On the other hand, the existence of the committee permits the President to disclaim personal knowledge of a covert operation if it should fail and prove embarrassing.

Former Secretary of State Dean Rusk has been quoted as saying: "Dirty tricks form about 5 per cent of the CIA's work—and we have full control over dirty tricks."[21] But the sheer size of the bureaucracy casts doubt on the effectiveness of the Forty Committee. As already noted, it is not plausible that a committee, most of whose members spend the majority of their time on other matters, can control every covert operation being conducted by the CIA around the globe. The size of the Directorate of Operations within the CIA lends support to this view. According to Victor Marchetti and John Marks, the Clandestine Services employ six thousand people, making it the largest single element within CIA with the largest budget ($440,000,000). Of this total,

Marchetti and Marks estimate eighteen hundred persons are assigned to covert action, with a budget of $260,000,000.[22]

There is simply too much going on at any given time to be controlled by a part-time committee. For example, in 1962 the S.S. *Streatham Hill*, a British freighter leased by the Soviet Union, limped into San Juan, Puerto Rico, for repairs with eighty thousand bags of Cuban sugar in her hold. She had struck a propeller on a reef. Many of the sacks of sugar were put into a warehouse during repairs. CIA agents managed to contaminate the sugar that had been unloaded with what was described as a "harmless but unpalatable substance." A White House official happened to see a report about the sabotage and informed President Kennedy. The President was not merely annoyed; he was "furious," and ordered that the contaminated sugar not be permitted to leave Puerto Rico.[23] It did not appear, in other words, that the Forty Committee had approved this particular covert operation. If it did approve, it did not inform the President.

Even when an operation is approved by the Forty Committee, important details must obviously be left to lower-level bureaucrats and operators in the field. For example, during the preparation for the Bay of Pigs invasion, CIA agents told members of the Cuban brigade that President Kennedy would not permit the invasion to fail, and that if it faltered, the President would commit American military power to assure the success of the operation. Did the Forty Committee authorize that such assurances be given to members of the Cuban brigade? It seems doubtful.

It also seems reasonable to speculate that certain covert operations are considered so sensitive that the CIA will not bring them to the attention of the Forty Committee. One former high official of the CIA told me, "There are some things that you don't tell Congress; some things you don't even tell the President." He apparently meant that some activities of the CIA are too sensitive to entrust to the President.

In addition to the Forty Committee there are two other possible or potential mechanisms of control of covert operations: the President's Foreign Intelligence Advisory Board (FIAB) and the shadowy CIA oversight committees in the House and Senate. But the available evidence does not indicate that either the FIAB or the congressional committees control these operations. The FIAB was originally established by Eisenhower in 1956 as a result of a recommendation of the Hoover Commission. It was permitted to lapse and then was revived by President Kennedy with its present name in 1961. Under President Nixon the board was headed by retired Admiral George W. Anderson, Jr. The eleven-member board consists of prominent businessmen, scientists, and others outside the government. While the board has from time to time investigated intelligence failures and made recommendations for organizational changes within the intelligence community, it does not approve covert operations in advance. The board is something of an anomaly in that it consists of private citizens privileged to know the innermost secrets of U.S. intelligence agencies, secrets that are denied to the public at large.

Four subcommittees of the House and Senate are supposed to serve as watchdog committees over U.S. intelligence agencies. They are the subcommittees of the Armed Services and Appropriations committees in the Senate and in the House. These committees give the appearance of control over the CIA without the reality. For the most part, they consist of senior members of Congress, many of whom are friendly to the CIA. The attitude of members of these committees toward covert operations may best have been summed up in a comment of former Senator Leverett Saltonstall of Massachusetts. To Saltonstall, the problem was that "we might obtain information which I personally would rather not have. . . ." CIA directors have insisted that the informal subcommittees exercise control over the agency; these claims may be tested against a remark made by Senator John C. Stennis, chairman of the Senate Armed Services subcommittee on CIA. In November 1971 he assured his colleagues that "this agency is conducted in a splendid way. As has been said, spying is spying. . . . You have to make up your mind that you are going to have an intelligence agency and protect it as such, and shut your eyes some, and take what is coming." Symington, a member of the CIA subcommittee, replied to Stennis, "I wish his interest on the subject had developed to the point where he had held just one meeting of the CIA subcommittee this year, just one meeting."[24]

III. A HISTORY OF COVERT OPERATIONS

No complete history of CIA covert political operations can be written, since the files relating to these operations remain classified. Moreover, intelligence organizations are traditionally compartmentalized, so that exposure of one operation or agent will not necessarily compromise other operations and personnel. Thus, even within the Directorate of Plans, knowledge of specific covert operations is denied to all but those persons with a need to know.

Nevertheless, over the years a substantial number of CIA covert operations have surfaced, in some cases because they failed and were publicized. Still other covert operations have come to light as a result of independent research by writers, journalists, scholars, and others, published in book form, and in newspaper and magazine accounts. In recent years, some former CIA employees have also disclosed details of certain covert operations.

The following brief compilation' of covert operations indicates that during the past twenty-five years there was no year in which some major secret CIA operation was not taking place in some country somewhere in the world. It is also safe to assume that if this many covert operations have become public knowledge, many others, both "successful" and unsuccessful, have not. But even a partial list would include the following:

Burma (1949–1961). The CIA supported some twelve thousand Nationalist Chinese troops who had fled to Burma in 1949 as the Communists gained control of mainland China. The Chinese Nationalist troops became heavily involved in the opium trade. The United States ambassador to Burma, unaware of the CIA role, answered Burmese protests of the presence of the troops by repeatedly denying U.S. involvement.[25]

China (1951–1954). During this period the CIA air-dropped guerrilla teams into the People's Republic of China. In November 1952 the Chinese captured two American CIA agents, John T. Downey and Richard G. Fecteau. The United States claimed that they were employees of the "Department of the Army." After twenty years of U.S. denials that the two men were CIA agents, Fecteau was released in December 1971, shortly before President Nixon's trip to Peking. Downey was freed in March 1973, soon after Nixon, at a press conference, finally publicly acknowledged him to be "a CIA agent."

Philippines (early 1950s). The CIA supported Ramón Magsaysay's campaign against the communist Huk guerrillas. The key CIA figure in this operation was Edward Lansdale, who later became an important CIA operator in Vietnam during the mid-1950s.

Iran (1953). The CIA organized and directed the coup that overthrew the government of Premier Mohammed Mossadegh and kept the Shah on his throne. The operation was run by Kermit "Kim" Roosevelt, the grandson of President Theodore Roosevelt. Mossadegh had nationalized the Iranian oil industry; one result of his overthrow by the CIA was that a group of Western oil companies signed a twenty-five-year agreement with Iran for its oil. For the first time, American companies were permitted into Iran, with a forty per cent share of the deal.

Guatemala (1954). In one of its most ambitious undertakings, the CIA overthrew the Communist-dominated government of President Jacobo Arbenz Guzman with U.S. arms and a CIA air force of World War II P-47 Thunderbolts. Colonel Carlos Castillo Armas crossed the border from Honduras with a hundred and fifty men. The operation had the full approval of President Eisenhower, who later confirmed the U.S. role in a 1963 speech and in his memoirs.

Cuba (1956). The CIA established and supported BRAC, an anti-Communist police force under dictator Fulgencio Batista. BRAC became well-known for brutal methods.[26]

Indonesia (1958). With a secret air force of B-26 bombers based at the Philippines, the CIA supported rebel elements in the Celebes who were fighting to overthrow President Sukarno. One of the CIA pilots, Allen Lawrence Pope, was shot down on a bombing run, parachuted, and was captured. President Eisenhower falsely claimed that the U.S. policy was one of "careful neutrality" and suggested that Pope was one of the "soldiers of fortune" who turned up in every war. Pope was freed four years later through the intervention of Robert Kennedy.

Tibet (1958–1961). The CIA established a secret base at Camp Hale, Colorado, nearly ten thousand feet high in the Rocky Mountains, near Leadville. There the CIA trained Tibetan guerrillas who were infiltrated back into Tibet to fight against the Chinese Communists. The CIA's clandestine operators later claimed that some of the guerrillas from Camp Hale helped to guide the Dalai Lama over the mountains to safety in India in 1959. The entire operation almost surfaced in 1961, when a group of civilians were held at gunpoint at an airfield at Colorado Springs while the CIA loaded some of the Tibetans on a transport plane.[27]

Singapore (1960). Two CIA agents were arrested in a bungled operation that resulted from a decision by Allen Dulles, then CIA Director, to infiltrate Singapore with CIA agents rather than rely on MI6, the British Secret Service, which was already established in Singapore. The agents were caught when they checked into a hotel room, plugged in a lie detector to test a spy recruit, and blew out all the lights in the hotel.

Secretary of State Dean Rusk was forced to apologize to Premier Lee Kuan Yew in 1961.[28] The State Department initially denied and then admitted the apology had been made.

Cuba (1961). A brigade of Cuban exiles trained and supported by the CIA on a remote coffee plantation in Guatemala was decimated when it invaded Cuba at the Bay of Pigs in an ill-fated attempt to overthrow Premier Fidel Castro. Many of the brigade members were captured. Four American pilots flying for the CIA died in the invasion. U.N. ambassador Adlai E. Stevenson recited the CIA's false cover story to the United Nations when the invasion commenced. The training of the Cuban exiles had begun under Eisenhower, but the invasion was carried out by President Kennedy, for whom it proved a major disaster.

Brazil (1962). The CIA spent a reported twenty million dollars in the Brazilian election in support of hundreds of candidates for gubernatorial, congressional, and state and local offices. A major objective was to deny leftist President Goulart control of the Brazilian Congress in 1962.[29]

Vietnam (1963). The CIA worked closely and secretly with the group of generals who carried out the coup against President Ngo Dinh Diem of South Vietnam on November 1, 1963. Diem was killed in the coup. A week before, the generals assured the top CIA agent concerned that the plan of operation marked "eyes only" for Ambassador Henry Cabot Lodge would be turned over to the CIA two days before the coup "for Lodge's review."[30] Other CIA activities in Vietnam are too numerous to be summarized here; perhaps the best known grew into the Phoenix Program, designed to "neutralize" the Vietcong. Over a three-year period, at least 20,587 persons were killed under the program, which was run by William Colby, the present head of the CIA.

Chile (1964 and 1970). The CIA spent an estimated twenty million dollars in 1964 in a successful effort to elect Eduardo Frei, the Christian Democratic candidate, over Salvador Allende.[31] Unsuccessful CIA efforts to block Allende's election six years later have been discussed earlier in this paper.

Congo (1964). Cuban exile pilots who had flown at the Bay of Pigs again flew B-26 bombers for the CIA, under the cover of a company called Caramar, to suppress a revolt against the central Congolese government.[32] The CIA was very active in the Congo in the early 1960s when that new nation became a center of Cold War rivalry; the agency threw its support to Joseph Mobutu, who became President.

Greece (1967). The role of the CIA in the coup that placed a military junta in power in Greece in 1967 remains murky even today; but it has been publicly acknowledged that the agency had worked closely wih Colonel George Papadopoulos, the colonel who led the coup. At his Senate confirmation hearing, Colby denied a London *Observer* report that the CIA had "engineered" the coup. Senator Symington asked whether Papadopoulos had been an "agent for the CIA." Colby replied, "He has not been an agent. He has been an official of the Greek government at various times, in those periods and from time to time we worked with him in an official capacity." When Symington asked whether Papadopoulos had been paid any money by the CIA, Colby replied, "I just do not know. I can say we did not pay him personally." Later Colby submitted a statement for the record saying that the CIA "never" paid Papadopoulos any money, a denial that would not, however, preclude payments through intermediaries.[33]

Bolivia (1967). A team of CIA covert operators was dispatched to Bolivia to aid the government of that country in tracking down Ernesto "Che" Guevara, a principal lieutenant of Fidel Castro's in the Cuban Revolution. Guevara disappeared from Cuba in 1965, then reappeared as the head of the guerrilla movement in Bolivia. Following Guevara's capture and death, Antonio Arguedas, the Bolivian Minister of the Interior, announced that he, Arguedas, had been an agent of the CIA for two years and had released Guevara's diary.[34]

Laos (1960–1973). CIA covert operations in Laos have virtually become a tradition in that small Asian nation. In 1960 the State Department and the CIA each backed different political leaders to be the head of the Laotian government. It was not the first time CIA covert activities have clashed with the overt policies of other branches of the U.S. government. In August 1971 the Senate Foreign Relations Committee published a staff report disclosing that the CIA for years had maintained a thirty-thousand-man army in Laos, consisting principally of Meo tribesmen operating under General Vang Pao. Air America, a CIA airline, provided air support for the secret war in Laos. The 1973 Laotian accord supposedly marked the end of this covert operation.

Italy (1958–1967). After World War II the CIA began covert financing of the Christian Democratic Party, with payments averaging as high as three million dollars a year through the late 1950s. In 1970 Graham A. Martin, then ambassador to Italy, unsuccessfully urged the CIA to resume its secret financing of the Christian Democrats, but his proposal was turned down.[35] As already noted, CIA concern over a possible Communist victory in the 1948 Italian elections marked the start of the agency's global intervention through covert political action.

Thus, even this limited list of secret political operations illustrates the wide range of CIA covert action, including dropping of agents by parachute, support of antiguerrilla activity, overthrowing governments regarded as unfriendly to Western political or economic interests, training of secret police, training of foreign guerrillas in the continental United States, full-scale paramilitary invasion, attempts to rig elections, training and financing of a secret army to fight a secret war, and clandestine support of friendly political parties. Although the techniques have varied in different countries and at different times, the basic objectives have remained the same: to manipulate the internal politics of other countries by secret action in ways that can, and have, often been denied by a succession of American Presidents.

IV. CONCLUSIONS AND RECOMMENDATIONS

Like the CIA itself, covert political operations are a direct outgrowth of the expanded American world role that developed during and after World War II. And, as in the case of the security-classification system that facilitates the secrecy surrounding these operations, secret political action grew in a vacuum, with insufficient public debate or questioning.

Covert operations may be viewed most clearly against the background of the Cold War, which provided their justification in the eyes of the policymakers. For two decades, Americans were warned of the perils of a monolithic international communism; to preserve the Free World it was deemed necessary, in the words of Allen Dulles, to "fight fire with fire." The external enemy was the rationale for the establishment of a vast secret-intelligence bureaucracy, its operations subject to none of the usual checks and balances that the American system imposes on more plebeian government agencies. Thus, history could be manipulated in favor of the good guys—us. The United states could wage secret war against what Dean Rusk liked to call "the other side." Or, as Allen Dulles contended in *The Craft of Intelligence*, the United States could not wait to act until "we are invited in by a government"—by then it might be too late.

What might have seemed logical and necessary in the era of the Cold War does not seem justified today. The world has changed; the Communist "monolith" has become fragmented; the superpowers seek détente, but covert political action goes on.

Yet it is difficult to discover any moral or legal basis for such operations, and they are, at best, of doubtful constitutionality. Morally, no one appointed the United States to intervene in the internal affairs of other nations. Such operations violate the charter of the United Nations. And one can imagine the reaction in this country if a foreign intelligence service launched an invasion of the United States in Florida, poured millions of dollars into the country to support a Presidential candidate or congressional candidates in order to influence the outcome of an American election, or attempted a coup to overthrow the President. A world groping for peace cannot afford secret wars.

Legally, the argument that the "other functions" clause can justify large-scale covert operations is extremely tenuous. There is no indication that Congress intended the "other functions" provision to justify such operations, and if Congress did, the language of the statute would be overly broad. Moreover, covert operations—at least those involving paramilitary action or the overthrow of governments—would appear almost by definition to be unconstitutional. The Constitution vests the war power in the Congress, and operations on this scale are clearly the equivalent of undeclared war. Yet they are undertaken by executive action alone; Congress and the public, which Congress represents, have no opportunity to debate or approve such operations in advance.

The President, it is true, has a constitutional responsibility to protect national security, but this does not extend to waging undeclared wars. If there is no moral, legal, or constitutional basis for covert political operations, it may be argued that there remains a practical basis—that such operations are pragmatically necessary to protect American security. There is, however, a fatal flaw in such an argument.

A democracy rests on the consent of the governed, and the governed are not permitted to give their consent to covert political actions because of their very nature. Moreover, when secret political operations are exposed, the government lies to protect them, by denying responsibility. The price has proved too high in terms of public confidence in the system of government. It does not work.

The road to Watergate was paved with government lying, often to protect covert political operations. The result was the greatest crisis in the American political system since the Civil War, the impeachment vote by the House Committee on the Judiciary, and, for the first time in almost two hundred years, the resignation of a President while in office. The standard of "plausible deniability" has no place in the American constitutional system. For in plain language it means that the government can act as it pleases if it can get away with lying about its actions to the electorate. Covert operations have not proved workable in the American system; they are like a transplant rejected by the democratic host.

The damaging effect of covert operations on the American political system is the crucial and overriding consideration. But even from a practical standpoint, covert operations often have had the opposite effect of that intended. The Bay of Pigs strengthened Castro's position and weakened President Kennedy's. The governments of Iran and Guatemala were overthrown but the reputation of the United States in Africa, South America, and Asia has been tainted precisely because of such covert operations. As a result, the United States has sometimes been blamed for activities for which the CIA has *not* been responsible.

Since covert operations are by definition secret, the problem of control can never be solved in a democracy. If the Forty Committee does exercise control, it cannot be demonstrated, because its deliberations in turn are secret. Again, there is no way to graft secret political action onto the body politic in a system that rests upon consent.

The inescapable conclusion is that the United States should cease covert political operations, for all the reasons listed above. Congress, which has been struggling to regain its war powers from the President, should assert its right to end secret political intervention and secret wars as well. Congressional debate and national debate and legislation to accomplish these ends are required. The "other functions" clause should be rewritten specifically to exclude covert political operations. Congress should improve its control over the CIA and the intelligence community generally and establish a joint committee or more broadly based committees in the House and Senate for this purpose.

The Watergate crisis was a dramatic illustration of where the covert mentality can lead us when applied to American domestic politics. Watergate also proved something about the resiliency of the American system, for the impeachment proceeding and the resignation of Richard Nixon in one sense marked the drawing of a line by the people. Thus far—but no further—America showed that it was not ready for totalitarianism. The impeachment vote and Nixon's resignation represented a cleansing of the American political process domestically. The people and the Congress can and should assert themselves just as powerfully in the field of foreign affairs. We need have no more Vietnams, no more secret wars in Laos or Cambodia, no more Bays of Pigs. American foreign policy can be carried out openly, without covert manipulation of the affairs of other nations.

The fact that other nations may engage in covert political action is not sufficient justification for the United States to do so; for if we adopt the methods of our adversaries we will become indistinguishable from them. In time covert operations will change the character of the institutions they seek to preserve. Covert operations may be dangerous to other nations, but ultimately they impose the greatest danger to ourselves.

ROGER MORRIS AND
RICHARD MAUZY

Following
the Scenario

2

REFLECTIONS ON FIVE
CASE HISTORIES IN THE
MODE AND AFTERMATH
OF CIA INTERVENTION*

Beyond its most publicized activities, from the Bay of Pigs to the long-lasting mercenary wars in Southeast Asia, there is gathering evidence that over the last two decades the Central Intelligence Agency has secretly intervened as well in nearly a score of countries around the world. The successes or failures of such involvement, much less its foreign-policy justification, have been hidden from public view, buried behind official secrecy in a bureaucracy that rarely examines its conventions, and largely neglected by both the Congress and press. Yet these relatively obscure examples of CIA intervention are important precisely because they are widespread, routine, and unaccounted for. Far more common than proxy invasions or strategic overflights, a vast traffic in bribes, blackmail, and propaganda has become the daily staple of the CIA's covert intelligence operations. It is that traffic which rationalizes the existence of an equally vast intelligence bureaucracy and poses some of the most disturbing questions about the future role of the CIA in American foreign policy.

What follows is a survey of five case histories of such CIA interven-

---

* This piece is based upon both written sources and many oral conversations. Both authors have had extensive personal contact with decision-makers and foreign policy officials who supplied—on the basis of commonly shared knowledge—many of the previously unpublished details.

tion in the 1960s—in Ecuador, Brazil, Zaire (formerly the Congo), Somalia, and Indonesia. The history of these episodes is still fragmentary at best. But from interviews with official sources as well as from public documents, the main outline of CIA involvement seems clear enough. It is a record worth recounting for what it shows of CIA methods and of the ironies, sometimes bitter, in the aftermath of the intervention. But these five examples are more than an account of intelligence operations somehow detached from other national actions; they are also a somber reflection of how the United States conceives and executes its foreign relations.

Nor are these cases merely historical or in any sense academic. Though they belong to the 1960s, much of the policies, techniques, and mentality they exhibit still shape our foreign affairs. According to official sources, the CIA now maintains, with White House approval, close relations with regimes in four of the five countries, including substantial financial retainers for leaders in at least two of the states.

Moreover, these operations, carried out mainly from 1962 to 1967, were authorized by senior political appointees in past Democratic administrations. They are thus the responsibility of men who, if now out of government (and righteously pronouncing on the excess of the incumbents), might well hold office in some future administration. Finally, just as little has changed within the executive since these operations were conducted, there is still no reliable constitutional or political restraint on such intervention. A largely quiescent Congress, an often indifferent press, and a distracted, uninformed public continue to surrender their responsibilities in the making of a democratic foreign policy.

ECUADOR: PROMOTING COMMUNISM

"It was tribute to what a six-man station can do," said one former intelligence official of CIA operations in Ecuador in the early sixties. "In the end, they owned almost everybody who was anybody." Remarkable documentation of that claim—including the identity of "everybody" and how much he cost—appeared in *Inside the Company: CIA Diary*, the London-published memoir of Philip B. F. Agee, a former CIA case officer in Latin America who served in Ecuador from 1960 to 1963. But whatever the accounting details, CIA efforts in Ecuador during Agee's period there have long been regarded within the government as one of the CIA's most impressive successes.

The intervention in Ecuador was rooted in the policy of the Eisenhower and Kennedy administrations to isolate the Castro regime in Cuba and, more broadly, to prevent the further spread of anti–American governments in Latin America. In the process, however, the principal target of covert action was neither Cuba nor the Ecuadorian Communist party, but rather the country's non-Communist civilian political leadership.

With twenty-seven presidents between 1925 and 1947, its history a veritable caricature of Latin American instability, Ecuador had gained by the late 1950s a period of rare governmental and economic calm. The respite was to be short-lived. Though traditionally conservative in domestic policies—President José María Velasco Ibarra was serving his fourth term—the Ecuadorian regime maintained friendly relations with Cuba through Castro's rapid move leftward in 1960. That policy may have been determined in part by an authentic sympathy for the new Havana government, in part as an act of defiance toward Washington, fueled by U.S. pressure in an Ecuadorian-Peruvian border dispute in the fall of 1960. In any event, the Velasco regime did not follow suit when the United States formally broke with Cuba in January 1961, and the stage was set for a concerted CIA campaign to change Ecuador's policy and, if necessary, its government.

The main instruments of pressure against the Ecuadorian regime included not only the customary CIA penetration of influential elements in politics, journalism, and the military, but also those U.S.-sponsored labor organizations that were later to play a similar role so often elsewhere in Latin America—chiefly the American Institute for Free Labor Development (AIFLD), publicly founded by the AFL-CIO in 1961, and its companion organization, the Inter-American Regional Organization of Workers (ORIT), also established under AFL-CIO auspices. It was for these labor organizations, ostensibly voluntary and independent institutions in Latin America, that Philip Agee served as CIA liaison in Ecuador in 1960–1963—channeling covert financial support, orchestrating "spontaneous" political activities, directing the Ecuadorian labor organization's policy toward its own government.

The initial decision to launch the CIA's campaign in Ecuador seems to have been made early in 1961. At this point, U.S.-supported labor groups—of the kind Agee and the CIA serviced—were already waging well-organized, highly financed, and largely successful campaigns to control the Ecuadorian labor movement. By mid-July, Velasco was under heavy pressure from his own cabinet and some elements of the military to abandon his Cuban policy. Diplomatic relations remained intact, but Velasco broke openly with his volatile Vice President, Carlos Julio Arosemena, when the latter returned from a summer 1961 visit to Eastern Europe, where he urged closer relations with the Soviet bloc.

The split between Velasco and Arosemena deepened into the autumn and ended in a sequence of crisis and violence from which Arosemena, with Air Force backing, emerged in November as the new President. He immediately reaffirmed the maintenance of relations with Cuba, and within a week of the takeover of the Arosemena regime, Ecuadorian affiliates of ORIT publicly opposed diplomatic ties with Soviet-bloc states and warned of "Communist demagoguery" in the new government.

When the Organization of American States voted to exclude Cuba on January 31, 1962, Ecuador joined Argentina, Bolivia, Brazil, Chile, and Mexico in abstaining. And over the following months, the internal pressure gathered. There was an extraordinary increase in anti-Communist press attacks and labor demonstrations. Indiscriminate charges of Communist sympathies were flung at scores of officials, many of whom were forced to resign. By late March Arosemena had put down an attempted coup by army officers, but his political support was badly shaken.

On April 3, 1962, Ecuador broke relations with Cuba as well as with Poland and Czechoslovakia, thereby ending all ties with Communist states. There was a brief resurgence by Arosemena, now drawing support from across the political spectrum but principally from a coalition of liberals, moderate socialists and, independents. By mid-1962 he had forced out rightist Ministers of Defense and Interior and transferred or ousted several high-ranking military officers who had brought pressure on the break with Cuba. But a year later, in July 1963, Arosemena's civil government was overthrown by a military coup in the wake of mounting unrest, with labor in the lead.

"President Arosemena didn't want to break relations [with Cuba] but we forced him," Agee was to recall in a recent interview with *The Washington Post*. "We promoted the Communist issue and especially Communist penetration of the government."

The Ecuadorian case has seemed worth recounting in some detail because it was to prove almost a prototype of the later "spontaneous" overthrow of other Latin American regimes similarly at odds with U.S.

policy. The steady flow of money purchasing opposition politicians and strident editorials, the accompanying "vigilance" of U.S.-affiliated labor organizations, the inevitable inspiration of the military to save the nation—all were to be repeated with varying emphasis and intensity. In Ecuador as elsewhere, however, the outcome of the CIA intervention, and the related overthrow of Arosemena, was more than a change in the country's diplomatic alignment, the ostensible goal of the covert action. After its interval of economic stability, when it avoided the inflation and devaluation plaguing other Latin American countries, Ecuador fell during 1961–1963 into a persistent depression stemming from the political turmoil and a resulting decline in banana exports, a main cash crop. Ten years later, despite a recent oil boom, the country remained one of the poorest in Latin America in terms of income distribution. From 1966 to 1970, U.S. development aid to Ecuador was less than twenty-two million dollars. A former U.S. official estimates that the CIA spent at least half that much bringing down civil government in Ecuador between 1960 and 1963.

For Ecuadorian labor, apparently so anxious to be rid of Arosemena and to sever diplomatic relations with Cuba, the new military regime was soon to be a dubious blessing. "The Ecuador military regime has launched a systematic and ruthless attack on Ecuador's trade unions," an ORIT publication bitterly complained soon after the 1963 coup. "There is every reason to fear that Ecuador is heading towards a full military dictatorship. . . ." The country returned briefly to civilian rule in 1968, albeit under military supervision, but a new constitution was suspended two years later and a military junta resumed power in 1972.

U.S.-Ecuadorian relations were comparatively untroubled after 1963, flaring only briefly in a 1971 fisheries dispute. American firms, including ITT, Standard Fruit, General Tire, and Dow Chemical, dominate foreign investment with some sixty per cent of foreign corporate holdings. Trade with the United States is not significant by Latin American standards. In 1974, as in 1960, what authentic U.S. national interest would justify CIA intervention in Ecuador seemed a fit subject for debate.

As a final irony, in November 1974 the Latin American states met in Quito to consider the reopening of relations with Cuba, which has finally started to benefit from the politics of détente. By mid 1975 Washington had quietly abandoned its long-standing fear that diplomatic ties with Havana endangered vital U.S. interests in the Hemisphere. For the people of Ecuador, however, there would be no escape from a decade of military dictatorship, labor repression, and unrelieved poverty that began in large part with one of the CIA's "successes" of the early sixties.

BRAZIL: "IT DID NOT JUST HAPPEN . . ."

As the pressure was mounting on the Arosemena regime in Ecuador, much of the same sequence was being played out in Brazil. There, as in Ecuador, the spearhead of antigovernment activity was to be labor organizations spawned by the United States, and the target was a nationalist, non-Communist civilian regime. Similarly, the result in Brazil was the institution of a military dictatorship that pursued foreign policies more congenial to Washington but that also savagely repressed domestic liberties, including the rights of labor.

The development of events in Brazil during 1962–1964 is perhaps more familiar than the parallel operation in Ecuador. The regime of President João Goulart clashed with the United States early in 1962 over the expropriation of an ITT subsidiary, the resumption of Brazil's diplomatic relations with the Soviet Union, and Rio's abstention (along with Ecuador and others) in the earlier OAS vote to expel Cuba. Agee has reported that the CIA poured over twenty million dollars into Brazil's 1962 elections in support of opposition candidates for governorships, senatorial and deputy seats, and even thousands of provincial and municipal offices. The election, however, in which communism was *the* issue, was disappointing to Washington. In a record turnout, pro-Goulart candidates won a number of positions at national and local levels.

In the aftermath of the 1962 election, events moved rapidly. In November 1962 Brazil demanded transfer of a U.S. diplomat for interference in domestic politics. By January 1963 Washington had decided to withhold fifty million dollars in development aid pledged two years earlier, ostensibly pending fiscal reforms by Goulart. Coincidentally, the Brazilian branch of AIFLD (presumably with a Rio counterpart to Agee husbanding its resources) began to step up antigovernment operations. Courses in "labor affairs," in Brazil *and* in Washington, were given to anti-Goulart Brazilian labor leaders—including the head of the vital Telegraph and Telephone union, who, reported an approving *Reader's Digest* later, "after every class . . . quietly warned key workers of coming trouble and urged them to keep communications going no matter what happened."

U.S. aid remained frozen through 1963. Ambassador Lincoln Gordon became sharply critical of "leftist" elements in the Brazilian government. Charges of Communist penetration were, again, as in Ecuador, widely aired in the Brazilian press. On October 11, 1963, the Goulart regime announced the discovery of a cache of U.S. weapons entering the country under Alliance for Progress packages and reportedly addressed to anti-Goulart figures.

In January 1964 Goulart signed a potentially far-reaching bill to curb corporate profits expatriated from Brazil by foreign investors, a bill mainly affecting the host of U.S. interests in the country, valued at nearly a billion dollars. By early March Goulart had moved to repair his shifting political position by forming a popular front with leftist support, and had retained a coalition majority in parliament. "He had staying power," recalled one U.S. official who watched these events, "and he was the popularly elected leader of the country."

On March 26, 1964, the first military units came out against Goulart and by April 1 an army revolt had replaced civilian government with a junta. But the coup was also the result of a carefully orchestrated effort by labor organizations and anti-Goulart middle-class groups as well as the Army. "Some democratic labor leaders," boasted an ORIT labor publication, "were involved in the planning of the popular revolution as far as six months ago." "As a matter of fact," AIFLD's William J. Doherty, Jr., later told a broadcast audience, "some of them (Brazilian labor leaders) were so active that they became intimately involved in some of the clandestine operations of the revolution before it took place on April 1. What happened in Brazil on April 1 did not just happen—it was planned—and planned months in advance. Many of the trade-union leaders—many of whom were actually trained in our institute—were involved in the revolution, and in the overthrow of the Goulart regime." In the event, a key role in the coup was played by telegraphers trained in AIFLD seminars. One of the first acts of the military regime was to name several AIFLD "graduates," many trained in the United States, to purge the labor movements of "subversives."

Scarcely twenty-four hours after the coup, the Johnson administration offered "warmest good wishes" to the junta and offered to resume aid. Once more, though, the scenario managed in Washington and the field had incongruous results. Within months, the junta harshly suppressed the labor movement, and even AIFLD was to break with the regime. "They're not too favorable to any movement that's too democratic," explained one labor official of junta policies. A decade after the overthrow of Goulart, Brazil stands accused before the United Nations of gross abuses of human rights, including torture of some fifteen thousand political prisoners and alleged genocide of Amazonian Indians.

ZAIRE (THE CONGO): "AN EXERCISE IN NATION BUILDING"

It was to be, promised President Kennedy, "a long twilight struggle." And nowhere did the struggle seem longer, or the light so dim, as in the chaotic politics of the Congo following its independence in 1960.

Fourteen years later, the train of Congolese governments, the exotic place names, the endless confusion of personalities and conspiracies, and even the violence have a dated, almost comic, quality. But in the 1960s, the United States government saw it all as deadly serious business, a test that would determine the destiny of a continent important and perhaps vital to American interests. The Congo was not only a wealthy nation strategically placed in the heart of Africa, it was also presumed to be a symbolic battleground between East and West, where the success or failure of one's clients would have repercussions throughout Africa and the developing world. Briefly then, for the first and last time, an African problem became a priority for the White House and the subject of a U.S.-supported action by the United Nations.

Bureaucratically, the Congo crisis was supposed to be the final triumph of anticolonialism in American foreign policy, residing in the authority of the State Department's new Bureau of African Affairs. As Roger Hilsman later remembered, "We're running this show" was the boast of one of State's new African experts. But if the thrust of U.S. diplomacy at the United Nations and elsewhere was anticolonial, the decisive American policy in the Congo itself was soon being executed not only by the State Department but by the new CIA station on the scene. From the fall of Patrice Lumumba in 1960 to the coup installing General Joseph Mobutu in 1965, CIA cash payments to politicians, manipulation of unions and youth or cultural groups, and a rising investment in planted propaganda helped establish increasingly pro-Western regimes, ending in the military dictatorship that has governed the country for the last decade.

Perhaps the most dramatic instance of CIA intervention came in the 1964 Stanleyville revolt, when Cuban Bay of Pigs veterans were contracted to fly vintage B-26 bombers and white mercenaries were recruited by the Agency in South Africa and Rhodesia. ("Bringing in our own animals," as one long-time CIA operative described the mercenary recruitment.) The revolt was crushed, though not before fifty-eight European hostages were killed by the rebels in the wake of the CIA bombings and the Belgian-U.S. airdrop on Stanleyville.

The mercenary action, however, was extraordinary. More often, the intervention continued quietly in the passage of money and advice. Mobutu succeeded in a bloodless coup in late 1965, and has reportedly kept up a close liaison with his former patrons. "Such relationships aren't terminated," said a former intelligence official.

By the customary standards of national policy, the Congo, now renamed Zaire, has been an obvious success story for everyone. The country is united and pro-Western, its history presumably an inspiration to other American client regimes in fear of disintegration or subversion. Diplomatic relations with the United States are outwardly excellent. American corporate investment, notably in copper and aluminum, doubled to about fifty million dollars following a 1970 visit by Mobutu to the United States. Investors include Chase Manhattan, Ford, General Motors, Gulf, Shell, Union Carbide, and several other large concerns. In many respects Zaire seems unrecognizable from the volatile, ungovernable mess of little more than a decade ago. "It's been a good exercise in nation-building," says a senior Foreign Service Officer.

But the success story in Zaire can also be seen in a different perspective. After a decade of authoritarian rule, despite comparatively heavy U.S. and European aid, despite vast natural wealth, Zaire remains one of the poorest countries in the world, its growth rate over the decade 1960–1970 less than 2.7 per cent, and its GNP per capita only ninety dollars. Its stability has been purchased at the cost of recurrent terror and repression. This model state of American policy in Africa has yet to conduct a national free election, to allow the free functioning of political parties or labor unions, or to condone a free press.

Mobutu, the Agency's most "successful" client in Africa, rules by decree with a grotesque impulsiveness that seems to shock even his former case officers. One recalled that in June 1971 Mobutu had forcibly enlisted in the armed forces the entire student body of Lovanium University. "He was put out by some student demonstrations," remembered the official. Mobutu finally relented, but ten of the students were sentenced to life imprisonment for crimes of "public insult" to the Chief of State. Nor has Mobutu been altogether a model for U.S. diplomatic efforts in Africa. While reportedly dealing covertly himself with South Africa, Rhodesia, and Portugal (presumably to secure his southern frontier if not African solidarity), he has steadily refused occasional U.S. requests that he intercede to halt genocide in neighboring Burundi or Uganda.

As for the CIA itself, the exercise has also had its drawbacks. One intelligence source recalls a fervent Mobutu approach, eventually deflected, that either Zaire with CIA help or the Agency alone undertake an invasion against "those bastards across the river" in the Congo Republic (Brazzaville). He's a "real wild man," said one former official, "and we've had trouble keeping him under rein."

SOMALIA: CAMPAIGN FINANCING
AROUND THE HORN OF AFRICA

If Zaire enjoyed its moment of chic in world politics, and the covert investment that flowed from it, Somalia by contrast seems an obscure backwater of international politics. But the CIA intervention there in the mid-sixties, as in Ecuador earlier, is reportedly another tribute to what a small CIA station can do, however remote from the national interest.

An impoverished land of less than three million along the northeastern coast of Africa where the Indian Ocean meets the Gulf of Aden, Somalia was of concern to Washington for a number of reasons. Irredentist claims threatened border warfare with both Kenya and Ethiopia, the latter a long-time U.S. client state under Haile Selassie and the site of a major intelligence base. Somalia was also an early recipient of Soviet aid in Africa, and its coastline held potentially strategic ports for any future rivalry in the Persian Gulf or Indian Ocean, an interest shared by France and Britain. At that, however, the country was apparently not an urgent concern in U.S. diplomacy. When Somalia predictably rejected a 1963 American offer of "defensive" arms, conditioned on the exclusion of all other supplies, the State Department leaked its "displeasure" but seemingly did no more.

Over the next four years, 1963–1967, official U.S.-Somali relations were distant and U.S. aid next to nothing while Somali leaders visited the Soviet bloc, Somali newspapers published anti-American forgeries planted by Soviet intelligence, and the country fought a brief but bloody border war with Ethiopia. Then suddenly, early in 1967, history took a turn for the better. President Abd-i-Rashid Shermarke was elected for a six-year term as President in June and in July appointed as Premier Muhammad Egal, American-educated and avowedly pro-Western. By fall, U.S. aid was resumed in amounts twice the previous total since independence, and Somalia had concluded a border agreement with Ethiopia. In 1968 Egal visited the United States, following a visit to Somalia by Vice President Humphrey, and was hailed by President Johnson as "enormously constructive in a troubled area of Africa." What the two leaders did not discuss, say official sources, was how "constructive" the CIA had been for Mr. Egal, whose rise to power was reportedly facilitated by thousands of dollars in covert support to Egal and other pro-Western elements in the ruling Somali Youth League party prior to the 1967 Presidential election.

In retrospect, this clandestine bankrolling in Somalia seems very modest by CIA standards, only a tiny fraction of what the Agency has spent in a month in Southeast Asia or even what it spent in the Congo in the early sixties. And its immediate benefits—in rising U.S. influence, in the détente with a grateful Ethiopia—no doubt seemed real enough at the time. In any event, several sources say the subsidies were discontinued in 1968. But the withdrawal was to be perhaps too late. On October 15, 1969, while Egal was again visiting the United States, President Shermarke was assassinated. A week later the Army seized power, dissolving the National Assembly and Constitution and arresting the entire Cabinet, including Egal. Among the charges against Egal would be corruption of the electoral process and complicity with foreign intelligence services. Ironically, the bizarre CIA political contributions before 1967 may have been a decisive factor in the eventual fall of the Agency's candidate.

Little changed for the people of Somalia as a result of the CIA intervention. They are still grindingly poor, with a *negative* growth rate in 1968–1970 and less than seventy dollars GNP per capita. The main beneficiaries of the covert action, Egal and his colleagues, are mostly in jail or dead. In the last five years the country has turned again toward the Soviet bloc, and there are reports of Soviet naval bases and airfields menacing the Indian Ocean. Perhaps it is out of some sense of bureaucratic defensiveness, rooted in memories of the Egal episode, as well as out of a valid difference of view that CIA Director Colby is now reported to be less alarmed by the Soviet presence in Somalia than are his Pentagon counterparts.

INDONESIA: THE BIGGEST DOMINO

Finally, one of the most familiar CIA "successes" has been the succession of a pro-Western military regime, that of General Suharto, in Indonesia. Though there is no clear evidence that the Agency was instrumental in the 1965 coup that eventually overthrew President Sukarno, there is also no doubt that it was precisely Sukarno's ouster from the Right that had been an Agency goal for nearly a decade. In that sense Indonesia seems another telling measure of the possible results of covert action.

CIA intervention against the Sukarno regime probably began as early as the 1956 Sumatra revolt and was brought drastically into the open with the downing in May 1958 of a CIA B-26 and its pilot, Allen Pope, who was released during a brief thaw in U.S.-Indonesian relations in 1962. Diplomatic hostilities soon resumed in 1963–1964 during Sukarno's confrontation policy toward Malaysia, and by mid-1965, following violent anti-U.S. demonstrations in Indonesia, the U.S. Congress adopted a resolution urging a total aid cut-off. Then, in September 1965, in the wake of an abortive coup by pro-Chinese officers, the Indonesian military began the purge of Indonesian leftists that was not only to displace Sukarno but also lead, within a year, to the death of as many as eight hundred thousand people—tens of thousands of them, by the Army's own investigation, wholly innocent bystanders.

Assuming no direct CIA complicity in these events per se, the Indonesian coup should be seen in the context of what the Agency was trying to accomplish by covert action in Indonesia and elsewhere. Thus the fear of Communist subversion, which erupted to a frenzy of killing in 1965–1966, had been encouraged in the "penetration" propaganda of the Agency in Indonesia, just as it was exploited in Ecuador or Brazil. So, too, the Indonesian military must have known that their replacement of Sukarno and the obliteration of the Indonesian Communist party would hardly be opposed by an American government whose own covert intelligence operations had long been directed at both. "All I know," said one former intelligence officer of the Indonesian events, "is that the Agency rolled in some of its top people and that things broke big and very favorable, as far as we were concerned."

By 1974 there were some signs that Indonesia might be moving toward some relaxation of the harsh military rule applied since 1965. But Indonesia, like Brazil, was cited in the United Nations for gross abuses of human rights, and several sources estimate as many as fifty thousand political prisoners are still being held without trial.

For all the clear differences in setting and events, these five cases have much in common. And viewed together, they seem to characterize (if not caricature) some of the main elements of the CIA's covert action abroad.

First, there are the obvious ironies in both the techniques of intervention and the outcome of events. In most of the five cases "success"—however temporary—came largely at the expense of the Agency's own instruments. They trained political organizers and found political organizations outlawed. They used a more or less free press to plant propaganda and were left with more or less rigid censorship. They spent thousands to buy elections from the Amazon to the Gulf of Aden and were left with dissolved assemblies and no more troublesome voting. Relying on labor unions for their purposes, they saw the labor movement suppressed.

Then, too, there were the ironies in tactics. Presumably to avoid "instability" in Latin America, the Agency deliberately fostered political turmoil and division that might easily have gone beyond its control. No one planned the frenzied slaughter by Moslem gangs and undisciplined troops in Indonesia, but it stemmed in part from a climate of fear and suspicion which the United States worked covertly to ferment. Or on a more subtle level, to combat Soviet influence in Somalia our covert policy lavishly (by Somali standards) embraced the few politicians who might have done that, and destroyed their local credibility in the process.

There is, of course, no record of amends to our clients who suffered these untoward results—no escape engineered for Egal, no covert campaign or case officers to re-establish labor rights in Ecuador or Brazil, and, we must assume, no sure exit for Messrs. Mobutu or Suharto or their many peers if it should come to that.

All this raises the often puzzling question of exactly who were the clients and what were the basic interests of covert policies in these cases or others. It is clear enough that the Agency's clients were scarcely the institutions or popular organizations spawned or exploited. Least of all is there evidence of a direct interest in the social or economic welfare of the mass of people in any of the countries. Intervention left untouched the substantial human misery in all five countries, and in varying degrees added the burden of political repression. But then that was hardly the Agency's mission or target.

In the end, of course, the CIA's only authentic client was itself. Regimes, labor leaders, obliging editors, moonlighting cabinet ministers, ambitious colonels all come and go. The station remains, altering its rolls as necessary and passing them along from case officer to case officer, with the power of manipulation the only real criterion of covert operational success.

Within the U.S. government, all five of these cases have been judged as a major credit to the CIA's bureaucratic stock. Even Somalia can be rationalized as a vindication of covert action; our men in Mogadiscio fell, after all, when they left the payroll. Yet even within the bureaucracy there are apparently doubts about the longevity of our success. The covert money continues to flow in many cases because the "stability" of the agreeable successor regimes never seems secure. Guerrillas in Brazil, leftists or anti-American students in Ecuador, the psychological aberrations in Zairean politics, the resurgence of opposition in Indonesia—a station's work is never done.

Beyond the sometimes bizarre measures of success, these five cases also obviously share the common mythology of covert action. All belong to the Cold War anxieties of the sixties. All reflect the abiding conviction that the United States should and could shape the politics and diplomacy of other countries by clandestine, if necessary, ruthless, and altogether extralegal means. The prevailing orthodoxy was that our security was at stake in some measure in virtually every capital of the developing world as well as in the industrialized states. And security was surely nowhere inconsistent with repressive regimes. On the other hand, in none of the five cases—Ecuador, Brazil, Zaire, Somalia, Indonesia—did the CIA or its political superiors ever make it a public issue that the national security was involved.

The offending element in all cases—even, again, in Somalia, where the Agency now tends to discount Soviet influence—was an uncontrolled or sometimes belligerent nationalism. It was the infectious power of independence that seems to have been most disturbing to U.S. policymakers in the pre-détente era. But then none of these cases are relics of the past. The techniques they illustrate were applied anew, albeit perhaps with more sophistication, to the Allende regime in Chile, with

similar results. (One wonders how many unionists or students or journalists who obliged us in deposing Allende are now—as their Ecuar-
dorian, Brazilian, Congolese, Somali, or Indonesian counterparts before
them—suffering second thoughts under the less tender rule of the
Chilean junta.)

But perhaps the central point of these experiences is that the Agency
was not really some autonomous evil machine, buying and selling countries by some hidden bureaucratic impulse simply to manipulate or exist.
In these five cases and many more, the CIA was truly, as Richard Bissell
once told the Council on Foreign Relations, "a responsible agency of
national policy." What we are talking about in each of these cases is
foreign policy, from that of the lowliest desk officer in the State Department to that of the junior staff of the station in the field. The CIA
ultimately carried out the operations in these five countries because it
was national, Presidential policy to have compliant regimes in Latin
America, a "stable," pro-Western rule in Zaire, a reversal of leftward,
irredentist politics in Somalia, and an end to Sukarno's volatile nationalism. In that sense, the CIA met *real* needs within the United States
government. And if it had not existed, bureaucratic imperatives and
interests included, in all probability it would have been invented.

For the same reason, it is clear what the Agency does *not* do covertly,
whatever its capabilities. It does *not* attempt to relieve the torture of
prisoners in Brazil, or to discredit the police there, or to undermine the
savage exploitation of the Amazonian Indians. It does *not* mobilize on
behalf of higher wages for the vast Indian population of Ecuador. It
does *not* pressure Mobuto for free elections in Zaire or for denial of his
own covert support of a genocidal regime in Burundi. It does *not* finance legal or journalistic pressure in Indonesia to free the prisoners
held since 1965. One searches in vain for any evidence that the Agency
has intervened anywhere in two decades on behalf of human rights. But
that is not only a matter of covert intelligence operations. An argument
could certainly be made on strictly practical grounds by the CIA (as
indeed officials say it has been) that some support for groups downtrod-
den by "friendly" regimes is simply a way to cover all bets. Covert
action is most often no more nor less than the way we do business with
the world, the ruling expediency and inhumanity of diplomacy as apart
from the hypocrisy of rhetoric.

Finally, each of the five cases shares to a large extent the common
process by which covert operations—and foreign policy—have been

and are decided. Most often recommended by the field or desk, then approved by the highest level of government, mainly by the predecessor of the current Forty Committee, these cases proceeded with no visible trace of bureaucratic debate. There is no record of opposition from the State Department or White House staff, no resignations on principle, no major leak to forestall action.

For most Foreign Service officers, one suspects, these operations are distasteful, embarrassing, and certainly bureaucratically annoying to the degree that *their* clients are in the action, but not essentially inconsistent with the accepted conduct of foreign policy. So too they were accepted by two Presidents and their men. It seems a banal yet still striking fact: a large number of people in the United States government unquestioningly accepted and supported—and accept and support now—the proposition that it was necessary for this country secretly to bomb and bribe in some of the most marginal precincts of the national interest imaginable.

An analysis of covert action by the CIA can only lead toward a most basic discussion of United States foreign policy, and beyond that to the standards and concepts of a democratic foreign policy that we expect of public officials at all levels.

But then it is not only the sinister executive branch that bears responsibility for these episodes and the mentality they mirror. Congressman Michael Harrington (Democrat from Massachusetts) in 1974 expressed dismay that his colleagues from the Senate Foreign Relations Committee seemed uninterested in the revelation that eleven million dollars had been spent to unseat Allende in Chile. It is not, of course, so surprising or merely a reflection of the congressional awe of Secretary Kissinger. In general the Congress has consistently ignored covert operations, in comfortable, earnestly cultivated ignorance, for as long as the Agency has existed. The exceptions, such as Harrington's letter or Senator Case's exposure of Radio Free Europe or the Senate hearings on AIFLD and ITT, are all too rare.

For its part, the press has tended to treat the subject with the same air of resignation or gingerly neglect. Beyond the familiar exceptions, journalism has found it just as hard, or unimportant, to follow the mundane rhythm of covert action abroad. The CIA, like the reputation of the incumbent Secretary of State, is a continuing beneficiary of the distaste for investigative reporting in foreign affairs.

There seems no facile answer to any of this. But a beginning could be made by the Congress to control covert action just as it has demanded control over war powers, and for the same reasons of constitutional responsibility and sanity.

A Foreign Intervention Control Act might include the following:

—That *all* covert actions be subject to a declaration of vital national interest by the President and prior consultation with representatives of both Houses of Congress.

—A total bar on funding for interference in elections, mercenary military acts, or assassination.

—That the membership of the Forty Committee include two senators and two representatives, and that the committee's minutes be available for executive-session review by the appropriate congressional committee.

—The creation of a fully staffed Joint Congressional Committee on Intelligence Supervision, and the augmentation of the Appropriations Committee staffs for review of all CIA operations.

—An amendment to vest the supervisory role in all foreign-intelligence activities in the Secretary of State on the grounds that any such action abroad is an act of foreign policy.

—A total bar on the exploitation of private institutions by the CIA. The Katzenbach Committee left broad loopholes for such action, and it continues to discredit private American institutions throughout the world.

—That station chiefs be subject to executive-session confirmation by the Senate, on the model of ambassadorial confirmation.

—The creation of a special staff for intelligence review to serve all members of the Forty Committee on all aspects and implications of covert activities abroad.

—An immediate, comprehensive review by a special congressionally appointed commission of all covert-action programs (CIA or otherwise) with a mandate to recommend change.

However unlikely the implementation of these changes seems amid the political realities of Washington, where the incentive to control the CIA and assume genuine responsibility for national security remains, as the bureaucrats say, "thin" in all quarters, there will be no answer to the abuses of covert action without such reforms.

But the ultimate reform must come in foreign policy. The most careful controls on covert action will be unavailing so long as we see our role in the world in the way we have seen it for the last two decades. Our vast national intelligence apparatus, besides protecting authentic security interests, could conceivably be directed to strengthen the capacity of governments to resolve the enormous human problems now beginning to break over them. But that is not a matter of intelligence technique or success. It could only come from a larger decision that the United States conduct at last a humane and open foreign policy.

FRED BRANFMAN

The President's Secret Army

A CASE STUDY—THE CIA IN LAOS, 1962–1972 *

3

SENATOR SYMINGTON: . . . so what you are saying is no activity of this kind is done without instructions from the President?

MR. COLBY: Correct.

SENATOR SYMINGTON: *What you can really call the CIA then is* "The King's Men" or *"The President's Army."*

MR. COLBY: I do not think that is the case, Mr. Chairman. I think the CIA is an intelligence agency, which has the capability of using intelligence techniques as directed by the President and by the Congress—by the National Security Council. . . .

SENATOR SYMINGTON: I know you know that much of the CIA operations in Laos had as much to do with intelligence as the production of carpets in the United States. It was the operation of a war conducted, at least in some cases, by the State Department and the Central Intelligence Agency to cover up what we were actually doing. That is what worries the American people. They find something going on for years, killing a lot of people, about which they had no idea. . . .

—*Senate Armed Services Hearings, Nomination of William E. Colby*, July 2, 1973, pp. 19–21, 28. (emphasis added)

* This essay is based primarily on several hundred personal interviews conducted during a four-year stay in Laos (1967–1971). A "strengthened two-source rule" has been used, namely, I have tried to insure that interview material is confirmed by two independent sources who do not come from identical bureaucratic backgrounds, and that it is not contradicted by either common sense or documented data.

INTRODUCTION: NEITHER CLOAK NOR DAGGER

> The only U.S. forces involved in Laos are the air. We have no com-
> bat forces stationed there. And I personally feel that although the
> way the operation has been run is unorthodox, unprecedented, as I
> said, in many ways I think it is something of which we can be proud
> as Americans. It has involved virtually no American casualties.
> What we are getting for our money there, as the Ambassador said,
> is, I think, to use the old phrase, very cost effective. . . .
>
> —U. Alexis Johnson, former Under Secretary
> of State, Senate Armed Services Hearings,
> July 22, 1971, p. 4289

For anyone who lived in Laos and saw firsthand what CIA operations
led to, much of the current debate over the CIA has something of an
Alice-in-Wonderland quality. The issue of what the CIA has become,
for example, is often conceptualized as involving a choice between its
"intelligence" and "covert action" activities. The CIA must be allowed
to continue its covert actions, but they should be brought under more
effective control, the most moderate critics say; the answer is separating
the CIA's intelligence-gathering and covert actions, other critics respond. The CIA should revert entirely to an intelligence-gathering
organization, with its covert-action arm entirely removed, say stronger
critics.

The term "covert actions," however, conjures up small-unit activities,
from such rather innocuous actions like bugging Soviet embassies to
more controversial activities such as periodic assassinations of political
figures or sabotage.

The CIA in Laos began organizing the Meo in the late 1950s. By the
summer of 1961, Edward Lansdale could report to Maxwell Taylor that
"about 9000 Meo tribesmen have been equipped for guerrilla operations, which they are now conducting. . . . Command control of Meo
operations is exercised by the Chief CIA Vientiane with the advice of
Chief MAAG Laos."

The Meo then, and now, have had a unique courting system. Young
men and women of marriageable age will stand in a group throughout
the day, throwing a ball back and forth, talking, watching each other,
seeing how a prospective partner handles setbacks, achievements, sad-
ness, and joy. It is a graceful, happy custom, one which has delighted
foreigners for generations. By the mid-1960s, however, few men were

left to be matched with the young women. The male side had to be filled up by young boys, often ten years old or younger. It was not uncommon during this period for boys any older to be already fighting in the CIA's "Secret Army."

One can argue indefinitely over the responsibility for this state of affairs, blaming the Communists or Americans, the CIA or North Vietnamese. What one cannot assume, however, is that the terms "intelligence-gathering" or "covert activities" apply to a CIA that, by the early 1970s, was directing a Laotian war which had led to the decimation of whole peoples, which involved a military force of over one hundred thousand men, and in which were dropped over two million tons of bombs, as much as had been loosed on all Europe and the Pacific theatre in World War II (see Tables 1 and 2 on pages 77 and 78).

There are those who argue that the CIA's warmaking role in Laos was exceptional, one reluctantly engaged in under orders of a series of U.S. Presidents. Our own information indicates that this is untrue, that the CIA quite enthusiastically moved into Laos. Too many well-informed sources, for example, have described scenes such as that of high-ranking CIA personnel in Washington bitterly criticizing Pentagon activities in Vietnam at Georgetown cocktail parties, while proudly describing the CIA success story in Laos. The notion of a CIA righteously obeying its Presidential orders, albeit reluctantly, is also contradicted by too many reports like that of one CIA operative who told us of his superior bragging that "we tell the White House what we want it to know," shortly after he had joined the Agency.

The growing literature on CIA activities around the globe, moreover, clearly indicates that Laos was hardly the only country where the CIA acted as a military force. CIA-controlled forces in Laos alone, for example, were an integral part of the much larger Secret Army, including KMT and irregular Thai forces in Thailand, Shan tribes in Burma, irregular units in Cambodia, and what was once a force of Montagnards, ethnic Cambodians, Vietnamese, and Nung, totaling at least forty-five thousand in South Vietnam. This enormous force recognized no national borders or sovereign governments and was responsible only to its CIA paymasters.

Given the information that emerges daily about CIA involvement from Indonesia to Zaire to Iran, it seems clear that Laos is the epitome of what the CIA has become, not an exception.

For the purposes of this discussion, however, such debates may be put to the side. For, at the very least, Laos conclusively demonstrates that the CIA today has the *capacity* to wage full-scale war anywhere in the world. Whatever degree of control is exercised over it by an American President, the most basic question becomes this: Should any American President have at his disposal a clandestine military force allowing him to wage war in foreign lands without the real knowledge or consent of the American people and Congress?

Laos also raises the most basic questions about the CIA's intelligence-gathering and covert-action activities. The Pentagon Papers, for example, were widely interpreted as making the CIA look good through its relatively realistic assessments of the weaknesses of American bombing and the like. (Although a strong case can be made that this is not an accurate assessment of CIA intelligence activities in Vietnam.) What has not been stressed enough, however, is that the Pentagon Papers contain only selected CIA intelligence assessments regarding Vietnam, where the CIA is known to have been bureaucratically opposed to Pentagon involvement.

What did CIA intelligence reports have to say about Laos, where the CIA was in charge? Informed sources say categorically that CIA intelligence reports on Laos were consistently misleading on CIA failures in that country, and that any criticisms that did emerge were in any event almost totally ignored by CIA operatives waging the war.

The CIA's evolution into a major military force in Laos raises far more basic questions, going to the very heart of our society. Consideration of CIA activities in Laos shows the following:

1. The CIA demonstrated the capacity to deceive public and congressional opinion consistently, both through secrecy and "disinformation" about embarrassing facts that leaked out.

2. The CIA evolved into a major warmaking body in Laos, with almost all its budget and personnel devoted to war, not intelligence or covert activities. (What intelligence was gathered was usually meant for military ends.)

3. Far from serving as an effective warmaking body, the CIA in Laos had a record of consistent failure by any rational measurement. This derived in part from its clandestine nature, demanding that it try to wage a war through other "overt" bureaucracies that represented their own interests. The CIA served the American interest badly in Laos, and only its secrecy allowed it to continue its wasteful, bungling operations.

4. The CIA in Laos was composed of a foreign expeditionary corps

of Americans who regularly engaged in activities that many Americans would find repugnant to their most basic moral beliefs.

5. The only possible means that Congress and the American people have of controlling CIA warmaking abroad is massive, across-the-board budget cuts, accompanied by far more serious congressional review than is presently occurring. Such budget cuts might take place both in terms of the CIA's own budget presentation, and in terms of such countries where CIA military involvement is known to be heavy. Congress could carry out budget cuts of seventy to eighty per cent in these areas without affecting the CIA's ability to either gather intelligence or engage in activities related to gathering intelligence necessary for this nation's defense.

Considered in the abstract, such conclusions often seem unfair or overly cynical to some. When one comes to truly understand and confront the meaning of CIA activities in Laos over the past decade, however, these conclusions seem quite tame.

The leaders of this country have taken unknown billions of dollars, dollars that could have been used to help the sick at home and feed the hungry abroad, and spent them instead on bringing massive death and destruction to a tiny corner of the earth that many Americans today still have not heard of.

And there really was a CIA in Laos which directed this war, a CIA unfettered in practice by public or congressional constraint, a CIA which became in reality the President's private, secret army. One can approve of such a CIA, if one must. But one cannot deny its having existed or the importance of the questions it raises.

No people in history has seen its rulers create their own secret-army organizations abroad without one day coming to rue it at home. And for many of us, the real question is not so much assessing the magnitude of the clear and present danger posed by the CIA, as it is devising the means to control it.

CIA COMMAND CONTROL OF THE PRESIDENT'S SECRET ARMY

SENATOR SYMINGTON: . . . This war is being conducted by the CIA for the State Department. . . .

AMBASSADOR GODLEY: . . . My personal view of the CIA role in Laos [is that] I am convinced that they are rendering a great service to our government, particularly the men involved.

You have less than [deleted] CIA men in Laos today and they are assisting and covering and supplying equipment for protecting our dollars and the force that numbers roughly 30,000 men. . . .

They have, for example, in Laos men [deleted] who speak the language, who know the terrain like the palm of their hand, and who do what I consider to be an outstanding job. . . .

—*Senate Armed Services Hearings,*
July 22 1971, pp. 4276, 4279

To hear some executive officials describe CIA men in Laos, one would think them to have been a few dozen miracle men combining the qualities of Tom Dooley and Frank Merriwell to help the thirty thousand guerrillas with whom they communicated in flawless native dialects. It is striking, however, that an entirely different picture emerges from interviews with sources who knew these CIA men, particularly some of its top leaders.

Pat Landry, for example, the powerful man who ran numerous CIA activities out of Udorn, was described thus by a reliable source whose other descriptions of individuals to me have always proven accurate: "The guy that's running the show in Laos, Landry, is an ex-Cincinnati cop, a police captain. Nobody even knows this guy exists. He's got steely blue eyes, big and hard. He carries a riding crop, and he scares everybody. I was in Vientiane a couple of months ago, talking to a key pilot with Air America. And *he* used to drink with Landry every night."

Ted Schackley, CIA station chief in Laos from July 1966 to December 1968, also evokes strong feelings in people. A CIA agent who served under him gets edgy in his chair as Schackley's name is mentioned. "Oh, man, was Schackley *weird*. Tall, thin, real tall. And cold, man, real cold. Calm, quiet, he just kind of looked at you in this weird way. And real white skin, real white." "White skin?" the listener asked. The answer came back softly, "He never went out in the sun, man, he never went out in the sun."

Lawrence Devlin, Schackley's successor in Laos from August 1968 to December 1970, had previously served with U.S. Ambassador Godley in the Congo during a period of heavy CIA involvement in that nation as well. A former CIA executive wrote: "Schackley has since been succeeded by Larry Devlin, former chief of station in the Belgian Congo, where, when things grew quiet, he once dropped everything for a clandestine foray in the French Congo in hopes of tracking down Che Guevara. These are the kind of men who have led the CIA in Laos, where the CIA has led the American nation into another humiliating, inextricable, international dilemma."

Devlin's successor, Hugh Tovar, who served in Laos from October 1970 through 1972, does not seem to touch off the same sparks at the mention of his name. A family friend, for example, described him as an upright man, a good Catholic, if somewhat dismayed at the spectacle of nude swimming at his daughter's dormitory at Radcliffe. The same CIA man who was so upset with Schackley and Devlin described Tovar as "a very intelligent and smooth individual, not at all like Devlin and Schackley."

Tovar, on the other hand, is hardly your Frank Merriwell type either. One of his posts before coming to Laos was serving as CIA station chief at the time of the Indonesia coup against Sukarno and the subsequent massacre of hundreds of thousands. He had also worked on the "covert-action staff at CIA headquarters in Washington, a group that specializes in propaganda, psychological warfare, the penetration and manipulation of student and labor groups, and so forth. Characterized as "very sophisticated and clever," he is said to have been the head of this section at Langley.

This, then, is how the men who ran the President's Secret Army in Laos are described. These descriptions are important precisely because so little is known publicly about these powerful men who consumed so much of our treasure and national effort.

Describing CIA Secret Army generals in Laos, one realized quickly that one of the greatest sources of their power was that they were accountable to no one in theory but one man, the President. One of the most important checks on the power of the United States Army, after all, is that its leaders and actions are relatively exposed. A Westmoreland knows he must justify his actions publicly and, if he fails, must pay the consequences.

A CIA Secret Army, whose leaders are unknown, as are its true costs, its many Tet-like failures, and its ever-increasing escalations, is subject to few such constraints. As long as a President stands ready to provide it with the necessary funding, personnel, and, above all, bureaucratic primacy among other American organizations, an organization like the CIA Secret Army can continue indefinitely, checked only by final battlefield disaster.

This lack of public accountability was one of the most important factors that contributed to the evolution of the CIA from a rather small intelligence-gathering agency into a secret army organization in Laos.

An Executive Mandate

> Don't do anything you know doesn't come from us. I don't care
> what Seventh Air Force wants . . . they aren't running the show up
> here. We take our orders directly from the President.
> —CIA Station Chief to Air Attaché,
> *Laotian Fragments*, p. 64*

Few Americans have ever even thought of the CIA as an actual army, complete with tens of thousands of foot soldiers, air power, and logistics command. One reason is that the CIA has a relatively small number of known direct-hire employees. Marks and Marchetti, for example, estimate that full-time CIA employees number only about 16,500, with only some 11,300 involved in clandestine services and back-up. Such figures are relatively tiny compared to the two and a half million Pentagon employees. How did so tiny an organization go about the business of actually waging a massive covert war?

Part of the answer is, according to Fletcher Prouty, that the CIA actually employs a far higher number of personnel. Prouty, whose job from 1953 to 1963 included the creation of Air Force covers for thousands of CIA employees, argues that numerous CIA personnel are planted in every government agency, although they are often unknown to their own co-workers. He points out, for example, that he maintained on his books 605 separate army units alone, involving some four thousand men, who appeared to the outside world as military men but were actually directly working for and paid by the CIA.

In addition, of course, the CIA also employs on contract tens of thousands more U.S. personnel, either through proprietary companies or its own operations. As a result of being given the authority to run the war in a place like Laos, it has also acquired the right to call upon the services of a wide variety of Americans whose salaries were actually being paid by other U.S. organizations; and, most important, its lavish funding allowed it to hire tens of thousands of foreign mercenaries, even rent whole tribes.

Although it has been common to speak of a "few dozen" CIA men who ran the war in Laos, for example, the truth is that the CIA on a

---

* *Laotian Fragments* (New York: The Viking Press, 1974) is a book about the United States Mission in Laos, written by John Pratt, a U.S. Air Force officer who was head of an Air Force historical project known as Project Checo at Udorn Air Force Base during 1969 and 1970. During this period Major Pratt had occasion to visit Laos frequently. His book, though technically a novel, gives a picture of the American mission remarkably similar to that given by sources interviewed by the author of this paper.

typical day in 1971 had direct control of over two thousand Americans and forty-five thousand Asians fighting the war within Laos; could call upon another sixty-five thousand Americans and Asians in Laos indirectly involved in the war; and was supported by another fifty thousand Americans outside Laos, mostly involved in the air war, who were directly and fully involved in waging war against Laos (see Table 2).

Bureaucratically, the key factor in allowing this structure to be built up was a Presidential decision to turn the war over to the CIA in Laos. When President Kennedy decided that the CIA would be the major warmaking body in Laos after July 1962, he also permitted a structure to be set up to allow it to do so.

The CIA was set up as the command control center for the American war effort in Laos. In addition to being allowed to fund sufficient installations and personnel of its own, the following decisions were also made:

1. The CIA would fund directly an irregular ground force of hill-tribes people and others; this force would, in turn be on the front lines and be expected to bear the brunt of the fighting.

2. The CIA would be given direct control over a number of key organizations, allowing it to provide *air transport* (Air America, later Continental Airlines also), *bombing, and other air services.*

3. Above all, the CIA would be in operational control of Army (ARMA) and Air Attache (AIRA) offices established in Laos.

The Company (CIA) over All

Officially, the CIA was just one of several equal agencies operating under an all-powerful United States ambassador. It was necessary to set up a formal structure that had the U.S. ambassador running U.S. activities in Laos because of the political desire to give the overt appearance of adhering to the Geneva Accords (thereby allowing the Kennedy administration to reap the political benefit of having made peace, as well), and the bureaucratic wish to have a CIA wage war free of public accountability.

In Laos the CIA became the controlling agency of the American side of the war. Beginning small, the total number of people involved in Laos had grown to some one hundred thousand on an average day in 1971 (see Table 2). This force, which included two thousand Americans in or over Laos, was directed by the CIA "Command Control" structure described in this section.

In general, we use the term "CIA Secret Army" to refer to this entire force of one hundred thousand, which includes U.S. Air Force units, in addition to irregular forces on the direct payroll of the CIA. We do this because one of the most important things about the CIA in Laos is that by 1968, at the latest, U.S. Air Force bombing had become the key aspect of its war, a *sine qua non* without which its troops would often not move.

The CIA and the American Embassy

During January and February 1966 I was engaged in trail-watching on the Ho Chi Minh Trail. We were flown in, under direction of the CIA. Our only contact was with a CIA guy. All we knew was that his name is Al. . . . While in Northern Laos later we were also under the jurisdiction of the CIA. . . . The CIA had a very powerful position out there. Many of the military deferred to the CIA. In general, everyone had a lot of respect for them, thought they really knew what they were doing.

—Former Green Beret who fought in
Laos, 1965–1967 (interview)

It's the CIA who makes policy at Long Cheng—and in Laos. The embassy political section doesn't do anything. They don't have any real power.

—USAID Official, Laos (interview)

The CIA waged war in Laos through its dozens of operatives deployed at all key strategic points on the front lines. As a result, almost all information about activities behind Pathet Lao lines came from the CIA; CIA personnel were in charge of planning ground actions and coordinating air support and logistics for them; military personnel under AIRA and ARMA were given operational tasks involving implementation and technical backstopping of strategy.

If the ambassador or his staff needed to know something, they generally went to the CIA, which had the most up-to-date information available.

The only State Department employee on the ambassador's immediate staff who had a formal military role was the U.S. embassy "bombing officer." In principle, he was in charge of okaying all proffered targets put forward to him for strike from CIA, AIRA, or Seventh Air Force sources. In practice, however, this job was relatively meaningless. For one thing, the State Department official handling it generally had no knowledge in the field.

More important, however, former bombing officers have revealed that the job was virtually impossible. Targets were presented for approval identified only by their coordinates, sometimes dozens daily. It was simply impossible to request each target folder, look at the reconnaissance photos with the untrained eye, and come up with rational reasons for approving or rejecting each target. The CIA, by contrast, had gradually built up its own team of twelve to fifteen highly paid and highly professional photo interpreters at Udorn.

All this insured that the CIA had a major say in determining what targets would be proffered to the embassy, more than holding its own with Seventh Air Force and AIRA experts. By contrast, the inexperienced Foreign Service officer serving as the sole U.S. embassy "bombing officer" was little more than a rubber stamp.

As far as is known, CIA officials within Laos and the U.S. ambassadors there were of a like mind on all major issues. Informed sources suggest that, given the fact that the executive had charged the CIA with fighting the war, it would also consult the CIA before assigning any new ambassador to Laos. And from any vantage point, it would certainly seem pointless for a President to assign an ambassador to a country like Laos who was likely to start a major fight with the President's Secret Army.

Tony Poe: Field Commander in the President's Secret Army

> Now the old special forces, marine paratroopers, OSS-types—World War II types—they're getting old and they're pretty well beaten up and there just aren't that many coming along to take their place. . . . They've got some real legends, old Tony Poe in Laos for example. He's a great guy, who I really respect. But I'm not sure how he can justify the slaughter of the Meo tribe and love them as much as he does. Maybe it's about time Tony should get out of it.
>
> —Former U.S. agent in Laos (interview)

Tony Poe is a legendary CIA agent in Southeast Asia. A tall, rawboned man now about fifty, it is said that Poe was among the Marines at Iwo Jima in World War II. His subsequent top-secret exploits for the CIA are said to have included training Tibetans in the mountains of Colorado to wage war in China during the 1950s, whereupon he wound up in Laos. The late 1950s and early 1960s saw him set up the Meo as the nucleus of the CIA Secret Army. Known for his heavy drinking, Poe's ability to move on the ground in the remotest parts of Laos for months at a time, his numerous escapes from death, and a fanatic anti-Communism made him an object of awe and fear alike throughout northern Laos.

After setting up the Meo operation, Poe got disgusted with the vast influx of Americans into Long Cheng in the mid-1960s, it is said. He then moved to northwestern Laos, where he ran all western operations for the next five to six years.

To carry out his military duties, Poe had at his direct disposal during this period: seven or eight Americans funded by the CIA, mostly former U.S. Green Berets; dozens of CIA-trained Thai special forces known officially as PARU (Police Aerial Resupply Unit), based at Xieng Lom; full aerial support from Air America and Continental aircraft, used for everything from transporting troops to spotting for bombers to dropping grenades themselves on villages, particularly in the early years; Royal Thai and Royal Laos Air Force aircraft operating out of Houei Sai, as well as U.S. Air Force bombers; hundreds, possibly thousands, of Lao Theung and Yao tribesmen organized into village-based fighting units.

In addition, for the civilian side of his operations—including caring for troops, their dependents, and refugees—Poe could count on the support of several dozen other Americans in the region, ranging from the U.S. Agency for International Development (USAID) officials to International Voluntary Services (IVS) volunteers to Dooley Foundation medical personnel (although the Dooley hospital was notorious for being without medicine, and most sick or wounded were sent to the Chieng Rai hospital in Thailand).

They tell dozens of stories about Tony Poe: the time he was supporting Burmese insurgents while the U.S. military was supporting the Burmese government; the time he carried a wounded Laotian officer on his back for dozens of miles to safety, despite the fact that he was seriously wounded himself, the time he started offering a bounty for enemy ears, which could be deposited by his local troops in a big plastic bag hanging on his porch—and how he had to discontinue the practice when he found that his "boys" were getting "too ambitious" for the money, killing people needlessly.

Such agents as Tony Poe were the key to the CIA's operations in Laos, so key in fact that they often operated within their own areas like local warlords of old. For they were the field commanders, in charge of waging the CIA's war on a daily basis.

CIA direct-hire personnel like Poe formed the nucleus of the Secret

Army, from which radiated the numerous branches necessary for modern war.

In visualizing the structure of the CIA Secret Army in Laos it is useful to imagine three concentric rings. The smallest, in the center, was composed of the CIA itself. Its heart was in Thailand, with CIA stations inside Laos being forward command posts. The second ring was key CIA-controlled organizations in USAID, the Air Force, and such private companies as Air America, which are under direct CIA control. The third ring was a wide variety of other American and Asian units, which were directly involved in supporting CIA Secret Army activities on a daily basis. Outside this three-ring structure was a wide variety of other supporting organizations and personnel, serving as a technical and human pool from which the CIA could draw.

CIA Secret Army Organization: The Inner Circle

The CIA's regional office in Bangkok, Thailand, was in over-all charge of CIA activities in Laos, which must, of course, be conceived of on a *regional* basis.

For fighting the war in Laos demanded a logistic chain going from Thailand into Laos and involved recruiting Thai to fight in Laos, and training both Lao and Thai in Thailand; and numerous units used in Laos also found themselves militarily engaged in other countries as well. Thai special forces not only fought in their own war in Thailand, but were also sent into Laos and Cambodia.

The most important CIA installation for Laos operating under the Bangkok regional office, however, was the 4802nd Joint Liaison Detachment, which functioned as the operational command post for the CIA Secret Army in Laos. Headed by Pat Landry, the 4802nd JLD operated out of a large compound at Udorn Air Force base in Thailand. It was the command post to which CIA operatives like Tony Poe in Laos reported.

The CIA station in Vientiane, Laos, was a large one. Hugh Tovar (and his predecessors, Larry Devlin and Ted Schackley) worked out of the second floor of the American embassy in Vientiane. The exact division of duties between the CIA station chief in Vientiane and in Udorn is not known. The CIA station chief in Vientiane also had his own targeting officer for representing the CIA in targeting discussions, and was also known to play a direct role in planning military strategy, with representatives from CIA-Vientiane frequently visiting other CIA stations around the country.

In addition, there were a series of CIA installations in each of Laos's other four military regions.

The principal task of CIA men in Laos was serving as field commanders for Secret Army operations in their area of control. Over-all CIA responsibilities included planning and directing offensive and defensive military actions by Secret Army troops in the area, insuring an adequate supply of military and nonmilitary supplies, coordinating air strikes and aerial troop deployments, arranging for payment, recruitment, and training of all troops.

In addition, CIA personnel in Laos engaged in a wide variety of other military tasks.

On occasion, for example, CIA men would direct large numbers of bombing strikes for specific purposes other than supporting their own ground troops. One such incident occurred when CIA personnel ordered and supervised "shock" bombing operations on the Ho Chi Minh Trail. A shock bombing area was about thirty miles in length and would be subjected to roughly two hundred air strikes a day, for seven or eight days at a time. Such shock operations were generally run out of the Boloven Plateau sites at the beginning of the dry season, in an attempt to slow down truck traffic along the Trail into South Vietnam.

CIA personnel were also in charge of certain key sites in Laos, known as TACAN sites, which gave off signals to help American bombers fix their location while in Laos. The other key military task played by CIA personnel in Laos besides directing the Secret Army was conducting entirely separate small-unit and top-secret operations behind Pathet Lao lines, often going into North Vietnam as well.

In addition to engaging in missions themselves, CIA personnel are also known to have supervised the insertion of purely Asian teams behind enemy lines for spying, sabotage, or assassination. It is widely assumed, for example, that Prince Souphanouvong's son, Prince Ariya, was assassinated by such a team.

The "inner circle" of CIA personnel involved in directing the war in Laos, then, included people working out of the Bangkok Regional office in Thailand, the 4802nd Joint Liaison detachment, also in Thailand, the CIA station chief Vientiane's office and a half-dozen major CIA stations in Laos, and special stations located in South Vietnam.

Such people would not be identified in public and never be known at all except through word of mouth; they would not be listed in a U.S. embassy or USAID telephone book (with the exception of the Bangkok and Vientiane station chiefs, designated as "Special Assistants" in Bangkok, or "Political Officers" in Vientiane). The total number of such personnel is hard to estimate, but given the scope and magnitude of their operations, we would put the number at one to two hundred, with a majority operating out of Thailand.

THE CIA AND NATIONAL SECURITY

Speer is, in a sense, more important for Germany today than Hitler, Himmler, Goering, Goebbels, or the generals. . . . Speer is very much the successful average man, well-dressed, civil, non-corrupt, very middle class in his style of life, with a wife and six children.

Much less than any of the other German leaders does he stand for anything particularly German or particularly Nazi.

He rather symbolizes a type which is becoming increasingly important in all belligerent countries: the pure technician, the classless, bright young man, without background, with no other original aim than to make his way in the world, and no other means than his technical and managerial ability.

It is the lack of psychological and spiritual ballast and the ease with which he handles the terrifying technical and organizational machinery of our age which makes this slight type go extremely far nowaday.

This is their age.

The Hitlers and Himmlers we may get rid of, but the Speers, whatever happens to this particular special man, will long be with us.

—Editorial, *London Observer*, April 9, 1944 (excerpts)

Bill Colby . . . is a lawyer by training. He looks like a lawyer, also like a teacher, a minister, a banker, a doctor, anything except what he is—the nation's chief spooksman who for years was deputy director of the CIA's "black operations" directorate. . . .

He was born . . . the only child of . . . an Army officer. . . . The most controversial segment of William Colby's intelligence career concerns his involvement in . . . the operation code-named Phoenix. . . . Phoenix . . . involved the capture, imprisonment, defection and murder of the Vietcong. There were abuses . . . as Colby conceded. . . . But there are excesses in all wars and it seems manifestly unfair to brand Colby "a mass murderer and war criminal." . . . No one ever called him such names in World War II when he was killing Germans. . . .

A practicing Roman Catholic, a pillar in community affairs, a hard-working civil servant who earns $42,000 a year, a good and understanding father to his four surviving children . . . a loving and dutiful husband, William Colby . . . could be earning three times in civilian life what he earns in government service.

"But it wouldn't give me the satisfaction," he says, "that I find in this job."

—Lloyd Shearer, "William Colby, New Director of the CIA: He's Changing the Agency's Image," *Parade* magazine, July 21, 1974 (excerpts)

We have seen, then, that the CIA functioned as the President's Secret Army in Laos for over a decade. By the early 1970s there were one hundred thousand persons directly involved in the CIA's Secret Army war effort, and another sixty-five thousand persons indirectly supporting it. This effort was possible only because Congress and the American people were deliberately deceived, which left the CIA without any public mandate for its activities and in practice accountable to no one but the President.

The essential fact demonstrated by this experience is that *one man,* the President of the United States, can unilaterally use the CIA today to wage secret war anywhere in the world. This fact alone makes it clear that discussing the lessons of the CIA Secret Army in Laos is no mere historical exercise.

The fact is that CIA actions in Laos bore directly on the present and future of this nation in a way that few of our other foreign adventures do. For although U.S. military involvement in Vietnam is widely regarded as a failure in executive circles, CIA involvement in Laos is even today still regarded as a success. As such, the story of the CIA in Laos has become a kind of mirror whose reflection tells us much about the behavior and values of our leaders. Indeed, it can be argued that the CIA in Laos became a kind of archetype for some of the central political phenomena of our day, governmental developments that affect the life of every American almost as much as they have every Laotian.

Had more of us looked more closely and honestly at what Presidential actions in Vietnam told us about executive value systems, for example, the American public might have been better prepared for Watergate. Indeed, Watergate might have been prevented. Or, for another example, we might today look more closely at what executive leaders like Mr. Colby brought to Vietnam: the issuing of ID cards linked to computerized bio-dossiers to all Vietnamese over the age of fifteen; the establishment of a nationwide system of surveillance through informers and a U.S.-created police force that grew from ten thousand in 1961 to one hundred and twenty thousand in 1974; Mr. Colby's practice of setting quotás on the number of Vietnamese civilians to be assassinated or arrested per month per district, a decision that resulted in tens of thousands of murders under Operation Phoenix; the setting up of special "administrative detention" procedures whereby special "Councils" imprisoned tens of thousands without benefit of trial or representation by lawyers but solely on the basis of police dossiers prepared after brutal tortures on all those picked up in mass roundups of men, women, and children, often in postcurfew raids in the dead of night.

For if we could understand that Vietnam was just America writ large, that the mind-set exhibited by executive leaders in Vietnam was the same mind-set they brought to solving problems at home, not only might we be better prepared for understanding the growing "privacy invasion" in this country—the data banks, the surveillance, the wiretapping, the use of informers—but we might have an alerted American citizenry far more ready to combat such a threat than is at present the case.

We will not dwell at length on the moral question here. It is clear to all who care that the human costs of the CIA Secret Army effort in Laos were a monstrous affront to the conscience of humanity: massive bombing of civilian centers and a deliberate strategy of sending in ground sweeps afterward to take out the survivors, killing and wounding tens of thousands and wiping whole Laotian societies off the face of the earth; an estimated one million refugees generated; whole tribes fighting for the CIA, like the Meo and numerous Lao Theung tribal groupings, decimated as the CIA forced them to continue fighting long after they wished to stop.

For although the immorality of the CIA is widely understood, it is often rationalized or passed over on grounds of "national security." Since the CIA is working in the national interest, it is felt, its excesses are understandable—if distasteful.

If there is any one major question posed by the CIA Secret Army experience in Laos, however, it is whether the CIA indeed helps national security.

We have come to believe not only that the CIA in Laos made no contribution whatever to national security, but that in many ways its behavior in Laos and elsewhere reached the point where the CIA, rather than protecting the nation's interests, itself became one of the major threats to our long-term national security.

Lesson Number One: The Human Dimension

SENATOR HUGHES: Published reports also give you a key policy role in decisions to involve the U.S. in clandestine operations in Laos in the late 1950s and early 1960s—operations which grew into a secret, CIA-run war.

On reflection, do you believe it was wise for the Agency to get involved in such military operations? . . . Where should the line be drawn between CIA and Defense Department activities involving the use of armed force?

MR. COLBY: . . . Despite the difficulties for CIA [in Laos], I submit the Agency fulfilled the charge given it efficiently and effectively. . . . In general, the line should be drawn . . . at the point in which the U.S. acknowledges involvement in such activities. . . .

Any activity which could be construed as interfering in the internal affairs of other nations . . . are only conducted under specific direction of the National Security Council. With this approach, it would be unlikely that the CIA would play a role of this nature in any nation whose policies pose no conceivable threat to U.S. interests.

—Senate Armed Services Hearings,
Nomination of William E. Colby,
July 2, 1973, pp. 28, 29

When William Colby, the Director of the CIA, told the Senate during his confirmation hearings that the CIA was justified in interfering in the internal affairs of other nations if ordered to by the National Security Council, that the NSC had the right to give such an order if it determined that another nation posed a "conceivable threat to U.S. interests," and that the point at which the CIA should not engage in military activities was when the United States wished to "acknowledge" military involvement, he was revealing the mind-set of today's CIA.

Particularly revealing was his response to Senator Hughes' question of whether it was "wise" for the CIA to get involved in the war in Laos. For Mr. Colby, it was enough that the CIA had been ordered to by the NSC. The only point he had to add was that once under orders the CIA had performed its task "efficiently" and "effectively."

For if there is any one lesson that CIA involvement in Laos taught, it is that this attitude characterized the vast majority of CIA personnel in Laos.

When I went out to Laos, I assumed that the CIA there was made up

primarily of people—right-wing, adventuristic, violence-prone, courageous, tough ideologues.

As time went on, however, and I began to ask around, an entirely
different picture began to form.

Shortly after my arrival, for example, Tony Babb, a USAID com-
munity-development official gave me a ride out to a village in southern
Laos. Babb had worked with the NSA international affairs section in its
CIA-funded heyday and was later to work with the McGovern campaign
on his return from Laos. What kind of guys were they (the CIA officials),
I asked him. "Oh, not too different from anyone else," he responded.
What motives did they have? "You'd be surprised how many of them are
in it for the money."

The comment was typical. An Air America employee, for example;
once explained, "The CIA is just like anything else. There are a number
of benefits over here, and while there are some rough things about it, all
in all it's an appealing kind of life: the power it gives you, the money
you make. I'd say that none of the CIA guys make less than twenty
grand a year; they also get Air America travel benefits, PX privileges,
good vacation time, and time-off programs."

Criticism about the kind of job most of the CIA men were doing was
constant. The overwhelming consensus was that few were motivated by
ideals, that they just put in a day's work. "The CIA is no good. Most of
the guys in it are very stupid and lazy. They just don't want to get out
there and do the job the way it should be done. That's why we can't
win," was the way one USAID official who had worked with them for
years put it.

It became clear that although the Tony Poes, the Schackleys, the true
believers still existed, they were a dying breed. Instead they had been
replaced by a new kind of CIA man—a Hugh Tovar, a Vince Shields.

There is no mystery where this kind of mentality developed, of
course. This new CIA man was little different in personality from a
major personality type of twentieth-century America: the technicians
and bureaucrats who build our space ships, design our automobiles, run
our computers, staff our government agencies.

It is no coincidence that *Parade* magazine found William Colby a
perfectly normal gentleman: civil, pleasant, friendly, hard-working. He
no doubt is.

What must be noted also, however, is that these new men of the CIA
were not simply designing automobiles. They were waging war, engaged
in attempts to control the political behavior of whole populations, and

this fact changes the nature of war as we know it. Two major implications can be seen by looking at the war in Laos.

The first is the degree to which this new CIA man became part of an insulated, technocratic elite, isolated from many of the normal crosscurrents of popular opinion.

During the Vietnam war, for example, the United States Army in Vietnam, made up largely of conscripts, came to mirror many of the dominant popular values of the time. Peace signs, long hair, and pot began sprouting up. American troops began writing letters home to their parents about their disillusionment with the war, often with devastating effect. And hundreds of thousands of American GIs returned home from Vietnam very different men from when they had left—adopting a new life style and new values, determined never to become "part of the machine" again.

It is no coincidence, however, that in all those years of CIA warmaking in every corner of the globe there was not one CIA field warrior who went public with his story, let alone began active political organizing against the war or the CIA. The story of the CIA in Laos makes it clear why: the older, right-wing ideologues became, if anything, more committed with age; the younger majority—volunteers, largely in it for the money, isolated from contact with the outside world by the need for secrecy, protecting their identity, serving in an organization which rarely emphasizes any kind of values, enjoying a high degree of personal power—had no reason to "go public," and plenty of reasons not to.

The second consequence of warmaking by this new breed of CIA men was the degree to which technical solutions to human problems were sought, the manner in which human beings were reduced to objects to be bought if possible, physically controlled or eliminated if not.

The CIA in Laos, for example, successively recruited Meo, Yao, numerous Lao Theung groups in north and south Laos, lowland Lao, and then, most seriously, Thai, to fight in Laos. In virtually every case, moreover, the CIA manipulated the people in question—originally getting them involved through money and/or the threat or use of force and/or promises of independent kingdoms which it had no intention of fulfilling, and then keeping them fighting long beyond the point when they wished to stop.

When this ground strategy failed, the CIA continually pushed for increased bombing—bombing that, for whatever reason, resulted in heavy strikes against population centers.

After taking the Plain of Jars in September 1969, the CIA decided first to resettle its former inhabitants in two strategic hamlets there—either because it did not expect a counteroffensive or because it hoped that this would deter one. When the counteroffensive started anyway, a new strategy was decided upon: the people would be eliminated to clear the way for massive B-52 strikes. Tens of thousands were flown to Vientiane and a once-ancient society of fifty thousand no longer existed.

From these and other examples, the point perhaps is clear: the behavior of the CIA in Laos reveals that it became a largely professional, apolitical, amoral, technically oriented force of mercenaries who waged war as a technical exercise, were largely impervious to public opinion, and were obedient to orders from above.

It is not necessary, one hopes, to spell out in detail why such a secret force was hardly a reassuring guardian of the national security. One may not choose to believe the well-known writer who, in response to this description of the CIA, explained that by chance a member of his church had been a high-ranking official in Phoenix. When some of his fellow churchgoers asked the man how he rated Phoenix, he responded that while it hadn't been a success in Vietnam, because of faulty intelligence, the important thing was the experience they had gotten for use back at home.

And one may not be alarmed at the systems analyst from Route 128 in Boston, whom I was interviewing about the air war in Laos, who asked me, "But why stick with the past? I mean, ten years from now you won't be interviewing Laotian peasants, you'll be interviewing ghetto dwellers in this country." He went on to explain that the same CIA-linked systems-analysis firms that had gotten the contracts for Vietnam in the early 1960s had switched their emphasis to the nation's major cities in the late 1960s. City councils and mayors, using money that had trickled down from "Great Society" programs, were hiring these same firms to advise them on urban problems. Just as these firms had seen the problem as isolating "the Vietcong terrorist" from the rest of society in Vietnam, he explained, they also saw the solution to the crime problem in the United States as isolating the urban criminal through surveillance, identification cards, or other programs. "Why, ten years from now, there'll be helicopters over every major city on a regular basis, TV cameras everywhere, computerized ID cards, the whole works!" he went on.

But Watergate has taught us nothing if we have not learned that *no* President can be trusted with his private secret police and military force, which he can count on to carry out his orders obediently, not subject to public knowledge let alone review, and that the members of such a police and military force are little more than apolitical, amoral technocrats and bureaucrats of murder makes the issue even more compelling.

There is no notion more grotesque or bizarre than one that holds that the present members of the CIA, men who are beyond the reach of public opinion, men who have shown the most callous disregard for human life and democratic values, should remain the most trusted guardians of the American national security, free to wage war as they wish once one man, a President, has given them the go-ahead. To suggest that our national security lies in the hands of such men is more than folly. It is to invite the loss of what remains of our democratic traditions.

Lesson Number Two: The Foreign Policy Dimension

SENATOR SMITH: Why (should) an operation be carried on in Laos under . . . the State Department through the Ambassador (deleted).

UNDER SECRETARY U. ALEXIS JOHNSON: Under the Geneva Agreements we were prohibited from having American military personnel in Laos and that is the brief answer. . . . *CIA is really the only other instrumentality that we have. . . .*

—*Senate Armed Services*, July 22, 1971, p. 4293 (emphasis added)

SENATOR SYMINGTON: If Congress wishes to limit CIA [to] intelligence collection, would it be necessary to redraft the 1947 Act?

MR. COLBY: . . . The interpretation of the Act to date is that it is a bit beyond pure intelligence. . . . It would be appropriate to leave the Act as it is. . . . The Agency might be fettered . . . by some broader proscription. . . . *I think the basic point is that the Agency overseas is going to follow U.S. policy.*

SENATOR HUGHES: . . . Do you believe it was wise for the Agency to get involved in such military operations [in Laos]?

MR. COLBY: *The Agency's activities in Laos were undertaken in direct response to Presidential and National Security Council direction in order to carry out U.S. policy. . . .*

—*Senate Armed Services Hearings*, July 2, 1973, pp. 20, 28 (emphasis added)

One of the central political phenomena of our time is the astounding increase in power on the part of the U.S. executive branch since the end of World War II. Due in part to a proliferation of technology controlled by federal agencies beyond the grasp of Congress, as well as an increasing concentration of capital, more and more power has been steadily moving into fewer and fewer hands.

For the past twenty-five years, also, the U.S. executive has consistently intervened in an attempt to put down revolutionary movements by guerrilla armies. There is no reason to doubt that this policy continues in force today, and that the executive continues to practice counterinsurgency from Thailand to the Philippines to wherever guerrilla movements exist.

There has been one basic change, however. Public and congressional opinion are strongly opposed to *open* U.S. intervention with American ground troops. Where, then, is an American executive committed to intervention but unable to use U.S. ground troops to turn?

The answer, as Laos teaches us, is the CIA.

William Colby, during his confirmation hearings, made it clear that he felt that the CIA had a mandate to carry out Laos-like activities (though he also made it clear that he felt the size had been too large) if ordered to by the National Security Council.

A close look at past actions in Laos, moreover, reveals the first basic foreign policy lesson of CIA experience there: the existence of a CIA with the capacity to act as a Secret Army greatly increases the possibilities of both executive intervention and executive warmaking.

It should thus be remembered that CIA military involvement in Laos did not begin with the July 1962 accords. It began earlier, in a fashion similar to CIA presence in dozens of other countries around the world: a few dozen agents, covertly assisting small armies organized along tribal, political, or gangland lines.

But, back in July 1962, it was *the very existence* of the CIA as a paramilitary body that was a major factor in the choice to continue American intervention in Laos. It was, again, the *only executive instrumentality*.

One can speculate on what might have happened had there been no CIA. One likely possibility is that a Pathet Lao–dominated coalition might have taken power and demanded a halt in the bombing of the Ho Chi Minh Trail. U.S. leaders might have ignored the request on the grounds that a Communist country was helping the Communist National Liberation Front and North Vietnamese—and kept on bombing. In this case, the situation in Laos would not have materially affected the outcome of the Vietnam war.

Even in the event that the U.S. war effort in Vietnam had been materially affected by a neutral or even pro–Pathet Lao Laos, the worst that could have happened is that American leaders might have felt forced to negotiate for an end to war far sooner—thereby saving unknown numbers of American and Asian lives without materially affecting the final outcome.

Wherever speculation of a United States without a CIA leads you, however, there is no possible alternative that could have been worse than what actually happened. For what Laos teaches is that not only does the CIA offer a major impetus to executive intervention abroad, but it offers a brand of intervention which is, sooner or later, doomed to failure.

The basic issue in Laos was, of course, political. In the end, that party which could command the greater popular support would win.

CIA involvement in Laos, however, was characterized by an original choice of corrupt, warlike leaders (such as General Vang Pao) and the encouragement of such individuals by giving them lavish sums of money without insisting on any kind of internal reform.

The fact that by 1968 the CIA Secret Army had been fundamentally defeated by the Pathet Lao, tells the tale. In the early years, the Pathet Lao could count on the support of the people for food and shelter in places where they were fighting. Later, when the U.S. policy of depopulating their zones was in full swing, the Pathet Lao could count on thousands of their supporters from the rear lines (for example, Sam Neua), to support the troops as porters toward the front line (for example, the Plain of Jars).

The CIA Secret Army, however, could not count on that kind of popular support. Its troops had to have vast American support—indeed, such American support itself often became a means of control over the population, as when a village that would not fight would not get rice drops—and, by 1968, simply would not move without it.

This political maladroitness, moreover, was the direct cause and genesis of the period of automated slaughter that followed. By November 1968 the U.S. executive and CIA had made a sizable commitment to the war in Laos. With their ground army in disarray, it was inevitable that they would turn to mechanized means to try and hold their positions, a bombing campaign that saw 1,700,000 tons of bombs fall on Laos by March 1973, almost fifty per cent of them in carpet-bombing B-52 raids.

CIA political failures were also at the root of the disastrous decision to import tens of thousands of Thais into Laos. This decision added nothing to CIA Secret Army ground capabilities, since the Thai were notoriously hopeless as soldiers in Laos, where they were purely mercenaries without a cause. It alienated and discredited most of the Royal Laotian Government (RLG) government leaders, who knew full well that the Thais were the oldest historic enemies of their country; demoralized Lao units on the front lines; and increased the Thai political and military stake in Laos. While perhaps this helped the CIA in the short term by gaining them their only real political support, it added tremendously to the long-term problem of ever finding a workable political solution to the war in Laos.

To the extent that a rational foreign policy contributes to national security, then, the experience of the CIA in Laos suggests that it is more of a hindrance than an asset to such national security. The paramilitary involvement of the CIA with corrupt elements in countries around the world at this very moment gives strong impetus for executive intervention should local pro-U.S. regimes in a country be threatened; and such intervention will, sooner or later, fail because of the CIA's proven inability to promote political reform and its proven capacity for encouraging and maintaining weak, unpopular, minority elements that cannot stand on their own.

In that hypothetical instance in which the U.S. executive found itself allied with a strong, popular, indigenous national government or movement, of course, there would be no need for a clandestine CIA. Such a government or movement would likely not need help or, if needed, such help could be given openly, since it would be opposed neither by most Americans nor by most local inhabitants of the country in question.

Lesson Number Three: The Bureaucratic Dimension

CHAIRMAN STENNIS: These operations that the CIA are conducting in Laos were not initiated by them. They were started originally by the then sitting President of the United States. . . . The CIA as presently operated has a good record and has handled the money appropriated in a fine way. . . . The more I get into this, the more I am impressed with the effectiveness and the great value of this operation.
—*Senate Armed Services*, July 22, 1971, pp. 4278, 4280

The notion that a "relatively unbureaucratic" CIA is "flexible" and "well-equipped" to fight a Laos-like war, advanced by persons ranging from writer Robert Shaplen to former Ambassador Godley to Senator Stennis, is a rather bizarre description of the CIA Secret Army.

The CIA's inability to field a motivated hill-tribe ground force to fight the Pathet Lao in Laos insured that it would have to enlarge both the Asian and American component of its forces.

This led to an unusually high degree of feuding within the Secret Army among Asians: Meo versus Lao Theung; Meo versus Lao; Thai versus Lao, Meo, and Lao Theung; it also created tremendous tensions between Americans and each Asian group just mentioned.

This weakness of the Asian component, moreover, made it inevitable that American involvement would have to be increased. Since the CIA's first need is secrecy, this meant that it could not integrate large numbers of Americans into it. Instead, the CIA would see added to its effort parts of other bureaucracies, like Army and Air Force Attachés, AID, International Voluntary Services, U.S. Information Service, and, above all, airmen of the U.S. Air Force, Marines, and Navy.

By attempting to wage war *through* such organizations, however, the CIA inevitably wound up in a situation that produced unnecessary bureaucratic rivalry, jealousy, and confusion. CIA secrecy, moreover, not only inflamed jealousies and rivalries within the U.S. Mission in Laos; it encouraged factionalism within the CIA itself, a kind of warlordism that saw each CIA station put its own interests first.

As a bureaucratic model, then, the CIA's one-hundred-thousand-strong Secret Army was characterized by bureaucratically produced factionalism, personal hatreds, lack of information, absence of coherent goals, both horizontally and vertically, between every component part.

What is even more striking is that there was a paucity of means to straighten out these bureaucratic problems—internally or externally. The major spur to bureaucratic efficiency, such as it is in today's sprawling technocracy, is the media—which, as we have seen, had no access to CIA activities. Congress's investigating arm, the General Accounting Office, was not allowed even to refer to CIA's bookkeeping for most of the war, let alone go out in the field and assess its efficiency.

Internally, there was little spur whatsoever to increase CIA effectiveness. The CIA, after all, was the dominant bureaucracy in Laos. Members of other bureaucracies found themselves being transferred out of Laos with alacrity for criticizing the CIA—if they were lucky. A U.S. ambassador who did not have the means of determining the real nature of targets the CIA was bombing, as we have seen, was hardly in a position to make any major overhaul in CIA performance—even if he were so inclined.

In fact, then, what American officials are talking about when they praise CIA "flexibility" in fighting a war is the flexibility it affords in hiding itself from public scrutiny. And yet this very secrecy is one of the major factors making the CIA so inefficient at running a war. The conflict of interest between the executive-branch bureaucrat and the American public was never so clear.

From the executive's point of view, a CIA bureaucracy that could maintain the public image of a Meo general, Vang Pao, as a courageous leader of a beleaguered people fighting a vicious enemy for more than a decade does indeed allow maximum "flexibility" in both getting money out of Congress and using it as the executive wished in Laos.

There is no doubt that if the American people found out that Vang Pao's Meo had been forced and bribed into fighting, were finished by the mid-1960s when Vang Pao himself had enough, and were replaced first by Lao Theung, then by Lao, then by Thai, all of whom were successively weaker on the ground, and that the only way the whole thing was maintained was through a devastating bombing campaign which leveled every village and town for hundreds of miles, executive flexibility would have been reduced.

Once again, however, the CIA's performance in Laos showed itself at odds with national security. The last thing this nation needs is a secret, faction-ridden bureaucracy not open to correction obtaining domination over other bureaucracies through back-door politicking and creating personal bitterness and bureaucratic bickering leading to a great loss in concentration on the mission at hand.

The CIA's performance as a bureaucracy is perhaps its weakest, not strongest, point. It shows why, from the point of view of efficiency or the national interest—as opposed to executive-branch self-interest—the CIA is the very last organization to which one would wish to entrust the fighting of a war or anything other than intelligence-gathering, where secrecy is perhaps an advantage.

Lesson Number Four: The Public Dimension

MR. COLBY: The appropriate committes of the Congress and a number of individual senators and congressmen were briefed on CIA activities in Laos during the period covered. In addition, CIA's programs were described to the appropriations committees in our annual budget hearings. . . .

SENATOR SYMINGTON: . . . I have been a member of the CIA sub-committee. . . . The day before yesterday, Tammy Arbuckle had a story about [CIA] representatives fanning out, you might say, from Phnom Penh into various parts of Cambodia. . . .

MR. COLBY: . . . I would say that those are only intelligence operations.

SENATOR SYMINGTON: That is what they said in the beginning in Laos when I was there . . . that they were intelligence people. . . . The large majority of Congress was deceived by Laos. . . . We now get reports that Americans died in Laos and that we had been lied to, because we were told they died in Vietnam. We are getting pretty sick of being lied to. . . .

I learned most of my information about Laos from the newspapers. . . .

I just want to say for the record that the CIA is an intelligence agency. I was in on the creation of it. It was not an agency to conduct a war; it was an agency to gather intelligence.

> —*Senate Armed Services Hearings,*
> *Nomination of William E. Colby,*
> July 2, July 25, 1973, pp. 28, 151–54

SENATOR ELLENDER (*late Chairman of Senate Appropriations Committee*):

I did not know anything about [the CIA secret army in Laos]. . . . I never asked, to begin with, whether or not there were any funds to carry on the war in this sum the CIA asked for. It never dawned on me to ask about it. I did see it published in the newspapers some time ago.

> —*Senate Colloquy,* November 23, 1971

It might seem strange at first glance that William Colby could testify blandly that Congress had been fully briefed on CIA activities in Laos to Senator Symington, member of the CIA oversight committee in Congress, who had been complaining for nearly a decade that the CIA was illegally conducting a secret war in Laos without informing him or Congress.

In fact, however, such has been par for the course. The CIA and its spokesmen have long operated on the theory that by not varying from their basic line they can reduce arguments over the CIA role to two irreconcilable extremes, thus forcing the listener to choose between the unofficial critic or official CIA. As we have seen in this essay, time and again, official U.S. spokesmen have argued that the CIA was particularly effective in Laos, that CIA-supported Thai soldiers were not mercenaries, that the U.S. role in South Vietnam's police and prison system was actually to *improve* conditions, providing more humane treatment and better legal guarantees to those arrested.

The end result has been a public immobilized from putting concerned public pressure on Congress to curb the CIA, and a Congress too worn down and deprived of the facts—and perhaps a bit scared—to try.

The basic fact is that the CIA will not tell a Senator Symington when it decides to deploy agents in the field in Cambodia. Should Symington find out about it from a newspaper report, he has no independent means of checking the CIA's answer that the men are just "intelligence-gathering"; any questions he asks, given the fact that he has no independent evidence, are essentially pointless; and, in the end, he must let it pass, with the weak admonition, "I do not want to get into any dogfight about it. My advice would be to cut it out."

A similar practice has, of course, also been noted in relation to journalists and writers. The basic technique is simply not to allow them access to information about CIA operations, installations, or personnel, but to feed them selective "disinformation" that puts CIA activities in the best possible light.

What all this means, as we have noted, is that the CIA is today beyond effective control of the public. Although supported by taxpayer funds appropriated by Congress, the CIA has in practice become the private force of a few top officials in the executive branch, the President's private army.

But the real meaning for the public of CIA activities in Laos goes far beyond this. For it is not only that the CIA Secret Army in Laos was beyond public control, but there is also a strong argument that can be made that it was acting *against* the American public's interest.

The question of funding alone evokes this point. In September 1969, for example, Senator Fulbright stated that "I do not believe any of my constituents are deeply concerned about whether Laos is independent or whether it is not . . . But they are very concerned about their taxes, and the taxes are very bad. . . ." Fulbright left no doubt that he believed the people of Arkansas had little interest in supporting U.S. expenditures in Laos.

Two years later, however, the administration finally made public the first figures that began to approximate the total. Senator Symington, in a secret July 1971 hearing that was later declassified, put it this way:

> The only figure the people of the U.S. know we are putting into Laos is some fifty million dollars in economic aid; but when you add up the figures . . . exclusive of the bombing of southern Laos and the Ho Chi Minh Trail, you get nearly half a billion dollars, of which a large part is for the Thais that we are financing and training in Laos. If you add to that the bombing of the Ho Chi Minh Trail cost, over a billion, it is over a billion and a half dollars annually that we are spending, one way or the other, in Laos.

This one and a half billion dollar sum is itself only a partial cost, moreover. In all, one can estimate the U.S. executive spent something between *ten and twenty billion dollars* on fighting the war in Laos over the past decade.

It is, of course, open to debate whether most Americans, if they had the full information before them, the pros and cons on both sides, would have agreed to spend this kind of money on killing and maiming in Laos, thereby neglecting so many urgent needs.

What is not open to question, however, is that the fact that a tiny handful of executive officials took it upon themselves to spend ten to twenty billion dollars of public funds in Laos without fully informing the American public is a betrayal of public trust and the national interest. For to defend how the CIA functioned in Laos is to attack the very democratic process that we are taught is the only guarantee of our liberties. In the end, even the rights and wrongs of American intervention in Laos are secondary to this most basic lesson of the CIA Secret Army in Laos.

Out of public control the CIA today continues to serve as both means and incentive for the executive branch to intervene militarily and covertly in foreign lands; its bureaucratic structure unchanged and still unworkable, it offers no more chance of ultimate success than in Laos; its employees technicians of power and violence, it continues to offer neither hope of internal reform nor susceptibility to public guidance.

Any American President still has the capacity to intervene abroad without the knowledge of public or Congress—at whatever the ultimate cost in U.S. and foreign dollars, lives, and interests. Not until this capacity of the CIA to serve as a Presidential Secret Army has been dismantled will this threat to the American public interest abate.

Solutions

The question of how to insure that the CIA serve, and not betray, the interests of national security is a complex one.

The real answer, of course, is that the CIA can never serve the national interest until there is an executive branch that has turned away from war abroad to healing at home, has learned to accept wars of liberation by ending support for the dictatorships that make such wars so long and messy, has changed its relationship to the major corporations and the Pentagon so as to begin the process of economic reconversion: cleaning up the environment and learning to live with less, more equitably shared.

In the interim, the most intelligent solution would be to dismantle the present CIA entirely and start a new body that would, through congressional review and budget limitations, be strictly limited to gathering intelligence.

Failing this, the often advanced suggestion of simply removing the capacity of the present CIA to engage in clandestine operations by sharply cutting its budget and personnel, changing the 1947 act to limit it strictly to intelligence-gathering, and writing into *law* strict provisions allowing for intimate congressional review of every phase of its operations makes the most sense. Indeed, as some have suggested, this would even allow us to expand the present CIA Directorate of Intelligence by incorporating in it the wasteful military intelligence services that at present do little but produce intelligence designed to put military services in the best possible light.

The technical problem of how to eliminate the capacity of the CIA to wage secret war is not great, as those who advocate this solution point out. For one thing, we would start by simply eliminating the Directorates of Clandestine Services and Support. There are enough ex-CIA people and others to direct such an operation should Congress have the will to do so. The reality, of course, is that for the time being the most that can be realistically hoped for in the short term is a beginning of public and congressional oversight of CIA activities.

The first and most basic principle from which to begin, in our opinion, is that the CIA derives its right to clandestineness solely from its intelligence-gathering mandate.

Any activities that in any way involve CIA advice or funding to police, prison, paramilitary, or military forces abroad, or any CIA in-

volvement, either direct or indirect, in such activities, must be made public.

Second, a respected body of congressmen and senators must be allowed full access to every aspect of CIA activities to insure that in fact such full public disclosure has been made.

The time has long since passed when we had the luxury of allowing the present CIA "briefing" system, in which CIA spokesmen tell congressional oversight committees what they feel like telling them.

But we will not spend too much time on defining solutions to the CIA's operations here. For this is the least of the problem. Congress has numerous avenues open to control the CIA abroad and at home, most especially blanket funding cuts. What is needed is not suggested mechanisms but a broad public-education campaign designed to mobilize as much public support and action as possible for the purpose of controlling the CIA.

TABLE 1
U.S. Bombing in Laos

	Fighter-Bomber Tonnage		B-52 Tonnage	B-52 Tonnage as Per Cent of Total		Total	Per Cent of Total
1965		(12,599)*		469	3.6		13,068	
1966		60,552		13,068	17.8		73,620	
1967		82,911		45,114	35.2		128,025	
(Jan.–Oct. 1968	88,975		58,811		39.8	147,786		
(Nov.–Dec. 1968	56,059		35,772		39.	91,831		
1968—Total		145,034		94,583	39.47		239,617	
1969		356,551		159,491	30.9		516,042	
1970		235,080		232,025	49.7		467,105	
1971		216,987		230,016	51.5		447,003	
1972		77,406		61,392	44.2		138,798	
Jan.–Mar. 1973		33,935		42,790	55.8		76,725	
TOTAL		1,221,055		878,948	42.		2,100,003	
Summary:								
1965–Oct. 1968		245,037		117,462	32.		362,499	17.3
Nov. 1968– Mar. 1973		976,018		761,486	43.8		1,737,504	82.7
TOTAL		1,221,055		878,948	42.		2,100,003	100.

Source: Insert by Senator Symington, *Congressional Record*, July 18, 1973, S 13848.

* Chart gives sorties for 1965, but not tonnage. Therefore, estimate was made of tons/sorties for 1966, then multiplied by the number of 1965 fighter-bomber sorties.

TABLE 2
Secret Army Personnel Directly Involved
in Laotian War on an Average Day in 1971*

In or Over Laos

I. United States

Unacknowledged and unlisted CIA personnel, at field stations, clandestine sites	50
AIRA-ARMA-Project 404	127
Active-duty U.S. Military on temporary duty—technical-support operations	100
Unacknowledged Air Force and Army commandos behind Pathet Lao lines, at CIA station	100
U.S. Air Force, Navy, Marines, in air over Laos	1000
U.S. ground missions by regular troops into Laos from South Vietnam	50
Air America and Continental Airlines	514
USAID "Requirements Office"	34
USAID "Public Safety"	5
USAID "Research Management Branch"	41
Various USAID/IVS/USIS personnel directly involved in Secret Army support	50
Subtotal, U.S. Personnel In and Over Laos	2071

II. Thai

Thai Special Forces	200	
Thai regular units fighting for CIA Secret Army	15,000	
Thai pilots	20	
Thai civilians	250	
Meo, Lao Theung, Laotians		
"Lao Irregular Forces"	30,000	
Civilians	1000	
Others		
Philippinos, Black Thais, Nungs, Taiwanese, Vietnamese	250	
Subtotal, Non-U.S. Secret Army Personnel In or Over Laos		46,720

Outside Laos

I. United States

a. DEPCHIEF/JUSMAG Thailand	123	
b. 56th Special Operations Wing	1000	
c. 4802nd Joint Liaison Detachment	50	
d. Other U.S. Air Force, Navy, Marines involved in Laos air campaign daily	48,000	
e. Air America-Continental Airlines	250	
Subtotal, U.S. Warmaking Personnel against Laos from Outside		49,423

II. All Other   5000

Subtotal, Non-U.S. Personnel Making War against Laos from Outside	5000

Total Forces Directly Involved in Lao War Daily	103,214

* Figures approximate, meant only to illustrate order of magnitude.

ROBERT L. BOROSAGE
AND JOHN MARKS

Destabilizing Chile

4

"I don't see why we need to stand by and watch a country go Communist due to the irresponsibility of its own people."[1] With those words uttered at a June 1970 meeting of the top-secret Forty Committee, Henry Kissinger summed up his and the Nixon administration's attitude toward Chile in general and Salvador Allende in particular. Kissinger and Nixon obviously perceived the election of Allende, an avowed Marxist, as somehow threatening American interests, and they were not about to "stand by" and let the people of Chile decide their own political future. Their response was, in part, to unleash the CIA.

The 1970 election was not the CIA's first intervention in Chilean politics. Twice before—in 1958 and in 1964—Allende ran for president, and on both occasions the CIA worked clandestinely to block his election. CIA Director William Colby, testifying before the House Armed Services Committee on April 22, 1974, noted that his Agency dispensed three million dollars to insure Allende's defeat in 1964; other reports put the figure as high as twenty million dollars. Philip Agee, who was a CIA operative in Uruguay in 1964, has described how some of this covert money was funneled into Chile through the Montevideo branch of the First National City Bank, with the help of the assistant manager, John M. Hennessy.[2] Five years later Hennessy was named the Assistant Secretary of the Treasury for International Affairs and in that post helped to coordinate the economic aspect of the Nixon administration's anti-Allende campaign.

Hennessy's dual role vividly illustrates the interlocking, overlapping nature of American corporate and government involvement in Chile—and, indeed, in all Latin America. U.S. corporations dominated the key sectors of Chile's economy, and by 1970 loans by government-controlled financial institutions (AID, the Export-Import Bank, the Inter-American Development Bank, the International Monetary Fund, and the World Bank) had given Chile the highest per capita foreign debt in the world. With the knowledge of the U.S. government, companies like Anaconda Copper and ITT contributed money to Allende's opponents, and in the summer of 1970 ITT offered the CIA one million dollars to help prevent Allende's election. That offer was conveyed by John McCone, a member of ITT's board of directors, formerly the head of the CIA, and still on the rolls as a CIA "consultant."

With his past Agency experience, McCone must have known that the CIA had "penetrated" virtually every sector of Chilean life. In intelligence parlance, the CIA for years had been steadily "building its assets" —placing and recruiting agents—throughout the society. In cooperation with—and often under cover supplied by—the AFL-CIO, the CIA had infiltrated the labor movement. Agency operatives had bought their way into the local press; the country's largest newspaper, *El Mercurio*, was a regular recipient of CIA funds. Other operatives maintained regular "liaison" with the Chilean military and police services. Indeed, according to a CIA source with direct knowledge, as early as 1969 the CIA operatives in Chile were actively working to "politicize" the armed forces and the police in hopes of provoking a coup before the 1970 elections.

These "asset-building" operations were part of the workaday routine for the dozen or so fulltime CIA operatives assigned to the U.S. embassy in Santiago and for the other CIA men in the country under cover as students or businessmen. (U.S. multinationals, including Pan American Airways, ITT, and W. R. Grace, have long hidden CIA officers on their payrolls.) This permanent intervention in local politics had become a fact of life in Chile and was not insignificant. Ex-operative Philip Agee, in his book, *Inside the Company*, described how a smaller CIA contingent in Ecuador, operating on a budget of about a million dollars a year, was able to penetrate without great effort every major political party, the police, the military, the cabinet, the media, and the trade unions in that country.

The routine level of covert activity in Chile was supplemented by extraordinary expenditures in 1969. According to Director Colby's own congressional testimony (as described by Congressman Michael Harrington), $500,000 was approved that year "to fund individuals who could be nurtured to keep the anti-Allende forces active and intact."[3]

As the 1970 elections approached, the Agency again sought additional funds from the Forty Committee. At the June 1970 meeting of the Forty Committee—whose membership, in addition to Kissinger, included the Director of the CIA, the Under Secretary of State for Political Affairs, the Deputy Secretary of Defense, and the Chairman of the Joint Chiefs of Staff—an additional $500,000 was allocated for anti-Allende operations. This was a small amount compared with the secret funds spent in previous Chilean elections. Although more money could have easily been obtained from the CIA Director's contingency fund (an unvouchered "slush" fund that fluctuates between fifty and one hundred million dollars), Washington policymakers apparently feared that greater sums could not be spent discreetly and that disclosure of CIA involvement could work to Allende's advantage. Nevertheless, as Henry Kissinger's statement to the Forty Committee indicates, there was no lack of will among high Nixon officials to intervene.

Washington's interest was illustrated by the almost slapstick "Navy Band" incident in mid-1970. At that time, someone in the Chilean embassy in Washington noticed that some eighty-seven visa requests had been received from the U.S. Navy, and that all the visits *apparently* coincided with the upcoming Chilean elections. When asked about the purpose of the visas, the State Department informed the embassy that the men were members of a Navy band. Yet, there was obviously a little too much brass for one band (no fewer than three captains, three commanders, and fifteen lieutenant commanders). Further inquiry brought a two-man delegation from the State Department to the Chilean embassy. The American officials apologized for the previous error and informed the Chileans that the Navy group was traveling to Chile to take part in previously scheduled United States–Latin American military maneuvers. When the Chileans explained that their country had months before canceled its participation, the State Department men beat a hasty, and rather undignified, retreat.

In that summer of 1970, with the elections slated for early September, Henry Kissinger turned his personal attention to events in Chile. From his perspective as a global manager, any major challenge to the American-sanctioned order in Latin America was of concern, and Kissinger obviously viewed the Unidad Popular, Allende's popular-front movement, as a threat to that order. In a briefing to Midwestern newspaper editors, Kissinger stated that an "Allende takeover" (that is, a victory in a democratic election) was not in America's interest. "There is a good chance that [Allende] will establish over a period of years some sort of Communist government," said Kissinger, and that could pose "massive problems for us and for democratic [sic] forces and pro-U.S. forces in Latin America." In a stretch of his geopolitical imagination, Kissinger specified Argentina, Bolivia, and Peru as countries that would be adversely influenced by an Allende victory. Moreover, Kissinger feared that the "contagious example" of Chile would "infect" the NATO countries of Italy and France, too.[4] Kissinger was worried about dominoes, "infection," and Western stability; and Chile, like Indochina before it, became a test case for America's imperial will. Not surprisingly for the man who urged the "carpet bombing" of Hanoi, Kissinger seems to have had no interest in either the conditions of the Chilean people or the fate of Chilean democracy. Kissinger reputedly looked upon Allende's over-all adherence to democratic methods as a threat to American interests. A former member of Kissinger's National Security staff reported, "Henry thought that Allende might lead an anti-U.S. movement in Latin America more effectively than Castro, just because it was the democratic path to power."[5] By June Kissinger began, in the words of a former State Department official, to act like the "Chilean desk officer. He made certain that policy was made in a way he and the President wanted it made."[6]

Thus, at the June 27, 1970, meeting of the Forty Committee, Kissinger unequivocally supported the CIA's relatively limited secret campaign against Allende and apparently approved further contingency planning for CIA intervention on a larger scale. According to reports, Kissinger's staff, working with the CIA and the State Department, in July and August drew up a National Security Study Memorandum, NSSM 97, which outlined the American response to a possible Allende victory (which secret CIA polls predicted would not occur). The central recommendation included plans for a credit squeeze and covert support for opposition elements, leading to instability and disorder. The plan was not original; a similar U.S. strategy had been used against President Goulart of Brazil before his overthrow in 1964.

When the Chilean elections were held in September, the covert activities financed by the CIA, American corporations, and other foreign groups failed to prevent an Allende victory by a small plurality. The absence of a majority forced a runoff in the Chilean Congress—thus providing another occasion for CIA intervention. The Forty Committee reconvened, and again, according to Colby's testimony as reported by

Congressman Harrington, "$350,000 was authorized to bribe the Chilean Congress." This money apparently was not spent because inside the CIA the vote-buying techniques were seen to be "unworkable."[7]

But the CIA did not give up. The CIA began to move on a number of fronts. Internal ITT memoranda, originally published by columnist Jack Anderson, show that during September and October, William Broe, chief of the CIA's clandestine operations for Latin America, met several times with high ITT officials to propose a four-part plan for economic sabotage which was calculated to weaken the local economy to the point where the military would intervene to prevent chaos. ITT officials have testified before a Senate investigating committee that Broe wanted them to sound out other American corporations on this plan but claimed that ITT and the others found the CIA's plan "not workable."

The Forty Committee seems to have also approved a secret political-military strategy for the CIA. According to an ITT memo of September 18, sent by the company's representative in Chile, the American embassy in Santiago was given the "green light to move in the name of President Nixon." The ITT memo stated that U.S. Ambassador Edward Korry had been given "maximum authority to do all possible—short of a Dominican Republic–type action—to keep Allende from taking power."[8] In the same period, Korry boasted about his fight to cut off all U.S. aid "in the pipeline" for Chile and his efforts to line up support for Allende's opponents. The CIA, under Korry's general supervision, apparently intensified its efforts—started as early as 1969—to provoke the Chilean military into action. Now confirmed reports link the assassination of Chilean General René Schneider to this campaign. Another ITT document sums up the strategy: "A more realistic hope among those who want to block Allende is that a swiftly deteriorating economy will touch off a wave of violence leading to a military coup."[9]

Considerable violence certainly occurred in Chile in the postelection period, but the Chilean armed forces retained their traditional respect for the democratic process. In October Allende was formally ratified by the Chilean Congress as President. The U.S. government's open and covert actions had failed—for the time being.

DESTABILIZATION

Even while U.S. officials were pledging noninterference with the new government in Chile, the Nixon administration was putting together a program designed to make it impossible for Allende to govern. With Kissinger providing over-all guidance, various U.S. government agencies, including the CIA, contributed to the campaign against the new Chilean government. A major element was the credit blockade, orchestrated by John Connally and John Hennessy at the Treasury and supported by the major corporations and banks dealing with Chile. This "invisible blockade" was perhaps the most disruptive of the administration policies.

The second major element was the courting of the Chilean armed forces through increased military assistance and advice. Military aid to Chile rose from $800,000 in fiscal 1970 to $5,700,000 in 1971, to $12,300,000 in 1972. American advisers played an important role in encouraging their Chilean counterparts to see themselves as a force for "stability" against the "disorder" caused by Allende's rule.

The third major element in the Kissinger plan was CIA covert action within Chile itself. According to one of the CIA's own high strategists, Richard Bissell, speaking at a secret Council on Foreign Relations meeting in 1968, "Covert intervention is probably most effective in situations where a comprehensive effort is undertaken with a number of separate operations designed to support and complement one another and to have a cumulatively significant effect."[10] This philosophy was put into action in Chile from 1970 to 1973 with devastating effect.

Kissinger moved to create a new "country team" in Chile. Henry Hecksher, the CIA station chief who had predicted Allende would lose, was replaced in October 1970 by Raymond Warren, a career Agency operative with past experience in Bolivia and Chile itself. In 1971 Ambassador Korry, an independent if hard-line political appointee, was moved out in favor of Nathaniel M. Davis, a career State man. Davis had served as ambassador in Guatemala at the time of the ongoing "pacification" program there in the late 1960s, but his most valuable asset was reportedly his willingness to follow Kissinger's orders.

Following Allende's election, the Forty Committee authorized five million dollars for a "destabilization" program. (Congressman Harrington, after twice reading—and taking notes from—CIA Director Colby's secret congressional testimony affirms that Colby used the word "destabilization," although Colby himself now denies it.) That money was augmented by another one and a half million dollars in secret funds authorized by the Forty Committee to influence the outcome of the 1973 municipal elections. Congressman Harrington's summary of the

Colby testimony states that "funding was provided to individuals, political parties, and media outlets in Chile, through channels in other countries both in Latin America and Europe."

Although even Colby himself probably does not know exactly what schemes his operatives used to dispense their secret millions, some rough outlines can be divined. The CIA used its already established assets and recruited new ones across Chile's social spectrum. The following dialogue between Colby and Congressman Dante Fascell at a secret House hearing in October 1973 illustrates the scope of the CIA's efforts.

> FASCELL: Is it reasonable to assume that the Agency has penetrated all of the political parties in Chile?
> COLBY: I wish I could say yes. I cannot assure you all because we get into some splinters.
> FASCELL: Major?
> COLBY: I think we have an intelligence coverage of most of them. . . . We have had various relationships over the years in Chile with various groups. In some cases this was approved by the National Security Council and it has meant some assistance to them. . . .[11]

CIA "assistance" was, of course, supplemented by aid from private American business, sympathetic Brazilian allies, and other right-wing Latin Americans. Indeed, Brazilians trained by the CIA for their own 1964 coup seem to have played a major role in the disruption. The head of a Brazilian "think tank," Dr. Glycon de Paiva, boasted in a late 1973 interview with *The Washington Post*, "The recipe exists and you can bake the cake any time. We saw how it worked in Brazil and now in Chile."[12] Working both with CIA coordination and independently, Brazilian business leaders helped to finance and advise their Chilean counterparts, and Brazilian intelligence operatives were also quite active. In Chile, as in Brazil, right-wing think tanks were established to distribute propaganda, organize paramilitary units, coordinate intelligence, and train demonstrators and saboteurs. In Chile, as in Brazil, massive amounts of money poured into the country to support strikes, demonstrations, and other antigovernment activities. In 1973 Frederick Dixon of the CIA's Office of Current Intelligence told a House subcommittee that "there is some evidence of cooperation between business groups in Brazil and Chile."[13]

The CIA tried to coordinate these private efforts while running its own operations. The Agency put considerable effort into funding right-wing media. President Ford has noted that the money went "to help assist the preservation of opposition papers and electronic media."[14] Contrary to the President's seeming defense of a free press, the CIA money was used in large part to finance "disinformation" designed to increase confusion and panic in Chile. In addition to paying $25,000 (according to Colby) to help "an individual purchase a radio station," the CIA spent large sums on *El Mercurio*, the shrill conservative daily that openly advocated insurrection against the Allende regime. *El Mercurio* was financed, Colby said, because it was "the only serious political force among the newspapers and television stations there."[15]

Some of the CIA's money flowed into paramilitary and terrorist groups in Chile. Other funds went into support of the strikes and demonstrations that plagued the Allende regime. One hundred and eight leaders of the white-collar trade associations received training in the United States from the American Institute of Free Labor Development, an organization which, according to former Agency operative Philip Agee, was set up by the AFL-CIO under the control of the CIA.

In October 1971 Ambassador Davis arrived in Chile with instructions to "get a little tougher." Six weeks later, five thousand women, organized by the Christian Democratic and National Parties, marched through Santiago banging on empty pots to protest food shortages and the scheduled visit of Fidel Castro. The women, noticeably well dressed and well fed (some even attended by maids), sparked counterdemonstrations that led to rioting. This March of the Empty Pots was modeled on a similar demonstration that took place in Brazil in the Agency-managed campaign against Goulart in 1964. Although Colby has denied involvement in the march, former State Department Intelligence and Research Director Ray S. Cline admitted in *The New York Times* that the Agency provided "direct funding of a number of anti-Allende trade groups and labor unions," including this specific march. (After the article appeared, Cline issued a formal denial of his original statement.)[16]

In the summer of 1972, the organizers of the Confederation of Truck Owners strike also received CIA money, enabling them to pay strike benefits during the twenty-six-day nationwide truck strike. In the summer of 1973, direct subsidies were given to middle-class shopkeepers, taxi drivers, and truckers. Colby has repeatedly and heatedly denied that the Agency was directly involved in financing the August 1973 truckers' strike, which provided immediate backdrop for the coup. But in "deep background" he has admitted that it is possible that such money was received by the truckers. A "high Agency official," undoubtedly Colby himself, provided Seymour Hersh of *The New York Times* with the classic espionage dodge, "If we give it to A and then A gives it to B and C and D, in a sense it is true that D got it, but the question is, Did we give it to A knowing D would get it?"[17] Since the CIA seldom gives money directly to any group, this explanation allows for intervention without responsibility—"plausible denial," however implausible it may be. Plausible denial provides a protective covering inside the government as well as outside. Colby's sensitivity to the financing of the truckers' strike may be connected with reports that the Forty Committee decided against an Agency plan to finance the summer strikes. Cline, who had access to some Forty Committee proceedings, has been less evasive. He noted that "some of the money was intended for financial support of the small businessmen and the truckers in their resistance strikes against the Allende government."[18]

The CIA was also a major donor to right-wing political candidates in Chile. In the March 1973 municipal elections, the CIA spread some one and a half million dollars around to its favorite sons. In those elections, in spite of the ruinous economic blockade, the increasingly disruptive strikes and demonstrations, the CIA-financed political campaigns, right-wing propaganda, and paramilitary activities, the Allende party improved its position in the polls, gaining some forty-four per cent of the vote.

By the fall, however, another summer of strikes and increasing violence made the coup inevitable. In the surgical language of bureaucracy, Colby informed a House committee in October 1973 that the CIA "had an over-all appreciation" of the "deterioration" of the economic and political situation, and with the Navy pushing for a coup, knew that it was "only a question of time before it came."

Henry Kissinger testified in 1973, under oath, "The CIA had nothing to do with the coup, to the best of my knowledge and belief, and I only put in that qualification in case some madman appears down there, who, without instructions, talked to somebody."[19] Colby has also repeatedly disclaimed any responsibility for the coup: "The CIA had no connection with the coup itself, with the military coup. We did not support it, we did not stimulate it, we didn't bring it about in any way. We obviously had some intelligence coverage over the various moves being made, but we were quite meticulous in making sure there was no indication or encouragement from our side."[20] Even if Kissinger and Colby are telling the truth about the direct participation of the CIA in the coup d'état, it is at best disingenuous for them to claim that the United States, and the CIA specifically, had nothing to do with the overthrow of a government which it had worked to destabilize for three yars.

At a public conference held by the Center for National Security Studies in September 1974, Colby was asked if he thought the CIA's intervention in Chile was a success. Colby refused to make a direct answer, stating that "it is hard to say whether it is successful or unsuccessful without talking about what [our operations] were."[21] Nevertheless, within the CIA, the Chilean operation was unquestionably viewed as a success, at least prior to its revelation. Even President Ford defended it by saying, "I think this is in the best interest of the people of Chile and certainly in our best interests."[22]

One wonders what the President had in mind. A brutal military dictatorship has replaced a democratically elected government in Chile. All political parties have been banned; the Congress has been shut down; the press is censored; supporters of the last legal government have been jailed and tortured; thousands have been killed; and elections have been put off indefinitely.

And what American interests have been served? Our government has once again aligned itself with a repressive junta. Our leaders have once again been caught telling a series of lies to Congress and the American people about their covert actions in a foreign country. The lawlessness and ruthlessness of the CIA's operations have brought us opprobium around the world. The terrorism sanctioned and even encouraged by the CIA will surely instruct others in its use.

Only American corporations seem to have profited by our intervention, but even their interests were poorly served. If corporate investment can be protected only by repressive regimes, then those investments are a poor risk. No country can long violate its own citizenry's sensibilities simply to preserve corporate investments abroad, and a Harris poll in October 1974 showed that sixty percent of the American people opposed their government's program to "destabilize" Chile, and only eighteen per cent approved.

The CIA's operations in Chile are not merely of historical interest. Congressman Harrington, after reading Colby's testimony on Chile, wrote that "the Agency activities in Chile were viewed as a prototype, or laboratory experiment, to test the techniques of heavy financial investment in efforts to discredit and bring down a government."[23] The "experiment" was a bureaucratic success in Chile (although the subject died). The next victim may be in Portugal, Italy, or Greece or perhaps Peru or Mexico.

President Ford, when asked at a September 1974 press conference about the legality of the CIA's destabilization operations in Chile, said, "I'm not going to pass judgment on whether it's permitted or authorized under international law. It's a recognized fact that, historically as well as presently, such actions are taken in the best interests of the countries involved."[24] The President did not specify which country would next have its "best interests" served by covert action.

II

Covert Operations at Home

THOMAS B. ROSS

Surreptitious
Entry

5

THE CIA'S OPERATIONS
IN THE UNITED STATES

The New York Times report in December 1974 of "massive, illegal" domestic activity by the CIA was just one—though the most startling— of a long series of indications that the Agency has been operating outside the law inside the United States.

In fact, it had been a matter of public record for more than a year that former CIA Director Richard M. Helms effectively condoned such spying when it was proposed by White House assistant Tom Charles Huston on behalf of President Nixon.

In documents uncovered during the Watergate investigation, Huston proposed a broad domestic intelligence plan, including breaking and entering—"surreptitious entry" as it was politely described.

The interagency intelligence committee, on which Helms sat as the CIA representative, had advised the President in advance: "Use of this technique is clearly illegal: it amounts to burglary. It is also highly risky and could result in great embarrassment if exposed. However, it is also the most fruitful tool and can produce the type of intelligence which cannot be obtained in any other fashion."

In other words, Helms must have been aware that the plan involved a double illegality—the simple violation of the constitutional rights of a citizen to his privacy and the intrusion of the CIA into domestic operations. And so Huston confided in a memo: "I went into this exercise fearful that CIA would refuse to cooperate. In fact, Dick Helms was most cooperative and helpful and the only stumbling block was Mr. Hoover."

Huston complained that the fabled FBI director was "bull-headed . . . gratuitous . . . inconsistent and frivolous . . . old and worried about his legend." In short, the old nemesis of the liberals, for whatever reason, refused to break the law. But Helms, the darling of many a liberal salon, was prepared to do so without coaxing.

Hoover ultimately prevailed, or at least Mr. Nixon said he did, and the plan was not put into effect, or at least Mr. Nixon said it wasn't. There is little doubt, however, that the President got his private political police force in another form, the White House "Plumbers" who—with equipment supplied by the CIA—broke into the office of Daniel Ellsberg's psychiatrist and some of whom—CIA alumni included—took part in the "surreptitious entry" at the Watergate.

It was a strange fulfillment of the worst premonitions of those conservative Congressmen who, at the moment of the CIA's birth in 1947, expressed fear that a "Gestapo" was being set loose in our free land.

In proposing the creation of the CIA, the Truman administration took great pains to emphasize that the new agency was to limit itself to overseas organizations. On April 25, 1947, during a hearing of the House Committee on Expenditures in the Executive Departments, the following significant exchange took place between Republican Congressman Clarence J. Brown of Ohio and Secretary of the Navy James V. Forrestal:

> BROWN: . . . Perhaps we have not been as good as we should have been and I agree with that, either in our military or foreign intelligence, and I am very much interested in seeing the United States have as fine a foreign military and naval intelligence as they can possibly have, but I am not interested in setting up here in the United States any particular agency under any President, and I do not care what his name is, and just allow him to have a Gestapo of his own if he wants to have it. Every now and then you get a man that comes up in power that has an imperialistic idea.
>
> FORRESTAL: The purposes of the Central Intelligence Authority are limited definitely to purposes outside of this country, except the collation of information gathered by government agencies. Regarding domestic operations, the Federal Bureau of Investigation is working at all times in collaboration with General Vandenberg [Air Force General Hoyt S. Vandenberg, Director of Central Intelligence]. He relies upon them for domestic activities.
>
> BROWN: Is that stated in the law?
>
> FORRESTAL: It is not; no, sir.
>
> BROWN: That could be changed in two minutes, and have the action within the United States instead of without; is that correct?

FORRESTAL: He could only do so with the President's direct and specific approval.

BROWN: I know, but even then it could be done without violation of law by the President or somebody who might write the order for him and get his approval, and without the knowledge and consent or direction of the Congress. Do you think it would be wise for the Congress of the United States to at least fix some limitation on what the power of this individual might be, or what could be done, or what should be done, [so that] all these safeguards and rights of the citizen may be protected?

FORRESTAL: I think it is profitable to explore what you need for protection and I am in complete sympathy about the dangers of sliding into abrogation of powers by the Congress.

During a hearing of the same committee on June 24, 1947, there was this exchange between Democratic Congressman Henderson Lanham of Georgia and an administration witness, Dr. Vannevar Bush, Chairman of the Joint Research and Development Board of the War and Navy Departments.

LANHAM: Do you feel there is any danger of the Central Intelligence Division becoming a Gestapo or anything of that sort?

BUSH: I think there is no danger of that. The bill provides clearly that it is concerned with intelligence outside of this country, that it is not concerned with intelligence on internal affairs, and I think this is a safeguard against its becoming an empire. We already have, of course, the FBI in this country, concerned with internal affairs, and the collection of intelligence in connection with law enforcement internally.

To conciliate Brown, Lanham, and others, the bill was amended to provide that "the agency shall have no police, subpoena, law-enforcement powers, or internal security functions."

It is clear from committee hearings and floor debate that most congressmen thought that the National Security Act, as amended, would limit the CIA to intelligence work and, then, only outside the United States. There was nothing to the contrary in the express language of the act.

Even though the fifth paragraph of the act* refers specifically to "in-

---

* The act authorizes the CIA "to perform such other functions and duties related to intelligence affecting the national security as the National Security Council may from time to time direct."

telligence" and not to clandestine activity, it was seized upon as a loop-hole under which the CIA's role was secretly broadened beyond the evident intent of Congress to include covert operations at home and abroad.

Richard M. Bissell, Jr., former Deputy Director of the CIA for Plans (now the Directorate of Operations, the so-called dirty-tricks depart-ment), observed in a talk in 1968 that the National Security Act was "necessarily vague."*

"CIA's full 'charter' has been frequently revised," he said, "but it has been, and must remain, secret. The absence of a public charter leads people to search for the charter and to question the Agency's authority to undertake various activities. The problem of a 'secret charter' remains as a curse, but the need for secrecy would appear to preclude a solu-tion." He was alluding to several classified NSC directives authorizing CIA activity within the United States under certain conditions.

In short, the ambiguous "other functions and duties" clause of the National Security Act has been pushed to the limit at home as well as abroad. Even the express prohibition against "police, subpoena, law-enforcement, or internal security functions" appears to have been breached.

On December 17, 1972, *The New York Times* revealed that the CIA had secretly provided training to fourteen New York City policemen. The CIA's legislative counsel, John Maury, former station chief in Greece, admitted that "less than fifty police officers all told, from a total of about a dozen city and county police forces, have received some sort of Agency briefing within the past two years." In fact, according to ex-CIA official Victor Marchetti (in his book, *The CIA and the Cult of Intelligence*, co-authored by John D. Marks), the "police training had been going on for considerably more than the two years cited by the CIA—at least since 1967, when Chicago police received instruction at both the agency's headquarters and at 'The Farm' in southeastern Vir-ginia . . . and if the CIA had confessed to the full extent of its pre-1971 police-training activities, the figures would have been much larger." The CIA also supported and participated in the training of foreign officials at the International Police Academy in Washington, which was ostensibly run by the Agency for International Development.

In addition, the CIA maintained a secret base in the Colorado Rock-

---

* The talk, sponsored by the Council on Foreign Relations in New York, was supposed to be off the record. But a report on the meeting leaked out in 1971.

ies where, as late as 1961, it trained Tibetans to return home and wage guerrilla warfare against Communist China.

As part of the training program for its own agents, the CIA evidently has staged a regular series of illegal break-ins. Daniel Schultz, lawyer for Watergate conspirators Bernard Barker and Eugenio Martinez, revealed in court in June 1974 that they had engaged in a "penetration" of Radio City Music Hall in New York in the mid-1960s as part of a "training session."

In addition, Schultz said the two men later broke into the Miami home of a boat-crew member who was making trips to Cuba and into a Miami business office. These were said to have been CIA "security" operations within the Cuban community.

Perhaps the oldest of the CIA's domestic operations is its relationship with *émigré* groups, first the Eastern Europeans in the 1950s and then the Cubans in the 1960s.

During confirmation hearings on the appointment of John Alex Mc-Cone as director of the CIA in 1962, the following revealing exchange took place:

> SENATOR MARGARET CHASE SMITH OF MAINE: It has been alleged to me, Mr. McCone, that the CIA has been or is supporting the political activities of certain ethnic groups in this country, such as the Polish and Hungarian groups; is this true, and if so, what comment do you have to make?
> MC CONE: I can make no comment on it.
> SMITH: Is it true?
> MC CONE: I couldn't comment on it.

Senator Leverett Saltonstall of Massachusetts, an old friend of the CIA, sought to come to McCone's aid but made things worse.

> SALTONSTALL: Is it not true, Mr. McCone, in your understanding of the CIA, that any work on the ethnic groups in this country would not be within the province of the CIA, in any event; am I correct in that?
> MC CONE: I cannot answer that, Senator.
> SALTONSTALL: Perhaps that should not be answered.

Actually, for a decade, a $100,000,000 fund was available for this type of activity. A 1951 amendment to the Foreign Aid Act has provided the money for persons "residing in or escapees from" the Soviet

Union, the satellite nations, or any other Communist area of the world, either to form them into military units "or for other purposes."

In November 1964 Eerik Heine, a forty-six-year-old Estonian living in a suburb of Toronto, Canada, brought suit in federal court in Baltimore against Juri Raus, a thirty-nine-year-old Estonian of Hyattsville, Maryland, a suburb of Washington. Heine accused Raus of slander and demanded $110,000 in damages. Specifically, Heine charged that Raus had defamed him by publicly alleging that he was an agent of the Soviet KGB. Heine, a celebrated figure among the twenty to thirty thousand Estonians in North America, insisted he was an authentic freedom fighter who had spent seven years in Russian prisons, sometimes under torture, before escaping to the West.

Raus, national commander of the Legion of Estonian Liberation, admitted on January 3, 1965, that two years earlier he had publicly declared that "he was in possession of responsible information received from an official agency of the United States government to the effect that the plaintiff was a Soviet agent or collaborator."

Raus's lawyers submitted an affidavit from Helms, then Deputy Director, stating that Raus was a CIA employee acting on orders when he charged that Heine was a KGB agent. The lawyers asserted that because Raus was a government employee acting under orders, he had "absolute privilege." Under Supreme Court rulings, they contended, he could not be held liable even if it were proved that he spoke out of "actual malice."

Heine's lawyers objected and the judge, Roszel C. Thomsen, seemed at first to be deeply troubled. "Assume the plaintiff is a Communist," he said, "assume he is everything you say, everybody has some rights in this country. . . . In the United States, just as Mr. Justice Frankfurter said, 'There are some things you cannot do to a dog.' . . . You are not going to persuade this court that there is anybody in this country who does not have some rights."

Raus's lawyers responded by producing another affidavit from Helms, stating without elaboration that Raus had accused Heine in order to "protect the integrity of the agency's foreign intelligence sources." Declaring that any further disclosure "would be contrary to the security interests of the United States," he ordered Raus not to testify.

A third affidavit from Helms said Raus "was instructed to warn members of the Estonian *émigré* groups that Eerik Heine was a dispatched Soviet intelligence operative, a KGB agent. The purpose for this instruction was to protect the integrity of the agency's foreign intelligence sources, existing within or developed through such groups, in accordance with the agency's statutory responsibility of the Director of Central Intelligence to protect foreign intelligence sources and methods."

Finally, the Director of the CIA, Admiral William F. Raborn, submitted an affidavit supporting Helms and directing Raus to "respectfully decline to answer questions."

In the end Judge Thomsen sided with the CIA, restricted the testimony of Raus, and on December 8, 1966, dismissed Heine's suit. Thomsen overruled the contention of Heine's lawyers that the CIA had violated the provision of the National Security Act of 1947 which prohibited it from exercising any "internal security functions."

"It is reasonable," Thomsen declared, "that *émigré* groups from nations behind the Iron Curtain would be a valuable source of intelligence information as to what goes on in their own homeland. The fact that the immediate intelligence source is located in the United States does not make it an 'internal security function' over which the CIA has no authority. The court concludes that activities by the CIA to protect its foreign intelligence sources located in the United States are within the power granted by Congress to the CIA."

Judge Thomsen then revealed a remarkable series of events that had taken place in his court. During the proceedings, he said, he had asked the CIA "to submit a statement as to the legal authority of the CIA to engage in activities in the United States with respect to foreign intelligence sources." In response the CIA submitted an affidavit that included "particular paragraphs of a document which is classified 'secret' and which cannot be declassified for the purposes of this case."

The CIA had asked the Justice Department to submit the document to the court "under seal for in camera inspection." The agency said that if Heine's lawyers wanted to see the sealed document—evidently the "secret charter" referred to by Bissell—it would not object, but that they would have to go out to CIA headquarters to do so. What is more, they would not be permitted to disclose to their client "the excerpts thus made available to them."

Heine's attorneys refused to examine the excerpts under those conditions, stating that they would not look at anything they could not communicate to their client.

The CIA was created by a public law that most Americans assumed confined it to overseas operations. Now, however, it was saying that there were additional, secret provisos giving it the right to engage in certain domestic activities, but that these could not be disclosed to the American people.

While the Heine case was being argued in court, the CIA's extensive involvement in the academic community began to seep out in considerable detail. *Ramparts* magazine disclosed in April 1966 that Michigan State University had provided academic cover for the CIA police operation in South Vietnam. The magazine reported that the university ran a police training program for the CIA from 1955 to 1959 under a $25,000,000 contract and concealed five CIA agents in the project. John A. Hannah, president of the university and the chairman of the U.S. Civil Rights Commission, vehemently denied any knowledge of the CIA involvement. But Lyman Kirkpatrick, who had held a high position in the Agency during the period, said the university had signed a contract with the CIA and had full knowledge of its role in the project.

The Agency's connection with Michigan State was by no means unique. The CIA had worked out secret arrangements with individuals and institutes at dozens of colleges, universities, and research centers. The prototye for this kind of relationship was the Center for International Studies at the Massachusetts Institute of Technology. The Center was founded in 1951 with CIA money, and the following year Max F. Millikan, Assistant Director of the CIA, became its head. From the start, another key figure at the Center was former OSS man Walt Whitman Rostow, an economics professor who became President Johnson's personal adviser on national security and foreign affairs, as well as his principal link with the intelligence community. In a practice which subsequently became standard procedure at MIT and elsewhere, Rostow and his colleagues produced a CIA-financed book, *The Dynamics of Soviet Society*, in 1953. It was published in two versions, one classified for circulation within the intelligence community, the other "sanitized" for public consumption.

MIT declared in 1966 that the Center had severed all connection with the Agency, not on moral grounds but as a matter of "public relations" and "because of misunderstandings and unfounded suspicion of the character of our contracts with the CIA." In 1964, when the CIA connection was first revealed, MIT has airily implied it was a thing of the past. But when it publicly severed the CIA link it conceded that the Center was receiving fifteen to twenty per cent of its budget from Langley.

Scholars from MIT and elsewhere had complained that they were being taken for CIA agents even when involved in the most innocent research projects overseas. In an effort to remove the suspicions, Stephen T. Boggs, executive secretary of the American Anthropological Society, demanded the setting up of "an absolutely impassable barrier" between the CIA and scholars involved in foreign research. But the Agency clearly was determined to maintain its influence, direct and indirect, in the academic world.

The April 1966 issue of *Foreign Affairs*, the prestigious scholarly quarterly, contained an article entitled "The Faceless Viet Cong." It was a defense of the government's position that the guerrilla movement in South Vietnam was controlled by the Communist party of North Vietnam. It was written by George Carver, Jr., who was identified only as a "student of political theory and Asian affairs, with degrees from Yale and Oxford; former officer in the U.S. AID mission in Saigon; author of *Aesthetics and the Problem of Meaning*." In fact, Carver was an employee of the CIA. His contribution to *Foreign Affairs* represented only one of the hundreds of articles and books that the CIA had got into print at home and abroad without identification of their source.

The CIA has also been active in efforts to suppress critical books. In 1964, when *The Invisible Government*, a study of the CIA and U.S. intelligence by David Wise and Thomas B. Ross, was about to be published, McCone and other top CIA officials contacted Random House, the publisher, in an effort to stop or alter the book. The CIA also ran a legal study to see if it could buy up the first printing of the book. Finally, it weighed the possibility of prosecuting the authors under the espionage laws. But none of the efforts succeeded.

In 1972 the CIA asserted the right to censor Marchetti's and Marks's book, because they had signed secrecy oaths while working for the government. The courts upheld the CIA, and the book became the first in American history to be subject to prepublication censorship.

The CIA immediately proposed legislation that would make officials subject to a penalty of ten years in prison or a fine of ten thousand dollars for disclosing information the Agency judged would compromise "intelligence sources and methods." The bill would also give the CIA power to obtain injunctions against newspapers planning to publish the information.

In addition to its penetration of the book business, the CIA also gained a foothold in journalism. In November 1973 Oswald Johnston of the *Washington Star* disclosed that more than thirty-five American journalists working abroad—full-time reporters, free-lance journalists, and correspondents for trade publications—were on the Agency's payroll. Soon afterward CIA spokesmen said Director William E. Colby had ordered the practice stopped for full-time reporters for general news publications, but not for the rest.

The CIA also manipulated students and scholars in a similar manner, as became abundantly clear early in 1967, when *Ramparts* disclosed the Agency's long-secret links with the National Student Association, the nation's largest student group with chapters on three hundred campuses. Confronted by the magazine's detailed accusations, NSA leaders admitted that the CIA had subsidized the association for fifteen years. All told, it was estimated that the CIA had poured three million dollars into NSA.

Shortly after the *Ramparts* disclosure Sam Brown, a twenty-three-year-old Harvard divinity student and chairman of NSA's National Supervisory Policy Board, also accused the CIA of "trapping" association leaders into cooperation with it. Each year, he explained, the CIA picked out one or two NSA leaders to be informed of the secret relationship and to serve as liaison; they would be approached, advised that there were some secrets that they should know about, and asked to sign a security statement.

"Then," Brown said, "they were told, 'You are employed by the CIA.' At that point they were trapped, having signed a statement not to divulge anything. . . . This is the part of the thing that I found to be most disgusting and horrible. People were duped into this relationship with the CIA, a relationship from which there was no way out. There has been no physical intimidation, but it seems apparent that under the National Security Act—under the statements these people signed— there would be the probability of prosecution by the government . . . a twenty-year jail sentence to maintain your integrity is a very high price to pay."

The NSA disclosures led to a rash of revelations about the CIA's involvement with virtually every important segment of American life— business, labor, government, the churches, the universities, the news media, charitable organizations, book publishers, lawyers, teachers, artists, women's organizations, and cultural groups.

In response to the furor over the revelations, the President ordered an investigation by a three-man group, headed by Under Secretary of State Nicholas deB. Katzenbach and including Helms and John W. Gardner,

Secretary of Health, Education and Welfare and later head of Common Cause. Katzenbach said, "The President believes strongly that the integrity and independence of the educational community must be preserved."

Within a week, the President endorsed a preliminary finding by the Katzenbach group that absolved both the CIA and the administration. The CIA "did not act on its own initiative," the panel declared, "but in accordance with policies established by the National Security Council in 1952 through 1954."

In the unclassified portion of its final report, the Katzenbach panel recommended that the CIA and all other government agencies be prohibited in the future from providing covert financial support to any "of the nation's educational or private voluntary organizations."

The panel said there should be no exception to the ban on channeling covert government money to "any educational, philanthropic, or cultural organization." However, secret grants could still be made to private groups in other, unspecified fields when "overriding national security interests" were involved. (It was generally assumed that this loophole was included principally to permit continuing CIA subsidies to the international labor movement). The arbiter of the exceptions should be the same "interdepartmental review committee" that had invoked "national security" to approve the covert financing of private groups over the previous fifteen years. The Secretaries of State and Defense would also have to give their approval. The President adopted the panel's main recommendation and ordered all government agencies to sever their secret financial arrangements with private groups.

But the CIA was already well enough entrenched in other domestic areas. In fact, the Agency's home-front activity had become so extensive by 1964 that a special section, the Domestic Operations Division, had been secretly created to handle it. The very title of the division flouted the intent of Congress, which had been assured when it established the CIA—and over and over again since—that the Agency would not and does not engage in domestic operations.

The offices exercise control over a bewildering range of domestic operations, fronts, and "proprietary companies." In the 1960s the CIA ran its anti-Castro and Latin American network under cover of Zenith Technical Enterprises, Inc., located on the south campus of the University of Miami, and it had its own airport at Opa-Locka, near the Hialeah race track.

The CIA also set up the Gibraltar Steamship Corporation (which owned no steamships) in Miami as a cover for its broadcasts to Cuba from Swan Island in the western Caribbean, and it leased five ships from a real steamship company, Garcia Lines Corporation of New York, when it required its own navy for the Bay of Pigs invasion. Still another CIA corporation, Sea Key Shipping, operated attack boats against Cuba after the invasion failed.

In addition the CIA has set up a number of corporations in Delaware and owns probably the biggest fleet of "commercial" airplanes in the world. The airlines organized and financed by the Agency include Air America, Air Asia, Civil Air Transport, Intermountain Aviation, and Southern Air Transport, which it put up for sale in 1973 when it became hopelessly identified as a CIA front.

To run its fronts, corporations, and offices, the Agency's top officials have often turned to old friends and classmates, many of whom have served a tour in the OSS or the CIA. In the fall of 1966, for example, the CIA confirmed that its man in St. Louis for the previous fifteen years had been Louis Werner II, an investment banker, a graduate of St. Paul's School and Princeton, and a member of a prominent and wealthy St. Louis family.

In Boston a trustee for the Granary Fund, a conduit for CIA money to private groups, was another Agency Old Boy, George H. Kidder, who listed himself in *Who's Who* as "with Office General Counsel, CIA, 1952–54." When the CIA set up its clandestine radio on Swan Island, in the western Caribbean, to attack Fidel Castro, it turned to New York attorney Richard S. Greenlee, an old OSS hand who served behind Japanese lines in Siam, to act as a civilian front man.

The list of distinguished persons who have taken part in CIA cover activities reads like the roster of the American Establishment, that informal coalition of lawyers, businessmen, and financiers who, as Richard Rovere has suggested half facetiously, silently determine the course of public policy in the United States.

Morris Hadley, one-time head of the Carnegie Foundation, son of former Yale president Arthur Twining Hadley, and a senior partner in the prestigious Wall Street law firm of Milbank, Tweed, Hadley and McCloy,* permitted his family's Rubicon Foundation to be used as a CIA conduit.

Eli Whitney Debevoise, former Deputy U.S. High Commissioner in

---

* John J. McCloy, an intimate adviser of Presidents and, according to Rovere, the untitled chairman emeritus of the Establishment.

Germany and a member of the influential Wall Street law firm of Debevoise, Plimpton, Lyons and Gates, was one of the principal officers in the American Council for the International Commission of Jurists, a CIA conduit.

His partner, Francis T. P. Plimpton, former U.S. Deputy Representative to the United Nations, was a director of the Foundation for Youth and Student Affairs, a recipient of CIA funds.

John Hay Whitney, former ambassador to Great Britain and owner of the New York *Herald Tribune,* was founder of the Whitney Trust, a philanthropic organization financed in part by the Granary Fund, the CIA conduit.

The "nouveau" Texas Establishment has also been included in the CIA network. Oveta Culp Hobby, publisher of the Houston *Post* and Secretary of Health, Education and Welfare in the Eisenhower administration, allowed the Agency to use the Hobby Foundation as a conduit. John W. Mecom, the oil tycoon, was one of the original incorporators of another conduit, the San Jacinto Fund. Sarah T. Hughes, the federal judge who administered the oath of office to President Johnson, was a trustee of the Hoblitzelle Foundation, which handled CIA money.

Leon Jaworski, a Houston lawyer friend of Johnson's and later the Watergate Special Prosecutor, was a trustee of the M. D. Anderson Foundation, another recipient. In Boston a law partner of James D. St. Clair, Nixon's impeachment lawyer, also served as an officer on a foundation conduit for the CIA. In an ironic twist, the two major legal protagonists in the Watergate affair, already rife with CIA overtones, were both indirectly connected with the Agency.

Far from severing its connections with the business establishment after the foundation disclosures and the Katzenbach report, there are strong indications that the CIA deepened and broadened its relationship.

During the Council on Foreign Relations meeting in New York in 1968, Richard M. Bissell emphasized the necessity of a greater use of major international companies as a cover for CIA operations overseas.

"If the Agency is to be effective," he said, "it will have to make use of private institutions on an expanding scale, though those relations which have been 'blown' cannot be resurrected. We need to operate under deeper cover. . . . The interface with various private groups, including business and student groups, must be remedied."

Miles Copeland, an old CIA hand, was even more explicit in his recent book *Without Cloak and Dagger* (New York: Simon and Schuster, 1974). Claiming knowledge of the CIA's future plans, he predicted, "There will be greater cooperation with the multinational corporations. The Agency will step up its search for independent organizations with mutual interests through which it can operate. Agency officials believe that whatever anyone may think about it, we are entering an era when the interests of the United States and those of frankly 'capitalist' institutions throughout the world so coincide that we have no choice but to take advantage of the fact. If this means cooperation with the unloved multinational corporations, ITT included, so be it."

Early in 1974 a high-ranking CIA official told a small group of reporters that more than two hundred U.S. intelligence agents were stationed abroad posing as businessmen. Since the CIA was engaged at the time in a campaign to persuade the public that it was cutting back on its clandestine operations, the figure undoubtedly was conservative.

In any event, it was clear that the CIA was deeply involved with American business and, as with its ties to labor, the universities, *émigré* and student organizations, publishing and the press, the involvement had an inevitable domestic effect. By subsidizing the various groups— even for foreign purposes—and by promoting the "capitalist" interests of major international corporations—as Copeland perceived it—the CIA was obviously developing a large lobby of support at home.

Those who benefit from a relationship with the CIA might be disposed to go along or look the other way when the Agency oversteps the legal bounds in the United States. When the CIA subscribed to the illegal Huston plan for domestic intelligence, it is reasonable to assume that large and influential forces in the private sector were prepared to cooperate.

The Watergate scandal exposed how willing the CIA was to be used —at least at the outset—and how close the White House came to turning the CIA and the FBI into a political police force.

When Huston solicited support for Nixon's illegal domestic-intelligence plan, Helms readily subscribed to it.

When the White House demanded a psychological profile of Daniel Ellsberg, a private American citizen, the CIA produced it.

When John Ehrlichman sought technical assistance for E. Howard Hunt and the "Plumbers," General Robert E. Cushman, the Deputy Director of the CIA and now Marine Corps Commandant, immediately complied. Later, when the Watergate prosecution requested a statement from Cushman, Colby told him to clear it with Ehrlichman, and Cushman complied with Ehrlichman's demand that his name be dropped from the formal affidavit.

Finally when H. R. Haldeman, on Nixon's instructions, ordered Cushman's successor, General Vernon D. Walters, to divert the FBI investigation of Watergate, Walters promptly did so. And Helms, who attended the meeting, with full knowledge that the CIA would not be compromised by an investigation, offered no opposition.

The Watergate inquiry was thus put off the track for a critical two weeks in its crucial opening stage. And only when Acting FBI Director Patrick Gray demanded that Walters put it all in writing did the CIA at last formally withdraw its original request for a diversion of the investigation and admit that it was completely uninvolved.

As the transcript of the pertinent conversation between Nixon and Haldeman shows, the President decided to bring the CIA into the cover-up with the full expectation that it would go along.

Nixon indicated that in his previous experience as Vice President and in the 1960 campaign the CIA had displayed a willingness to cooperate in a political cover-up at Presidential direction. Nixon alluded to his book *Six Crises* (New York: Doubleday, 1962), and how that "s.o.b." and (expletive deleted) Allen Dulles had reacted to it.

In the book Nixon alleged that during the 1960 campaign John Kennedy had exploited information provided him by the CIA for political advantage. During the final days of the campaign, Kennedy called for strong U.S. support of the Cuban exiles seeking to overthrow Castro. Nixon contended that Kennedy had been told in the traditional briefing of candidates by high-ranking CIA officials that planning was far advanced for the Bay of Pigs invasion.

Nixon said he was compelled to oppose Kennedy's position on Cuba —even though he had vigorously supported the invasion within the National Security Council—in order to protect the operation, and as a result, may have lost the election.

When *Six Crises* appeared, Dulles sided with President Kennedy and endorsed a White House statement claiming that Kennedy had been provided with only general details of the CIA's link with the Cubans and denying that he had been briefed on the Bay of Pigs.

But Nixon insisted, in his taped conversation with Haldeman, that Dulles "knew" that Kennedy had been fully informed, but lied to protect the President.

"Now what the hell!" Nixon explained. "Who told him to do it? The President."

Dulles and the CIA covered up for Kennedy, Nixon suggested; now the CIA would cover up for him.

"You call them [the CIA]," Nixon directed. "Play it tough. That's the way they [the Democrats] play it, and that's the way we are going to play it."

It came as a shock to many in Congress and the general public that a political leader of Nixon's broad inside experience should have expected the CIA to take part in illegal political activity. It came as no less a shock that the CIA satisfied Nixon's expectations at least in part.

But during the long struggle to unravel the Watergate scandal, Congress was wary of focusing on the CIA for fear of being diverted from its main purpose. After the truth of Watergate had been exposed and Nixon had resigned, however, the climate was right for a major congressional investigation.

The New York Times' report on domestic spying by Seymour Hersh provided the catalyst. President Ford sought to pre-empt an independent inquiry by setting up a traditional, in-house commission of the Katzenbach variety. He confessed, in an off-the-record meeting with a group of private citizens, that he was careful to fill the commission with men he could count on to limit themselves to the charges of illegal, domestic activities and not intrude into such ugly foreign practices as assassination.

But his strategy backfired. The commission was so loaded with tame, Establishment figures closely linked to the CIA—including the chairman, Vice President Rockefeller—that it only served to stimulate public demand for an aggressive congressional inquiry.

Within a month of the *Times'* report, both the Senate and House voted to establish special, Watergate-type committees, dominated by moderates and liberals, to investigate the CIA, the FBI, and the entire intelligence community. For the first time since its creation in 1947, prospects seemed good for a searching scrutiny of the CIA and particularly of its illegal activities in the United States.

HERBERT SCOVILLE, JR.

The Role of Technology in Covert Intelligence Collection

6

BACKGROUND

Beginning with World War II technological methods of collecting intelligence have become increasingly dominant over the traditional agent, informer, or defector as sources of information, particularly in areas affecting national security. Stealing plans, infiltration of agents into laboratories, visual observation of new weapons have become more and more difficult and unproductive. Even if a spy could succeed in getting a look at a new weapon, he might not be able to acquire important information since this might be obtainable only with a scientific instrument. Thus a person watching a nuclear explosion would learn little other than that it went off, with perhaps some estimate as to whether it was large or small; but a seismic instrument or an acoustic listening device halfway around the world could tell the explosive yield, and a filter in an aircraft at this same distance could collect particles from which the secrets of the internal design of the bomb could be determined.

Fortunately, as the usefulness of human beings for collecting intelligence has decreased, the science of technical intelligence collection has grown dramatically. Not only has collection technology improved, but the very nature of modern military weaponry has made the task easier to accomplish in less provocative ways. Nuclear explosions release tremendous amounts of energy, and modern missiles travel along trajectories observable hundreds or even thousands of miles away. Radars and communications systems frequently bounce energy off the ionosphere so that the signals can be received at long distances. Modern weapons and their logistic support are easily observable by aerial photography. As a consequence, available information on even the most secret military weapons and on the deployment of forces even in remote localities is far superior to what it was twenty years ago.

When President Eisenhower made his famous "open skies" proposal calling for unrestricted, but monitored, overflight of national territories on both sides of the Iron Curtain, we considered that its acceptance would have gone a long way toward thawing the Cold War. The Russians disparaged it as legalized espionage. Today, thanks to technological improvements, our capabilities for obtaining military information far surpass any that we dreamed of under the Eisenhower plan and, surprisingly, the Soviet Union in the 1972 SALT Agreements sanctioned the right of the United States to have pertinent military information provided that it was obtained by national technical means that were not in violation of international law.

In view of the overwhelming priority of technological intelligence collection in the over-all intelligence picture, it is most appropriate that the role of this technology be examined in considerable detail as a part of the entire intelligence process. This discussion will attempt to analyze the usefulness of the major technical methods of intelligence collection and consider the political risks and provocations which they entail.

COMMUNICATIONS INTERCEPT

One of the oldest forms of intelligence collection is the interception of other parties' communications. Early man undoubtedly watched hostile smoke signals and attempted to decipher the messages being transmitted. This form of intelligence collection, however, took on a whole new significance with the advent of radio communications, which not only heralded a tremendous increase in the volume of information communicated, but also presented valuable new opportunities for listening in on the messages being transmitted. Since such listening was so inherently easy, a new field of countermeasures was developed to protect the privacy of radio communications. Encrypting messages became a standard procedure for disguising the content, and this, in turn, promoted a science of deciphering the codes. The race was on as one side attempted to improve the security of its communications system while the other side attempted to break through these barriers. Because this was a game of countermeasures and counter-countermeasures, dark secrecy was applied to efforts in this area. Successes had to be concealed in order to prevent them from being countered in future situations. The classic publicized case was the U.S. breaking of the Japanese codes before World War II. The secrecy over this success was probably in no small part responsible for our failure to take advantage of it at the time of Pearl Harbor.

Today, there is probably little question that methods are available to insure that any specific communication can be made invulnerable to being read. One-time cryptographic techniques make breaking specific messages almost impossible. In the real world, however, there are practical barriers toward establishing such tight security on all communications. The volume of communications, even in the national-security area, is so large that it is not possible to use such methods for every message. Furthermore, the operation of any system is always subject to human or mechanical errors and, in cryptography, these can lead to the compromise of information.

Finally, even if a message is transmitted in an unbreakable code, the intercept of the communication may still produce meaningful intelligence information. For example, the fact that points A and B are communicating gives by itself a useful piece of datum since it shows some connection between the two points; this can often be a clue as to the nature of the work at A and B. During World War II the transmission of messages from Los Alamos, a deserted school site in New Mexico, and the War Department, to say nothing of the University of Chicago, Hanford in the state of Washington, or Oak Ridge, Tennessee, would have provided an important lead as to the nature of the activities being carried out in the Los Alamos area. Therefore, communications security has to go further than just establishing codes. It must control the volume and nature of the traffic on any communications link and frequently pass false messages in order to hamper traffic analysis. Thus it will be seen that communications intelligence is a vast game of cops and robbers in which each side is continuously trying to outwit the other.

There would seem to be little question that this form of intelligence collection is vital not only in the national security but in the political area as well. Intercepting communications can provide a wealth of useful information on governmental plans and thinking. Different parts of a modern bureaucracy must communicate to operate. While the most sensitive messages can be kept secret, many of the less critical ones can be intercepted and understood. Furthermore, much useful information must be transmitted completely in the open, and occasionally this can prove to be of vital importance. For example, at the end of August 1961, a woman listening to open radio transmissions within the Soviet Union at a receiver in the eastern Mediterranean heard an advance press release with a three-day embargo announcing that the Russians would resume nuclear testing. She recognized the significance of this message, pulled it out of the mass of transcripts that were being made routinely, and forwarded it by priority to Washington. This unclassified message gave President Kennedy advance notice of the Soviet intentions to terminate the nuclear-test moratorium and the opportunity to take political action to forestall this Soviet move. Unfortunately, the government decision-making bureaucracy was too cumbersome, and, in the end, the President docilely allowed the Soviets to recommence testing. An important political opportunity was lost. This is a good example of where intelligence was good but was of little value because of unwillingness to act upon it.

The usefulness of communications intercept in the national-security field is so great and all-encompassing that the selection of specific examples can be misleading. Almost all military activities both in peacetime and in war are heavily dependent on communications. If these can be read, then national security would be greatly enhanced. In the event that military forces were to be used in a surprise aggression, widespread communications would be needed between their various elements. Even if the content of the messages cannot be read, the increased volume of communications could frequently be the indication that some operation is imminent. It could be the difference between national survival or collapse.

What are the political implications of intercepting governmental communications? Secretary Henry L. Stimson is reported to have said before World War II that "nations, like gentlemen, do not read other people's mail." This highly moral attitude has long since disappeared from the conduct of nations, and no longer is the public horrified at the thought of such operations. All countries take for granted that attempts are being made to intercept their communications, and employ the best countermeasures of which they are technically capable. This, of course, works to the disadvantage of less-affluent and less-developed countries, since they have neither the resources nor the sophistication to carry out such operations on a sufficiently extensive scale.

The provocation from this type of operation depends primarily on the means and location by which the intercept is carried out. Much of this can be done from international waters or from friendly countries bordering the target area. In the latter case, political sensitivities can be raised, since most nations do not wish it known that their territory is being used as a base for intelligence operations against their neighbors. However, such operations are so widely practiced that they now are rarely the cause for international protest. The use of friendly countries as a base does, however, create a degree of indebtedness to that country which can sometimes be a political liability. We are prone to support regimes that allow us to use their territory even though the objectives of that regime may not be compatible with our basic political goals. This is a problem that applies to cooperation in intelligence-gathering generally and is probably less serious in the communications-intercept area than in more clandestine or provocative operations.

ELECTRONIC INTELLIGENCE (ELINT)

A similar type of technological intelligence collection is the intercept of radio waves of a noncommunications type, particularly those from radars. This type of intercept, known as ELINT in the intelligence jargon, first came into being with the advent of radar in World War II and has since blossomed into a very extensive intelligence activity. Radars are now the eyes of almost every aspect of military operations. In addition to detecting and tracking hostile aircraft and missiles, radio beams are used for guiding defensive missiles toward the incoming targets. Although many modern offensive missiles now rely on inertial or laser guidance techniques to avoid the chances of their being jammed, radars are often used for offensive missilery as well. Radars are critical to all manner of naval operations. Thus the collection and analysis of ELINT has become a very high-priority task of all military intelligence organizations.

Radars, if they are to be of any military use, must be continually exercised. An air-defense radar that is not turned on provides no defense at all. Furthermore, training must be continuously carried out to insure that they are operated properly. All of these factors provide frequent opportunities for carrying out ELINT operations. Countermeasures, such as with the coding used for communications transmissions, are not available to maintain security.

Despite the increased opportunities for ELINT collection, however, all such operations are not necessarily nonprovocative. In order to detect antiaircraft radars located along the periphery of a country, it is frequently necessary to fly aircraft and sail ships close to the borders in order to intercept the signals. Frequently, such operations are subjects of international incidents. The *Pueblo* seizure off the coast of Korea is an example of one in which the intercept platform, this time a ship, was seized in international waters, although operating in a perfectly legal manner.

Even when over international waters, such operations can be provocative and are often a potential source of international incidents. In order to insure that the radars will be turned on and functioning in a truly operational mode, aircraft frequently approach the coast as if intending to penetrate the national boundaries. It is not surprising that under such circumstances, trigger-happy air-defense personnel are inclined to take counteraction. Furthermore, the scale and number of such operations are probably much larger than can be really justified on the basis of military need. There is always a tendency in such a situation to repeat and repeat operations with the consequent increased probability that an incident will occur. Greater restraint on the part of those authorizing such operations would probably reduce international tensions without any serious loss to national security.

A related type of intelligence collection normally classed under ELINT is the intercept of telemetry signals from new-weapons-testing programs. In order to develop a new missile or carry out a space mission, a nation must equip its test vehicles with instrumentation to measure the functioning of various components, and the only way in which the data from these instruments can be relayed back to the test site is by radio telemetry. Since in many cases the telemetry signals will be receivable at long distances from the source, the opportunities for intercepting such signals from without the country are great. Interpretation of the signals may be more difficult than for the nation that was originating the telemetry, but, nevertheless, useful information can frequently be obtained on the nature of the test program. An example of conspicuously successful telemetry intercept was at the time of the first Soviet-manned space flight. U.S. receivers in the Aleutians were able to pick up the television pictures of the astronauts as they were being transmitted back to the Soviet Union so that U.S. authorities were in a position to know simultaneously with the Russians that the mission was a success. Soviet secrecy had led to considerable skepticism over their claims of space superiority, and these intercepts provided the data for an independent analysis of their achievements. Similar telemetry intercepts provided much of the information which Secretary of Defense Schlesinger and his predecessors have published on the details of the Soviet missile-test program.

Since most of this collection can be carried out at long distances and outside the territories of the testing country, it is not provocative and therefore not a source of international friction. Truly covert ELINT operations within the country are rarely needed or feasible, but in some areas the territories of friendly countries are required as a base of operations. This could on occasion lead to political embarrassment and an undue dependence on the good will of that country in order to obtain permission for the operations. A case in point is Turkey, which is strategically located opposite the southern border of the Soviet Union where much of the Soviet missile launching and other weapons testing occurs. It is no secret that the United States has many stations in that country for the collection of such information, and the continuance of these operations is dependent on maintaining good relations with the Turkish government. These relations were recently subject to strains as a result of our desire to persuade the Turkish government to halt the cultivation of poppies, a major source of the illicit drug trade in the United States. The United States could have been hampered in its representations to Turkey by the desire to keep these strains from reaching the point where we would lose our receiving sites there.

Unfortunately, satellites are not ideal platforms for intercept of signals from those portions of the test ranges in the interior of the Soviet Union because normal-altitude satellites traverse the target area so rapidly that the duration of any single intercept is very short. Thus it would be easy to schedule launchings so as to minimize useful coverage by the satellite receivers. The intercept from stationary satellites at a distance of more than twenty thousand miles is greatly handicapped because the long range reduces the strength of the signal to an intolerable extent.

RADARS FOR INTELLIGENCE COLLECTION

A final form of electronic intelligence collection is the converse of ELINT, that is the use of active radars to observe a missile in flight. This type of collection, known as RADINT, involves the transmission of easily detectable radio signals, so it cannot be done clandestinely. It has been used very successfully to observe missile-flight testing by operating high-powered radars within line of sight of the ballistic-missile trajectory. By this method the United States was able to confirm the first Soviet ICBM test flight in 1957 and to keep track of virtually all launchings of long-range missiles since that date. The deployment of such radars on native territory is of course nonprovocative, since radiation has no effect on the object in space. However, as in the case of the telemetry receivers referred to earlier, the radar had to be located in Turkey in order to observe the launch ends of the Soviet medium-, intermediate-, and intercontinental-range ballistic missiles. The more that such type of technological intelligence collection is recognized internationally as legal, the less will be the dependence on good will of the nation for its continued deployment. The United States and the Soviet Union have now endorsed such national technical means for use in verifying arms-control agreements.

NUCLEAR-TEST-DETECTION METHODS

A special class of technical intelligence techniques includes those which have been devised for the specific purpose of detecting and obtaining information on nuclear tests. Ever since the first nuclear explosion, an important intelligence goal has been to acquire knowledge of nuclear tests carried out by foreign governments and insofar as possible to gather information on the nature of the explosive used. As a consequence, over a period of years a series of highly sophisticated scientific methods were developed and put into operation. Fortunately, nuclear weapons produce such large-scale phenomena that they are easily observed at very long distances from the source and, therefore, do not require the intrusion into the territories of the testing country. The value and effectiveness of the various techniques of gathering this information were freely discussed in open negotiations which began in 1958 and led to the Limited Test Ban Treaty of 1963. There have been continued international information exchanges since then in attempts to negotiate a comprehensive test ban. Rather than being considered provocative, the collection of information on nuclear tests is looked on as a contribution toward reducing the risks of nuclear war.

PHOTORECONNAISSANCE

Although all the foregoing technological methods of intelligence collection are extremely useful for the maintenance of adequate information to protect our national security, they are dwarfed in importance by photoreconnaissance. A picture is worth a thousand words—and often many reels of recorded radio signals. Photography provides easily understandable evidence even when a skilled photo-interpreter is needed to describe the object on the film. It has applications in almost every intelligence area, whether it be scientific, political, economic, or military.

Even though photoreconnaissance has long been an important tool of intelligence, recent technological advances culminating in the capability to obtain useful photography using satellites as platforms have completely revolutionized the entire intelligence-collection process. No longer can any nation hide its military and industrial activities behind an Iron Curtain. Only those facilities, equipment, or forces that can be continuously kept under a nonrevealing cover, such as underground or in an innocuous structure, can be concealed; this can rarely be done. The mission of an agent to procure information on troop dispositions, missile deployments, or submarine construction has now been eliminated. An entire country can be photographed within a few days, the only limitation being the degree to which clouds interfere, and almost no area in the world is continuously cloud-covered. Thus, with persistence, any target is now subject to photo observation.

Aerial reconnaissance dates back to the first availability of the airplane, and probably the most valuable function of aircraft in World War I was to carry out visual reconnaissance. By World War II the sophistication of both the aircraft platform and its photographic systems was greatly improved, and aerial reconnaissance was an important combat mission. However, the risk of a single aircraft operating on a reconnaissance mission being shot down was very high so that its usefulness was somewhat restricted. With the end of open conflict the value of photographic reconnaissance became very limited because of the political and physical hazards of penetration beyond foreign borders.

In 1955 the effectiveness of the Iron Curtain in obscuring Soviet military developments became intolerable to U.S. security planners as the Russians gradually accumulated nuclear weapons of greater and greater power and sophistication. Under CIA direction a crash program was initiated to develop a very-high-altitude, long-range photoreconnaissance aircraft, equipped with the most advanced state-of-the-art photographic material. Its ability to fly above Soviet interceptor or missile defenses was its only protection; it could, however, be observed and tracked by Soviet radars so that its presence was known. On the other hand, it had no capability for offensive action. This new aircraft, nicknamed the U-2, was truly a revolutionary technological achievement and became operational in 1956 just at a time when fears were being aroused over the burgeoning Russian ballistic-missile program. Overflights of critical areas in the Soviet Union were carefully programmed, and for the first time the Iron Curtain was significantly lifted.

Although the Soviet leaders knew of these overflights, they refrained from public protest, since they did not wish to admit to the vulnerability of their air space—a good example of a most provocative intelligence-collection program that was protected by its immunity from counteraction. By May 1960, however, perhaps with the assistance of a bit of luck, the Russians finally managed to shoot down a U-2, and the international uproar that followed brought this program of overflight of the Soviet Union to an end. However, the useful reconnaissance life of U-2-type aircraft continued, and this type plane discovered the Soviet missiles being deployed in Cuba and has also provided photographic coverage in many troubled areas of the world even up to the present time.

Although the U-2 was invaluable in collecting the only information then obtainable on a wide variety of high-priority intelligence targets within the Soviet Union, it was still far from an ideal reconnaissance platform. Because of the political sensitivity of overflights, the number of sorties was kept very limited, perhaps of the order of thirty during the four years that it operated in that theater. More important, the area that an aircraft could cover in a single flight was limited to at the most a swath approximately one hundred miles across and about three hundred miles long. As a consequence, only the highest-priority locations could be targeted for coverage, and large areas of the Soviet Union remained completely blacked out.

Aircraft photoreconnaissance has tremendous value in some situations, since the vehicle can be easily directed on short notice to a specific location, can take a high-resolution picture, and can give a planner usable information within a few hours after the return of the plane. It has the disadvantages of the need for a base within range of the target, of limited-area coverage, of vulnerability to destruction, and, most im-

THE ROLE OF TECHNOLOGY | *119*

portant, of being extremely provocative. It is hard to tell whether a plane is carrying a camera or a bomb. This hostile characteristic frequently destroys completely its value as an intelligence tool in peacetime. Nevertheless, because of their flexibility, aircraft will probably continue to have limited utility as platforms for photoreconnaissance despite these drawbacks.

October 4, 1957, however, marked the beginning of a new era that culminated in the current revolutionary improvement in capabilities for photoreconnaissance.* On that day the Soviets orbited their first satellite, which traversed the United States and many other countries of the world and set the precedent for making legitimate space transit of national territories without permission of the states involved. No country has ever raised the question of legality, and thus the first steps were taken toward the establishment in customary international law of the freedom of access to outer space for peaceful and scientific purposes.

Of course, these early satellites did not contain any cameras for taking pictures of the territory over which they passed, but the precedent had been set. In 1960 the United States orbited weather satellites capable of making low-resolution photographs of the earth, that is, photographs that could define large geographical features such as lakes, but not smaller man-made objects such as buildings or vehicles. Still no complaints on the part of any nation. Admittedly, these early space flights were of no practical value for intelligence purposes, but they did help set the stage for international approval of satellite reconnaissance.

Early in 1960 fears of widespread Soviet ICBM deployment that could not be confirmed or put to rest by the U-2 or other intelligence sources resulted in the creation of the so-called missile gap, an important campaign issue in the Presidential elections of that year. By the end of 1960 satellite photography was starting to be available, during early 1961 the missile gap began to shrink, and by the end of 1961 U.S. authorities confidently discounted the existence of any missile gap. Apparently the Russians had deployed at the most a handful of their cumbersome first-generation SS-6 missiles. The ability to carry out satellite observation of large areas of the Soviet Union with sufficient photographic resolution to spot missile silos had proven that the launchers were not hidden even in the remote parts of the country.

* This material on satellite reconnaissance is drawn from a chapter by the author entitled "A Leap Forward in Verification" in the book *SALT—The Moscow Agreements and Beyond* (New York: Free Press, 1974).

The Soviet Union proceeded with a parallel development of observation satellites, and both nations improved the capabilities of their systems throughout the 1960s. By 1964 Secretary of Defense McNamara was regularly reporting publicly on Soviet strategic deployments, and in 1967 President Johnson extolled the virtues of the U.S. space program for protecting our security. In recent years Defense Secretaries Laird and Schlesinger have described the Soviet strategic posture in detail, frequently announcing new construction very shortly after it began and accurately describing the size of Soviet missiles. Neither country, however, publicly admitted the method by which this information was obtained, in order to avoid a political confrontation and a possible international uproar which might have raised questions as to the legality of such operations. Instead, there was a tacit recognition of photographic-satellite capabilities by both sides and perhaps an increasing realization that the availability of the information to the other nation provided a stabilizing influence.

Satellite reconnaissance has a number of major advantages over that carried out by aircraft in addition to its invulnerability and international acceptance. A satellite in orbit at an altitude of one hundred to three hundred miles can survey very large areas in a very short time period. If a satellite were launched in a north-south polar trajectory, then the entire earth could be covered, once in daylight and once at night, every twenty-four hours.

Apparently, at the present time, both the United States and the Soviet Union have two kinds of systems, namely, those that can photograph rapidly large areas with relatively low resolution, and other systems that can focus on specific locations deemed of interest as a result of the large-area surveys. Judging by the details reported on Soviet weapons systems, the United States and probably also the Soviet Union have a capability to resolve objects with a dimension of a few feet or even less. This would permit the observation of most items of military equipment exposed in the open. The information obtained can be relayed back to earth by TV transmission or by returning the photographic film to earth in a recoverable capsule. In the case of TV transmission, the time lag between observation and the availability of the information at a command center can be very short—hours or less—but if the film must be returned to earth, the delay can be days or even a week or more.

In the early 1960s, while the early reconnaissance satellites were being gradually improved, debate was simultaneously proceeding on the international legality of such operations. Although the principle of free access to space for peaceful purposes was universally recognized from the outset, considerable debate ensued concerning the definition of the term "peaceful."

An agreement between the United States and the Soviet Union was finally reached in the fall of 1963, when the Soviet Union suddenly dropped its insistence on including a ban on space reconnaissance and negotiated with the United States representatives a United Nations resolution (General Assembly Resolution 1884, XVIII, October 17, 1963) dealing with outer space which called upon all States to refrain from placing in orbit nuclear weapons or other weapons of mass destruction. The United States and the Soviet Union had just previously stated their intentions not to do so without including any reference to the issue of reconnaissance satellites.

The final seal of approval was placed on the use of space for photo-reconnaissance by the ABM Treaty and the Interim Agreement on Offensive Weapons signed in Moscow in 1972. In these agreements the United States and the Soviet Union agreed not only that national technical means should be used to verify the provisions of these arms-control agreements, but also that these information-collection methods should neither be interfered with nor have deliberate concealment measures used against them. Although satellite reconnaissance is not specifically mentioned in the treaty, the legislative history is clear that this was the key method of information collection being referred to. Even though these were bilateral agreements between the United States and the Soviet Union, no other country has ever objected to such reconnaissance, and thus one can say that it now has widespread international legality. At last we have available a technological intelligence-collection tool that is recognized as legal and, therefore, nonprovocative. Since space vehicles are not practical for launching weapons, overflights by reconnaissance satellites cannot be considered as hostile acts. Furthermore, such reconnaissance has the capability of satisfying such a wide variety of information needs that it should reduce the justification for intelligence collection by many much more provocative methods. For example, aircraft reconnaissance could be largely phased out and the capability maintained only for extraordinary situations or potential use in wartime.

NEW ROLE OF TECHNICAL INTELLIGENCE

A review of the over-all field of technical intelligence collection demonstrates with little doubt its overwhelming importance in the entire intelligence picture. No other intelligence methodology even approaches technical intelligence in the breadth of its applications or in the quality of the information provided. It produces a wealth of hard facts much less subject to alternative interpretations than the information from other sources. No one questions its reliability as a source, since it is not subject to manipulation like a human agent. Its data is invaluable for almost every aspect of military and national-security planning. Even such limited arms-control agreements as the partial Test Ban Treaty and the SALT treaties would have been impossible without technical intelligence data, and, more significant, disarmament will never be achieved without it. Even in the political arena, technical intelligence provides the factual background to assess the estimates of intentions derived from political analyses. It is similarly useful in the economic field, where it provides data on industrial and agricultural programs without which too often one would be dependent on suspect published reports.

Technology has not only improved the intelligence-data base but it has done so with increasingly less provocation and fewer political risks.

The important question that should be asked is whether our national-security planners and the intelligence community have adequately taken this new situation into account. We should not carry out politically risky agent operations when the incremental addition to data available by technical methods is not large. We should not carry out provocative peacetime aircraft missions when satellites can provide the same data even if the latter method is more expensive. We should not be negotiating arrangements with governments inimical to our democratic principles just to obtain a base for redundant information available from other sources. Aircraft and naval missions that run the risk of armed conflict should be carefully re-examined to determine their real priority in light of the new situation. Some of these new looks are undoubtedly taking place and may be behind the reported cutbacks and reorganizations in the intelligence community, but in light of the revolutionary changes wrought by improvements in the technology of intelligence collection, it is hard to believe that even more cannot be done.

III

The
Implications

ROBERT L. BOROSAGE

The Central Intelligence Agency

7

THE KING'S MEN AND THE CONSTITUTIONAL ORDER

The "Grand Inquest" into the crimes and abuses of President Nixon taught us what we should have learned from the war in Indochina: lawlessness is the prerogative of power. Now, the inquiry must turn from the usurpations of one man to the powers and policies of the institutions that form the basis of the "imperial Presidency" and imperil our freedom and liberty. No executive institution demands immediate investigation more than the Central Intelligence Agency, "the King's Men" or "President's Army" established in the White House, engaged in clandestine activities throughout the world, its gray and furtive realm hidden from public or congressional control by an unprecedented secrecy.

CONSTITUTIONAL ORDER AND DISORDER

Every form of government possesses certain essential traits, principles that distinguish it from others. Moreover, every country might be said to have its own "spirit of the laws," its own basis of legitimacy which inheres in its laws, in the opinion of its citizenry, in the actions of its leaders, in its traditions, history, and culture.

Our Constitution established a republican form of government for the nation. The republic was founded on a rather pessimistic view of political man, and a mechanistic, Newtonian scheme of government. Man was viewed as ambitious, corrupt, and corruptible, prone to unwise passions and foolish aspirations. To protect the polity from the designs of the ambitious or the corruption of the venal, the constitutional order established a system of checks and balances, a separation of powers and functions among the legislature, the executive, and the judiciary. The basic concept of checks and balances was designed, as Justice Brandeis reminded us, "not to promote efficiency, but to preclude the exercise of arbitrary power."[1]

A fundamental principle of the republic was that all would be subject to the rule of the law. As Corwin noted, "The colonial period ended with the belief prevalent that the 'executive magistracy' was the natural enemy, the legislature usually the natural friend of liberty."[2] Thus, in a republican order, "the legislative authority necessarily predominates."[3] The legislature would be the "engine" of the republic, passing laws for the executive to execute, laws that would empower the executive to act and would limit the scope of its discretion and the means of its action. The legislature would control the purse and the power of taxation. Moreover, the legislature would constitute a continuing inquest into the affairs and activities of the executive and the polity to insure that its laws were carried out, its provisions sufficient, and to guard against corruption, abuse of power, or usurpation.*

The spirit of the American laws reinforced these basic principles. Hannah Arendt, addressing Montesquieu's conception of a spirit of the laws, concluded that "consent, not in the very old sense of mere acquiescence with its distinction between rule over willing subjects and rule over unwilling ones, but in the sense of active support and continuing participation in all matters of public interest, is the spirit of American law."[4]

Active consent and participation requires that information about the government's activities be readily available. Beyond an injunction against secrecy, however, an active consent also requires arenas—town halls, clubs, associations, assemblies, demonstrations—in which the citizenry can meet, exchange their views on the subject of government and vote on matters of interest. Consent without information is acquiescence in ignorance; consent without discussion and decision is approval without citizenship or politics.

---

* For Montesquieu, a leading mentor of the colonial mind, the legislative and the executive were assumed to operate on different principles. The governing principle of monarchy (whether elective, constitutional, or hereditary) was honor—thus a.monarch would be concerned with grandeur, with putting his or her subjects to tasks of sufficient magnitude to bring glory and awe to the regime. The governing principle of a republic was virtue; a true republican would be satisfied with the development of virtuous men in the polity.

Needless to say, we have moved far from these basic principles of government. Madison's fear of legislative tyranny has now been replaced by the very real threat of executive autocracy. The Presidency—under Richard Nixon, virtually a fourth branch of the government unto itself—has become dominant and domineering. The executive has assumed the initiative in the legislative process and has slowly captured more of the power of the purse. Secrecy now far exceeds voluntary disclosure. The citizenry acts more like an audience than like a participant in government. Local assemblies have withered and died. And in national-security matters the executive acts with virtual independence, with a freedom and license a Tudor king would have applauded.

The historical basis for this profound alteration has been emergency: economic depression at home and war abroad. Its legal expression has been either claims of inherent executive power or broad delegations of power by the Congress. Its institutional base has been the burgeoning bureaucracies and the growth of national and multinational corporations. The United States has been in a state of national emergency since 1933. Presidential license, which grew to meet the economic crisis of the Great Depression, became supreme in World War II. Years ago, Tocqueville warned the young republic that "war does not always give democratic societies over to military government, but it must invariably and immeasurably increase the powers of civil government. . . . If that does not lead to despotism by sudden violence, it leads men gently in that direction by their habits. All those who seek to destroy the freedom of the democratic nations must know that war is the surest and shortest means." The experience after World War II illustrated the validity of his warning.

After World War II the emergency never ended: the wartime institutions were never dismantled, the prerogatives never surrendered. The powers exercised by the President during the emergency did not revert back to the legislature or the people.

Truman and his advisers had global aspirations, designs fueled by great ambitions and great fears. The executive would manage a global responsibility; America would, in Dean Acheson's view, inherit the mantle of Britain and Rome. Yet, imperial policies abroad—a policy of constant intervention and continuous engagement—required structural alterations in the "peacetime" executive at home. Thus institutions designed in the executive for total warfare during World War II were legitimized for the postwar period.

These institutions were purposely designed to isolate foreign-policy decisions from congressional and public control. One could hardly manage an imperial mission under what William Bundy disparagingly called "the klieg lights of a democracy."

The institutional structure gave a new bureaucratic reality to the executive claims of prerogative over questions of national security. When President Nixon claimed an inherent power to make peace or war, to dispatch troops, to make commitments, to hide information from Congress, to wiretap, or to break and enter under the banner of national security, which he would define to fit his purposes, he had some thirty years of practice to support his claim. The President was simply expounding the principles of a new constitutional order already inchoately established in the actions of the postwar imperial Presidency. As Ralph Stavins has suggested elsewhere, America was caught between two constitutional orders: the republican and the imperial.[5]

The Central Intelligence Agency exemplifies this imperial constitutional order. Its legal foundations, mission, secrecy, and relationship to the Congress provide a clear definition of a political form that violates our republican framework. A republican order is premised on the rule of law and requires that the legislature define the charter of inferior executive offices and agencies; the CIA's mission is defined by secret charter developed in the executive and dubiously pegged upon vague congressional statute. A republican order presumes disclosure and freedom of information; the CIA luxuriates in extreme secrecy. The former demands accountability to the legislature and the people; the latter avoids accountability as much as possible. The former is based on the assumption that peace is the normal state of affairs for the polity; the latter presupposes and supports continuous intervention, war and parawar. In every aspect of its existence, the Central Intelligence Agency represents an affront to the constitutional order of the republic and a monument to the imperial aspirations of the executive.

LAW AND PARA-LAW

The Constitution confers the "legislative powers" upon the Congress, a power extending to all laws "necessary and proper" for executing any provisions vested by the Constitution "in the Government of the United States, or in any Department or Office thereof."[6] As Hamilton put it, "The essence of the legislative authority is to enact laws, or in other words, to prescribe rules for the regulation of the Society."[7] Further, the law could not be excessively vague or overbroad; the Congress was proscribed from delegating "essential legislative functions with which it is vested" to another body.[8]

The executive power is a power and duty to execute the laws; indeed, the very premise of a rule of law is the proposition that the executive is subject to law, and this proposition is precisely what distinguished the new republic from the monarchies of Europe. The distinction between the legislative and executive functions need not be overdrawn. Congress has the power to delegate authority to the executive. It may pass legislation that, having established the goals and standards, empowers the executive to elaborate directives and procedures to guide enforcement. Anyone familiar with administrative agencies and their history understands that such delegations can, particularly since the New Deal, be very broad indeed.[9]

Recently, however, we have witnessed the spread of a new form of law, law based upon executive initiatives that can only be termed legislative. The growth of executive power and prerogative has been accompanied by the spread of what might be termed para-law. Para-laws are the internal regulations of the bureaucracy, premised either upon a claim to inherent power or a grant of a broad and unchartered power from the legislature or simply established without reference to any legal basis. The para-legal gives the appearance of legality and of regulation by law to executive agencies without the reality of legislative determination and definition. It might be said to represent a transitional form between the rule of law and the reign of a leader.[10]

The legal foundation of the Central Intelligence Agency provides a good example of the para-legal mode. The CIA traces its birth not to an act of Congress, but to an executive order issued by Franklin D. Roosevelt in 1941, establishing an Office of Coordination of Information (COI) in the White House.[11] Headed by William "Wild Bill" Donovan, a nonpareil bureaucratic entrepreneur, the COI was transformed into the Office of Strategic Services (OSS) with the outbreak of the war. The OSS soon became engaged in clandestine actions throughout the world, actions that, in the context of a war against fascism, were never questioned.

The OSS retained the same authority as the COI, and the Roosevelt executive orders gave no indication of the scope of its activities. The orders contained no reference to covert operations, merely empowering the new office to coordinate, analyze, and disseminate intelligence information and estimates. The standard bureaucratic catchall provision empowered the office to "carry out, when requested by the President, such supplementary activities, as may facilitate *the securing of information* [emphasis added]." From this phrase, Donovan and Roosevelt derived a rather dubious legal authority for covert actions throughout World War II.

After the war the OSS was disbanded, its functions transferred, divided, and reassembled—all by executive orders.[12] The intelligence office was reorganized as the Central Intelligence Group while Truman and his leading advisers negotiated truces between the different contending national-security bureaucracies. Only when the administration had lined up the various bureaucracies in support of a consolidated National Security Act, did it turn to Congress.

The National Security Act of 1947 sought congressional ratification of *ad hoc* wartime institutions for peacetime. Admiral Chester Nimitz testified that the bill was designed "to incorporate the lessons of the past war. It gives legal status to those co-ordinating and command agencies which were found most effective to the conduct of global war. This is a forward-looking bill [*sic*]."[13]

Title I, Section 102 of the bill established the Central Intelligence Agency under the direction of the National Security Council.

This procedure was characteristic of the post-Depression executive: executive initiative based upon emergency and necessity followed by congressional ratification, legitimation, or adoption. The procedure inverts the republican norm of congressional legislation and executive ratification. In a very direct sense, it forces Congress to act as a veto on executive initiative and legislation, rather than the reverse. Congress, in this course of events, is at a supreme disadvantage to a unified executive. It has no opportunity to render a considered judgment *ab initio*. For example, by the time the National Security Act of 1947 was referred to Congress, the Central Intelligence Group already possessed a glamorous wartime history and a galaxy of powerful friends and supporters. Moreover, the administration had lined up the whole national-security bureaucracy in favor of the compromise legislation, presenting Congress with one official after another attesting to its necessity. Since the intelligence agency already existed, the mystique of intelligence could be employed to limit debate and impress the impressionable. When General Hoyt Vandenberg, head of the Central Intelligence Group, testified in favor of the legislation, he apologized for having to limit his testimony to protect activities from disclosure. Congress was given the decision of repudiating an agency rather than creating a new one. Needless to say, Congress passed the National Security Act without extended discussion of the Agency, its powers, duties, or activities.

The 1947 act was to provide the CIA with the façade of legitimacy. As H. H. Ransom has noted, the "real constitution of the CIA is not so much the statutory authority, but the score or so of super-secret National Security Council Intelligence Directives."[14] Secret NSCIDs form the operative charter for the Agency, the para-legal basis for its activities at home and abroad. Thus the statutory basis of the Agency has no meaning for bureaucratic purposes: its direction comes not from the law, but from executive directives, which are open to neither congressional nor popular review and which may even conflict with other aspects of the 1947 bill.[15]

COVERT ACTIONS AND EXECUTIVE WAR-MAKING

To the framers of the constitution, the executive was to be particularly mistrusted in matters of war and peace, an axiom being that, in Madison's words, "The executive is the department of power most distinguished by its propensity to war: Hence it is the practice of all states, in proportion as they are free, to disarm this propensity of its influence." The history of European monarchies had impressed upon the colonists the dangers of empowering one man to commit the nation to war. Rulers tended to make war for reasons of personal ire or ambition, thereby wasting the lives and resources of the populace. As James Wilson wrote, the power to declare war must be lodged in the Congress as guard against "being hurried" into war, so that no "single man [can] . . . involve us in such distress."[16]

Thus Congress was given the war power. In Wilson's summary:

> The power of declaring war, and the other powers naturally connected with it, are vested in Congress. To provide and maintain a navy—to make rules for its government—to grant letters of marque and reprisal—to makes rules concerning captures—to raise and support armies—to establish rules for their regulation—to provide for organizing . . . the militia, and for calling them forth in the service of the Union—all these are powers naturally connected with

the power of declaring war. All these powers, therefore, are vested in Congress.[16]

Moreover, the legislature was granted a large role in foreign affairs short of war. The executive, characterized by the "unity, secrecy and dispatch" necessary for foreign negotiations, was to control the day-to-day management of foreign affairs. Yet the executive's powers were to be shared with those of the Congress. Treaties and commitments required the advice and the consent of the Senate, and it was assumed that the leaders of the legislature would participate early and frequently in negotiations. Thus Presidential license to commit the nation to alliances or to involve it in war was severely circumscribed by the Constitution.

Initially, the constitutional division of power was buttressed by institutional realities. The standing Army and Navy were small throughout our early history, and although active Presidents often chafed at constitutional restraints, little more than a skirmish could be fought without recourse to Congress. Also, the executive was still small and responsive, the Congress vigorous and, if not wise, at least cantankerous and jealous of its powers.

The purposes behind this separation of powers was most clear. The framers knew that for a republic to survive war would have to be an abnormal and temporary state of affairs. War, as Senator Fulbright has suggested, fostered traits alien to a republic: secrecy rather than openness, deceit rather than honesty, suspension of humanitarian impulse rather than its propagation.

Today we have virtually abandoned these careful restraints and guidelines. Senator Fulbright wrote, "It may not be too much to say that as far as foreign policy is concerned, our government system is no longer one of separated powers, but rather one of elected, executive dictatorship."[17] Every President since Roosevelt has waged war or para-war abroad without prior approval by Congress. Executive war can be undertaken in secrecy, funded through an array of secret monies, and planned in secret sessions in the White House, and a President may employ either overt or covert bureaucracies to carry out his designs.

Secret wars sponsored by the CIA are an important aspect of this executive dictatorship over questions of war and peace. The Agency sponsors continuous covert engagement abroad. It offers the President a variety of seductive clandestine alternatives—ranging from bribery to full-scale warfare—to gain whatever objectives may be defined for an area. Shrouded in secrecy and deception, the Central Intelligence Agency contributes a clandestine praetorian guard that the President can dispose of at his will (provided he can gain Agency concurrence).

Continuous engagement erodes the distinction—so important to the republic and the congressional powers—between war and peace, intervention and withdrawal. Engagement is constant; each escalation is based on a prior bureaucratic commitment. Congress can never be in the position to declare war or to make a commitment without being faced with a long bureaucratic history of meddling and promises. War or para-war becomes the constant state of the polity; the President ever speaks as Commander in Chief and the power of Congress and the energy of the people are diminished in executive interventions abroad.

SECRECY: THE BUDGET OF THE CENTRAL INTELLIGENCE AGENCY

In 1949 Congress passed the Central Intelligence Administration Act at the behest of the Truman Administration.*[18] The Act established the regulations that would direct the administration of the new agency. The legislation exempted the CIA from the general laws designed by Congress to regulate the affairs of executive bureaucracies. Thus the CIA was empowered to contract by negotiation without advertising, to bring up to one hundred aliens into the country annually without following immigration procedures, to hire and fire employees without regard to civil-service regulations or requirements, and so forth. Most important, the Act provided that appropriations or other monies made available to

---

* The procedures surrounding the passage of this bill once again exemplify the CIA's estrangement from normal legislative procedures. The hearings on the bill in both the House and the Senate were held in executive session. Both reports simply reprinted the provisions of the bill without further explanation or elaboration. Congressman Short of Mississippi expressed the common assumption, "We are engaged in a highly dangerous business. It is something I naturally abhor . . . [but] there is no way out of it so far as I can see, and perhaps the less we say in public about the Bill the better off all of us will be."

Only Victor Marcantonio, the firebrand New York congressman, recorded his objections for the record: "This is the first time in the history of Congress that members are being asked to vote on legislation about which not merely information is withheld, but also explanation as to the provisions of the legislation. . . . No member of Congress has been informed; . . . only the members of the Committee on Armed Forces. . . .

"Congress is suspending its right to legislate, and we are being asked to do this in furtherance of the cold war. . . . I refuse to believe that our nation is so unsafe from a security standpoint that we have to suspend . . . the legislative prerogatives of the representatives of the people in Congress. . . ."[19]

The bill passed 348 to 4.

the Agency "may be expended without regard to the provisions of law and regulations relating to the expenditure of government funds"; and that for "objects of a confidential, extraordinary or emergency nature," expenditures may be authorized solely on the certificate of the Director. Finally, it permitted the CIA to transfer to and receive from other governmental agencies such sums as may be approved by the Office of Management and Budget (OMB). These provisions gave legislative approval to an Agency budget, hidden in the interstices of the federal budget, which neither Congress nor the public could divine.

Since the passage of the bill, the budget figures of the Central Intelligence Agency have remained secret. In 1953 the Acting Director of the CIA, C. P. Cabell, in response to inquiry by Senator Mansfield, wrote that the "CIA appropriation figure is very tightly held and is known to not more than five or six Members in each House."[20] To this day the budget figures are known to only a handful of congressmen and bureaucrats, and the budget itself is sent to Capitol Hill with a *secret* classification for approval by Congress. In both the House and the Senate, the figures are shown only to a few generally sympathetic congressmen on the Defense Appropriations subcommittees of the House and Senate and not generally shared with all members of the subcommittees.

This secrecy directly contravenes Article I, Section 9, Clause 7 of the Constitution, which provides:

> No money shall be drawn from the Treasury, but in consequence of Appropriations made by Law; and a regular Statement of Account of the Receipts and Expenditures of all public money shall be published from time to time.

The clause placed a positive limitation and duty upon the legislature and the executive. In his commentaries on the Constitution, Story contrasted the provision with the practice "in arbitrary governments [where] the prince levies what money he pleases from his subjects, disposes of it as he thinks proper and is beyond responsibility or reproof. . . . [In a republic] Congress is made the guardian of [the public treasure]; and to make their responsibility complete and perfect, a regular account of the receipts and expenditures is required to be published, that the people may know what money is expended for what purpose and by what authority."[21] For the founders, the major question concerning the clause was whether the phrase "time to time" was sufficiently well-defined to insure a periodic accounting. The purpose of the clause was for the protection not of Congress, but of the people. During the Maryland debates on the Constitution, James McHenry said, "The people who give their money ought to know in what manner it is expended." In New York, Livingston reassured the delegates; the clause, he thought, would protect the people from a corrupt Congress, as publication of the budget from year to year would soon expose any corruption.[22]

The clause was directly related to the notion of informed consent, so important to American law. Consent could not be given unless the people could evaluate the cost, the purposes, and the activities of the government. To be sure, some matters might require secrecy. Mason, in the Virginia debates, thought that secrecy might be necessary (temporarily) "in matters relating to military operations and foreign relations," but "he did not conceive that the receipts and expenditures of the public money ought ever to be concealed. The people," he affirmed, "had a right to know the expenditures of their money."[23]

In 1967 William B. Richardson, an insurance-claims examiner in Greensburg, Pennsylvania, "a member of the electorate and a loyal citizen of the United States," brought suit in Federal District Court challenging the constitutionality of the secret funding of the CIA and demanding an accounting of its expenditures. In 1972, the Third Circuit Court of Appeals, sitting *en banc*, upheld his standing, finding that "if appellant, as a citizen, voter and taxpayer, is not entitled to maintain an action such as this to enforce the dictates of Article I, Section 9, Clause 7 . . . then it is difficult to see how this requirement, which the framers of the Constitution considered vital to the proper functioning of our democratic republic, may be enforced at all."[24]

The Court of Appeals' decision was overturned by a five-to-four decision of the Supreme Court on June 25, 1974. The Court did not reach the merits of the claim, but ruled that as a taxpayer Richardson had no standing to bring the suit. "Any other conclusion," wrote Chief Justice Burger, "would mean that the Founding Fathers intended to set up something in the nature of an Athenian democracy or a New England town meeting to oversee the conduct of the National Government. . . ."[25]

The Court's decision turned on standing to sue, rather than the merits of the case. In dissent, Mr. Justice Douglas touched upon the substantive issue, noting:

> The sovereign in this Nation are the people, not the bureaucracy. . . .
> The statement of accounts of public expenditures goes to the heart

of the problem of sovereignty. If taxpayers may not ask that rudimentary question, their sovereignty becomes an empty symbol and a secret bureaucracy is allowed to run our affairs.[26]

The reluctance of the least powerful branch to assert itself in the area does not diminish the stark contrast between the secret budgetary provisions for the Central Intelligence Agency and the spirit and letter of our Constitution.

SECRECY: THE CIA AND THE FIRST AMENDMENT

Every form of government demands its secrets, and a republic is no exception. Although the founders made no provision for executive secrecy in the Constitution (which provided only for congressional secrecy), some secrecy in operation was no doubt assumed as part of the process of government. In diplomatic negotiations, Jay observed in the sixty-fourth Federalist, "perfect secrecy and immediate dispatch are sometimes requisite . . . ; and the most useful intelligence may be obtained if the persons possessing it can be relieved of the apprehension of discovery."[27]

Yet secrecy was also inherently suspect. "A popular government, without popular information or the means of requiring it," Madison wrote, "is but a prologue to a farce or a tragedy or perhaps both. Knowledge will forever govern ignorance, and a people who aim to be their own governors must arm themselves with the power that knowledge gives."[28] Disclosure and freedom of information was, therefore, an important aspect of a government based upon consent and participation.

From the beginning of the republic, a continued tension between secrecy and disclosure was established. Repeatedly, the executive would seek to act secretly without informing the public; and time after time, concerned citizens would seek to learn the secrets and publish the information. As early as 1795, President Washington laid the Jay treaty before the Senate in secret session. Senator Mason of Virginia, in vehement opposition, sent the document to the Jack Anderson of his day, Benjamin Franklin Bache of the *Philadelphia Aurora*, who promptly published it to spark public outrage.

Government officials have made repeated attempts to squelch such activities, beginning with the infamous Sedition Acts of 1798, which provided the statutory basis for criminal prosecutions against newspaper editors. Out of this struggle grew a rather strong belief in free expression, particularly freedom of the press. At the core of this constitutionally protected area of activity was a historic commitment against prior restraint of speech. In 1931, this principle received a clear enunciation by the Supreme Court in *Near* v. *Minnesota*. Chief Justice Hughes, reviewing the adoption of the First Amendment, laid down the basic rule:

> . . . Liberty of the press, historically considered and taken up by the Federal Constitution, has meant, principally although not exclusively, immunity from previous restraints or censorship.[29]

Although subsequent criminal prosecution or civil damages might be available for abuses, prior restraint was not. Not even the Sedition Laws empowered the executive to impose a prior restraint upon publication.

Yet government secrecy itself represents censorship at the source or prior restraint. A system of military secrecy grew in the United States without clashing with the judicial rule against censorship. Truman extended the classification system to civilian agencies of the government in 1951. The system was formalized by a series of executive orders, issued by Presidents Truman, Eisenhower, and Nixon, which established the para-legal basis for a governmental classification system.[30] Congress added specific legislative guidelines for secrecy in atomic energy, communication codes, and other areas.

The legal and para-legal foundations for government secrecy never provided statutory authority for judicially enforced prior restraint. The Espionage Acts were basically aimed at providing criminal sanctions against spies. The special authority given to the CIA Director to "protect sources and methods" was accompanied by no criminal or injunctive remedy. Government classification was based almost completely on executive order and enforced more by threat of dismissal than of criminal penalty.

The CIA established an elaborate security and secrecy system under the authority of the Presidential executive orders, and every CIA employee signs a "secrecy agreement" upon entering and leaving the CIA. The employee pledges never to reveal any secret information to unauthorized persons, and recognizes a governmental "property right" in the "information or intelligence [not simply the documents] or any method of collecting it."[31]

For years this system worked quite effectively. Retired agents sent in their books for "clearance" by the Agency. The Agency's control over secrets was the best in town, its authorized leaks and tales almost as effective as those of J. Edgar Hoover. As long as the Agency's mission was clear and popular, as long as its officials enjoyed a high esteem and morale in the Cold War years, its only leaks were those authorized by its directors, employed in bureaucratic in-fighting (an unavoidable practice in Washington). More generally, the postwar classification system increased the level of information control but did not result in direct judicial infringement on the First Amendment right against prior restraint.

Yet on April 18, 1972, representatives of the Central Intelligence Agency entered the District Court for the Eastern Districts of Virginia seeking an *ex parte* temporary restraining order and a permanent injunction against Victor Marchetti, an ex-Agency official. The terms of the injunction required that Marchetti submit all his writings to the Central Intelligence Agency for "clearance" prior to publication, and that he cease violating his "secret agreement" in speech or writings for the remainder of his life. The District Court issued the permanent injunction on May 19; its decision was substantially affirmed by the Court of Appeals; the Supreme Court denied certiorari.[32]

The order constitutes the first prior restraint against publication of political speech in our nation's history. It resulted in a book, *The CIA and the Cult of Intelligence*, marred by the deletions of a government censor.

The District Court and, to a lesser extent, the Court of Appeals, essentially ignored arguments based on the First Amendment. The case was said to concern enforcement of an employment contract, not freedom of speech. The argument that the *government* could not enforce an agreement in violation of the First Amendment did not impress the Court. Both the District Court and the Fourth Circuit Court of Appeals ignored the standard established by *The New York Times Pentagon Papers* case, requiring "direct, immediate and irreparable injury to the United States" for an injunction to be granted.[33] The Court of Appeals instead substituted a bureaucratic test: the information had to be classified to qualify for censorship, obtained in the course of employment, and not previously in the public domain.* This standard would, if general-

---

* The Agency initially sought to limit the scope of this term. One official suggested only information disclosed by the executive branch be considered in the public domain. Congressmen, presumably, dealt only in rumor and speculation.

ized, empower the executive to enjoin and censor the writings of virtually any former employee.

A second extraordinary aspect of the Marchetti case was the basis for the decision. No statutory basis existed for injunctive relief demanded by the CIA. Congress had frequently refused to pass statutes aimed at providing such relief. The CIA could sue Marchetti for damages or it could attempt to prosecute him under the Espionage Laws, but it had no statutory basis for standing in a suit to enjoin. In fact, William Colby, in a legislative proposal to the OMB on January 14, 1974, complained, "There is no existing statutory authority for injunctive relief."

In proceeding against Marchetti, the Agency based its standing on "the government's interest in protecting the national security," a claim of inherent *executive* power to bring the action to protect the nation. To reach this unprecedented result, the courts first had to accept an assertion of an inherent executive right to bring suit.*

Chief Judge Haynsworth, writing for the Court of Appeals, was prepared to go even further. He suggested that had there been no secrecy agreement, "the law would probably imply a secrecy agreement," to enforce a system of prior restraints. The judge went on to suggest that the operations of the CIA, "closely related to the conduct of foreign affairs and to the national defense . . . , are an executive function beyond the control of the judicial power." Judge Haynsworth apparently did not see any contradiction between declaring a matter beyond the control of the judicial power and using that same power to enforce it.[35]

The CIA was not satisfied with its *ad hoc* victory over Marchetti. In January 1974 William Colby submitted to the OMB a draft bill to amend the National Security Act of 1947. The bill proposed essentially an Official Secrets Act to protect the secrecy of the Central Intelligence Agency. The legislation provides for criminal penalties against persons who have authorized possession of classified information and willfully disclose it to unauthorized persons. It also seeks statutory authority for the Marchetti injunction, an injunction to be levied upon a showing by the Director of the Central Intelligence Agency that a violation of CIA security is threatened.

---

* The step taken by the District Court in *Marchetti* was explicitly rejected by at least one judge in the *Pentagon Papers* case. Mr. Justice White concluded, "In the absence of legislation by Congress . . . I am quite unable to agree that the inherent powers of the executive and the courts reach so far as to authorize remedies having such sweeping potential for inhibiting publications by the press.[34]

This extraordinary legislation would give the heads of the CIA a virtual carte blanche in controlling information released about it. To be sure, the proposal is geared to the moderate temper. It provides for judicial review of the validity of the classification—no doubt in full knowledge that approval would be no more difficult than receiving a warrant from a magistrate is for the FBI. The proposed legislation also exempts information provided "upon lawful demand to any regularly constituted committee of the Senate or the House." Given the scope of modern claims to executive privilege, the standard could virtually end the flow of embarrassing information being passed to Congress and would certainly diminish a major source of congressional knowledge: the unauthorized leak of information to a concerned congressman.

CIA Director Colby claims the legislation is necessary in order to provide "adequate protection of the intelligence sources and methods. . . ." For some this argument in itself would illustrate the incompatibility of the Agency's mission with a republican constitutional order. Instead of a review of the arguments for and against secrecy, the question of why the CIA is proposing such legislation now should be considered.

The Agency's secrecy system was self-enforcing for twenty years. Some former Agency hands submitted their books for review, others (Thomas Braden and Miles Copeland, for example) did not. It was a matter of small importance, for all were loyal and proud of the Agency. Only when the Agency's role abroad came under widespread criticism, and the Cold War assumption that justified criminal activity abroad in the name of democracy was dispelled, did the secrecy system fail. Given a widespread societal debate, not even employees of the most secret of organizations could withstand the personal urge to reconsider and reassess and suppress the personal moral agony of a change in perspective.

For the citizenry, information must be available precisely at such moments so that a serious and informed review and reconstruction can proceed. Until a new consensus is formed, it is imperative that the much maligned "marketplace of ideas" be open to all points of view. Free access to facts, however, violates the "requirements" of a covert agency. Its sources are damaged by open debate; its effectiveness reduced; its agents may be endangered. Thus the CIA now seeks judicial and legislative support for its secrecy system. Its recourse to the courts illustrates both the need for and fear of public discussion, of public reconsideration.

Perhaps, as Judge Haynsworth suggested, secrecy is an executive function: the executive should try to keep secrets, and the press and people should try to expose them. Neither criminal nor injunctive sanctions should disturb this struggle. No doubt, this may not meet the requirements of a clandestine agency. Again, the dictates of a clandestine agency seem to conflict with the principles of a healthy polity, founded on the consent of the people.

RICHARD A. FALK

CIA Covert
Operations and
International Law

8

In one respect, international law has always been relevant to the conduct of illegal covert activities in foreign societies. The "guilty" government will not question the sovereign prerogatives of the target society to take appropriate punitive measures to apprehend and punish the perpetrators. The U-2 incident illustrates this relevance very vividly. After the U-2 was shot down and Francis Gary Powers captured on May 1, 1960, the United States, not realizing that Powers survived the crash, issued a cover story about a weather plane having accidently strayed from course. When Soviet Premier Nikita Khrushchev "blew" the cover story, catching the whole government from Eisenhower on down in a humiliating lie, the United States finally acknowledged that the U-2 was on a spy flight, that Powers was a CIA contract employee, and that the Soviet government was entitled to apprehend and punish Powers, as well as make an international protest about the violation of its sovereign air space. By the middle of May Eisenhower had promised the Soviet leader that U-2 flights over the Soviet Union had been permanently suspended.[1] Implicit in the American response was the recognition of the illegality—and consequent impropriety—of the U-2 flights. But perhaps more to the point was *the residual willingness* to comply with international law, *if and only if*, the CIA link was discerned by irrefutable evidence and the cover story blown. That is, so long as the secret is kept or the cover story holds, the inhibitions of international law are cast aside.

Perhaps even an additional set of qualifications are necessary. The Soviet Union displayed the capacity to shoot the U-2 down and, therefore, the flights would have become operationally untenable in any event. More remote, less territorial espionage satellites (SAMOS) were on their way toward being made operational in any event. Finally, the Soviet Union had geopolitical clout; U-2 overflights of other adversaries such as Cuba and North Vietnam, countries without shoot-down capabilities or political weight, continued even though their existence was discovered by the target governments and angry protests formally made. Therefore, we can safely conclude that *the residual relevance* of international law is both a matter of last resort and of only modest importance.

It is surprising that the international law argument against covert activities is so rarely raised.

Even critics of the impact of secrecy upon the conduct of foreign policy by the United States have refrained from arguing that the CIA should be curtailed because its activities are so flagrantly in violation of international-law standards. Rather, the argument for curtailment is made to rest exclusively upon domestic constitutional considerations of accountability and of the associated claim that dangerous erosions of democratic traditions take place because public officials are encouraged to deceive and lie to their own citizenry so as to maintain "the cover." For instance, in an influential article Nicholas deB. Katzenbach recommends: "We should abandon publicly all covert operations designed to influence political results in foreign countries. . . . We should confine our covert activities overseas to the gathering of intelligence information."[2] Katzenbach declares that he is "prepared to take some losses in our foreign policy if by doing so we can restore the fundamentals of representative democracy to our foreign policy."[3] In the background, also, is Katzenbach's more pragmatic concern to "gain that public consensus without which no foreign policy can hope to succeed,"[4] which he believes calls for an abandonment by CIA of its covert operations abroad. Katzenbach, although a former professor of international law, never sees fit, even *en passant*, to comment that "another reason" to give up covert operations is that they violate international law. Why is this?

There is not much doubt that several standard types of CIA covert operation violate international law standards to which the United States government is formally committed. If such violations were committed by rival governments they would be denounced by our officials as "illegal." Perhaps the illegality of secret operations is not noticed because there is no reason to expect governments to be responsive to international law when they are not even held accountable to domestic legal processes?

Undoubtedly, one reason for the neglect of the international-law di-

mension is that until recently, when more carefully documented disclosures made their way into the public arena, most of those with access
to the relevant patterns of conduct were themselves policymakers. Policymakers, whether of liberal or conservative persuasion, tend to
premise their evaluations of foreign policy initiatives on domestic arguments and on their degree of success, rather than on their degree of
conformity to moral or legal norms. Even the Bay of Pigs operation in
1961 was regarded as a fiasco not because the United States had taken
covert part in an aggression against a foreign government with whom we
were at peace, but because the CIA sponsored an invasion by anti-
Castro exiles that failed so miserably to accomplish its strategic mission.

Closer to a real explanation for the neglect comes from CIA enthusi-
asts who do not doubt that covert operations may, on occasion, be
"illegal" or involve "immoral" practices, but accept their occurrence as
essential to the furtherance of national purpose in the world or to offset
similar initiatives by America's geopolitical rivals. In effect, the pro-CIA
position, and I believe the only tenable rationale, is to say that for one
reason or another engaging in covert operations is more important for
the country's well-being than complying with international law. Is this
true?

THE INTERNATIONAL-LAW CASE AGAINST CIA
COVERT OPERATIONS

The international-law case is in a sense self-evident and is partially
conceded by the insistence of the CIA upon secrecy and its related
practice of defending itself against allegations by cover stories (that is,
lies). Part of the explanation for the secrecy/deception is that such
behavior is inherently objectionable to a segment of domestic opinion
and—even more—to world public opinion. Another part of the explanation implies an awareness that covert activities by the CIA in foreign
societies violate their fundamental international-law rights as sovereign
states. Surely the United States government claims the legal right to
insulate American society against covert activities carried out under the
direction of a foreign government, especially if that activity were to
cross the line of intelligence-gathering and involve attempted interference and manipulation of domestic political processes.

International law rests on the fundamental proposition that the government of every sovereign state has complete jurisdiction over events

taking place within its territory, and that, correspondingly, a foreign government has no legal right to act beyond such explicit grants of right as are made in the course of exchanging diplomatic representatives or agreeing to a foreign military presence. In a wide array of contexts CIA covert activities occur with the consent of foreign governments and are designed to sustain such a government in power against its domestic enemies. As Marks and Marchetti observe, "For the most part, the agency's aim was not to overthrow particular Latin American governments but rather to protect them from local insurgent movements."[5] In such a situation, then, the secrecy and cover story are maintained not to avoid a U-2 kind of confrontation, but to protect the *effectiveness* of the operation on behalf of the foreign government.

The international-law issue here is complicated and controversial. It is a special instance of the broader question as to whether a foreign government can legitimize intervention in its internal affairs by giving its *consent*. There are no very clear guidelines available in this class of instances. If there is an ongoing civil war, then some international lawyers consider foreign governmental intervention on behalf of either side, even if requested, as illegal. More broadly, the argument is made that any secret authorization of foreign military and paramilitary action violates the principle of national self-determination that inheres in a *state* (or society) rather than in its *government*.

Finally, if the covert activities to which consent has been given are themselves an aspect of conduct that violates international law, then the CIA is an accessory to the illegal behavior of the foreign government. For example, if the CIA, at the request of the government in state A, helps recruit and finance an army for an attack on state B, then the entire operation is illegal under international law, and the United States and the government of state A are the guilty parties.

Another more esoteric situation is created if the CIA, at the request of the government in state A, helps with commission of "crimes against humanity" (a Nuremberg offense category), that is, provides weaponry or counsels tactics that involve indiscriminate and inhumane destruction of civilians, even if the victims are citizens of the country wherein the action occurs. This situation existed for more than a decade, on a massive scale, comprising the so-called secret war in Laos.[6] The Phoenix Program—with its full panoply of counter terror—is the most celebrated instance of CIA involvement in the commission of crimes against humanity on a systematic basis.[7] *Therefore, our first category of in-*

stances involves the CIA role in aiding, abetting, and conspiring with foreign governments which are themselves violating rules of international law. (We are leaving aside—as not clearly enough covered by international law—the role of the CIA in helping governments defend themselves against internal and external enemies; the strongest international-law case is violation of self-determination, the weakest is where state A is engaged in valid self-defense or where there is forcign participation of a comparable scale on the side of an insurgency.)

A more familiar pattern of CIA conduct involves a spectrum of covert activities carried on without the consent of the constituted government in the foreign society or in direct opposition to its wishes. The spectrum ranges from intelligence-gathering activity to participation in a coup designed to seize political power from the government presently in power. In the middle are efforts to influence the outcome of elections in a foreign society such as "the green light" reportedly given on September 23, 1970, by the Nixon administration "to do all possible—short of a Dominican Republic–type action—to keep Allende from taking power" in Chile.[8] Bizarre cross-purposes are occasionally manifest, as when the CIA took some part in overthrowing the Diem regime in South Vietnam during 1963 even though the Saigon government was itself our ally whose existence was itself stabilized by earlier CIA interventions. Rather like the American soldier who made the famous remark at Ben Tre—"We had to destroy it to save it"—the U.S. government had come to the view that it had to destroy the Saigon regime in order to save it. The international-law argument here is unambiguous—it is clearly violative of nonintervention norms and prohibitions upon the use of force to engage in military or paramilitary activities in a foreign society for purposes hostile to the well-being of the constituted government. Published reliable sources make it plain that such a military and paramilitary role has been played by the CIA in a large number of countries since the formation of the Agency in 1947, especially since the Korean war allowed the Cold War mentality to dominate foreign-policy goals.

One extreme instance of such a CIA undertaking was the authorization of a paramilitary operation under the direction of Colonel Edward Lansdale to disrupt the public order of North Vietnam way back in 1954 in the immediate aftermath of the Geneva Accords. The illegality was compounded by the effort to disrupt an international peace agreement, negotiated after seven years of bloody warfare, which the United States had given its solemn pledge to support.

Among other significant instances of paramilitary intervention by the CIA to overthrow a legal government in a foreign society are the following: the anti-Mossadegh coup of 1953 in Iran; the anti-Arbenz coup of 1954 in Guatemala; the unsuccessful anti-Sukarno coup of 1958 in Indonesia; the unsuccessful anti-Castro invasion of Cuba at the Bay of Pigs in 1961; the unsuccessful harassment of Chinese administration of Tibet throughout the 1960s; the anti-Papandreou coup of 1967 in Greece; and the anti-Sihanouk coup of 1970 in Cambodia. These are among the most publicized instances, but there are growing indications that CIA covert activities occurred in many additional countries where the United States was eager to encourage a change of government policy and personnel. Therefore, *a second cateogry of instances involves the international-law violations that arise from the spectrum of covert activities carried on in a foreign society without the knowledge and consent of the territorial government and inconsistent with its political independence as a sovereign state.*

One of the major areas of development for international law over the past three decades has been the promotion of an international law of human rights. The general aspiration is proclaimed in Articles 55 and 56 of the United Nations Charter, and has been given more specific content in the Universal Declaration of Human Rights. The norms in these documents, supported by an overwhelming consensus of governments, including the United States, express a set of agreed limitations as to the limits of coercion a government may rely upon in relation to its own population. Although these legal documents cover a wide range of civil liberties associated with human dignity, the most minimal legal commitment is expressed in Article 5: "No one shall be subjected to torture or to cruel, inhuman or degrading treatment or punishment."

The CIA has also consistently adopted as a means the deprivation of human rights of individuals who stood in the way of CIA objectives. In a series of countries the CIA has opposed regimes that were basically upholding human rights and helped replace them with regimes that relied upon torture as a routine technique of governance. The instances of Guatemala, Greece, and South Vietnam are well known. The Chilean instance is still shrouded in doubt as to detail, but the basic thrust of CIA efforts is clear: first, if possible, prevent Allende from coming to power through the elective process; second, if the first line failed, encourage all developments that would lead to the downfall of Allende as soon and as decisively as possible. The tragic outcome is now familiar to all, graphically expressed by Gabriel García Márquez as follows: ". . . implanting the hell-dark seeds brought from Brazil, with all of the machines of terror, torture, and death, until in Chile there would be no trace of the political and social structures which had made Popular Unity [Allende's winning populist coalition] possible."[9]

The Chile case illustrates a general commitment of CIA policy to support right-wing governments that repress, no matter how mercilessly, human rights and to oppose progressive governments, no matter how respectful of human rights. The irony, of course, is that the CIA succeeds only in situations where the left-oriented regime has not moved in a totalitarian direction and allows political opposition to operate and mobilize its forces. Allende, for instance, was vulnerable to CIA tactics precisely because he upheld the human rights of his opposition.

The international-law contention here is relatively simple: in a series of separate-country situations, in a wide array of patterns, the CIA has directly and indirectly contributed to the violation of human rights of individuals and groups on a massive scale. Therefore, *a third category of instances involves the international-law violations of human-rights standards which are perpetrated in foreign societies with the knowledge, consent, and participation of the CIA.*

A closely related issue has to do with military conduct violative of the rules of war embodied in the Hague and Geneva treaties, which form the backbone of the law of war. As Marchetti and Marks document, the Special Operations Division (SOD) of the CIA carries out its paramilitary and military roles without any deference to the laws of war: "The paramilitary operator . . . is a gangster who deals in force, in terror, in violence. Failure can mean death—if not to the operator himself, then to the agents he has recruited. The SOD man wages war, albeit on a small and secret level, but none of the rules of warfare apply."[10]

A former CIA operative described his training experience this way: ". . . we received training in tactics which hardly conformed to the Geneva Convention. The array of outlawed weaponry with which we were familiarized included bullets that explode on impact, silencer-equipped machine guns, home-made explosives and self-made napalm for stickier and hotter Molotov cocktails. . . . What did a busload of burning people have to do with freedom? What right did I have, in the name of democracy and the CIA, to decide that random victims should die?"[11] The extent to which the CIA conducted and counseled paramilitary and military operations in violation of fundamental laws of war is well documented.

The laws of war are designed to protect "enemy" populations from cruel and indiscriminate modes of warfare. The violation of these laws was relied upon by the United States and its World War II Allies to prosecute criminally thousands of Germans and Japanese soldiers and civilians thought to be responsible perpetrators. The trials led to convictions, prison sentences, some executions.

Obviously, the CIA is not the only bureaucratic actor responsible for violating the laws of war and responsible for war crimes, but it may be the only part of the government whose policies are consistently so designed. The status of the Nuremberg Principles is in some doubt among international lawyers, but the United States government took the lead in trying to embody the war-crimes experience after World War II as a permanent feature of international law. Therefore, *a fourth category of CIA violations of international law involves various breaches of the laws of war and the commission of a wide array of offenses that would seem to qualify as crimes of war.*

Other related undertakings by the CIA seem to have a distinct status under international law. For instance, in relation to both the Geneva Accords of 1954 and 1962 and the Paris Agreement of 1973, the CIA was active in obstructing the implementation of a solemn international peace agreement. Roger Hilsman, a Kennedy official, and Peter Dale Scott show in great detail that CIA efforts in Laos immediately after the 1962 Geneva Agreements actually proceeded in defiance of White House policies to uphold the bargain so painfully negotiated.[12] The post-1973 role of the CIA in Indochina is difficult to depict in detail, but there is no doubt that the CIA has been active on a number of fronts to assure noncompliance with the Paris Agreements. Such efforts to induce noncompliance of peace agreements cut against the most fundamental legal thrust of the U.N. Charter "to save succeeding generations from the scourge of war" and constitute an instance of a crime against the peace that the Nuremberg Tribunal called the supreme crime against mankind that embodies within itself all other crimes. Therefore, *a fifth category of CIA covert activities worthy of separate notice is its active contribution in a number of different international settings to the violation of international peace agreements to which the United States was either a negotiating, guaranteeing, or endorsing party.*

A separate kind of CIA violation of international law is reported by Marchetti and Marks. Evidently Saipan in Micronesia has been used as a secret military base in connection with CIA activities in Southeast Asia. Micronesia is a Strategic Trust Territory administered by the

United States, supposedly for the well-being of the inhabitants, as a trust exercised for the organized international community as embodied in the United Nations. The U.S. government is obligated to give annual reports of its administration and to allow periodic inspection visits by U.N. representatives. Naturally, the discovery of a CIA base on Micronesia would produce an international incident of major proportions. Hence, the CIA apparently disassembles the base prior to scheduled U.N. visits and then reassembles it as soon as they are over.[13] This behavior violates the Trusteeship Agreement upon which United States administration rests. Therefore, *a sixth category of CIA covert activities involves the violation of the Trustee Agreement by which the United States administers Micronesia on behalf of the organized international community.*

There are undoubtedly other categories of CIA covert activities that could be isolated as violative of international-law standards. For example, the CIA role in sustaining the Laotian supply of heroin seems clearly incompatible with international regulatory efforts to which the United States is a party.[14] Our treatment has been sufficiently comprehensive to make out at least a prima facie case of international-law violations by the CIA over a wide range of instances, over a long period of time, in flagrant respects, and with serious repercussions for international relations.

ARGUMENTS AGAINST THE INTERNATIONAL-LAW CASE

John McNaughton, a Harvard law professor on leave to the Defense Department and a principal adviser at the time to Defense Secretary McNamara on Vietnam policy, wrote a draft memo dated October 13, 1964, entitled "Aims and Options in Southeast Asia,"[15] which proposes that the United States conceive of its role in Indochina as that of a "good doctor." McNaughton explains that being a good doctor means, "We must have kept promises, been tough, gotten bloodied, and hurt the enemy very badly." One of the critical questions that might mar this desired United States performance is posed as follows: "Is the United States *hobbled by restraints* which might be relevant in future cases (fear of illegality, of U.N. or neutral reaction, of domestic pressures of U.S. losses, of deploying U.S. ground forces in Asia, of war with China or Russia, of use of nuclear weapons)?"[16] On the basis of our assessment of CIA's covert activities I think we could have replied to McNaughton's question with a resounding No. But the issue of policy is one of judgment: should the United States be "hobbled by restraints" of the sort mentioned by McNaughton in the conduct of its foreign policy?

CIA supporters argue that such constraints would adversely affect America's national interests if they were to be enforced against the CIA. Miles Copeland, a former CIA official, insists "that most intelligent citizens would be relieved, not dismayed" to know that the United States government is not shocked by the reality of "Soviet perfidy" and possesses the means by way of American perfidy to counter it. Copeland wrote, "When we choose to violate any of our policies, from being truthful in our diplomacy to refraining from interfering in the internal affairs of a sovereign nation, we find means outside the normal machinery of government. Our Government has such means. It is able to define a problem, to release forces which, largely on their own power, can effect a solution, and to disclaim any responsibility."[17] These bland words include torture, murder, napalm, atrocities, deception, and official lies.

Thomas W. Braden, another CIA former official, speaking out against CIA detractors, wrote an article in 1967 under the provocative title "I'm Glad the CIA Is 'Immoral.' "[18] Like Copeland, Braden argues that the United States is engaged in "a game of nations" within which one technique used is to engage in CIA-type activity. After reviewing some of the CIA's more innocuous interferences in foreign societies— funding friendly unions, infiltrating student groups, financing anti-Communist cultural activity—Braden asks, "Was it 'immoral,' 'wrong,' 'disgraceful'? Only in the sense that war itself is immoral, wrong and disgraceful, for the cold war was and is a war fought with ideas instead of bombs. And our country has had a clear-cut choice: Either we win the war or lose it."[19] Of course, Braden, too, poses the question in a deliberately misleading way—it is one thing to counter Soviet politicizing and propagandizing activity with comparable means, but quite another to take part in paramilitary and military violence for a variety of purposes, many remote from any credible claim to be responding to covert interventions of the geopolitical rivals of the United States. Nevertheless, an issue of genuine moment is posed: namely, other major governments active in international relations are *not hobbled by restraints*, that is, do not respect international law. In such a situation, then, is it reasonable and desirable to expect the United States alone to be so hobbled? Why should the country penalize itself in playing the game of nations with unscrupulous rivals, in particular, the Soviet Union?

To assess this argument adequately it is necessary to determine the range, frequency, and character of covert activities by other governments, as well as to appraise their degree of effectiveness. Soviet covert activities in Eastern Europe cover a range of illegalities comparable to those of the CIA in Asia and Latin America, but it is precisely in this area that CIA activities are least evident. The CIA is most active in those spheres of influence wherein the United States seeks to acquire and to sustain its paramountcy; its activities seem more closely connected with neo-imperial diplomacy than with any genuine insistence on neutralizing the activities of other governments. It is still possible to maintain that since other governments do not accept the restraints of international law, the United States is also not obliged to comply. The absence of enforcement procedures, the widespread practice of covert activities, and the general quality of the state system mean that compliance with international law is a matter for *voluntary* determination by each government in each context.

A related, more restrictive, contention of the same general character is that the international legal norms of prohibition invoked in opposition to CIA covert activities are peculiarly "weak" and "soft" instances of law, even with respect to international law as a whole. The principal norms at issue—the prohibition of aggression, the principle of national self-determination, the doctrine of nonintervention, crimes against the peace, crimes against humanity—are so general in their character that it is difficult to achieve agreed definitions, much less agreed interpretation of their application to specific circumstances.

In effect, covert activity by the CIA occurs in a virtual "no law" area, where the character of the norms is not of sufficient authority to fill the vacuum created by notions of state sovereignty. In a way, the argument is directed at the basic flaws in the world-order system—namely, that there are still no legally significant qualifications on the discretion of a national government to the use of force in international conflicts, even when the force used amounts to the initiation of warfare.[20] Therefore, to complain about lesser-included instances is hypocritical and nonsensical; and CIA's covert activities constitute in general a lesser-included instance, perhaps rising on a few occasions to the status of a subspecies of war as in the "secret war" in Laos or the role taken in repressing the insurgency in the eastern region of Peru during the mid-1960s.

A final line of argument concerns the "double standards" used to assess covert activities. In effect, CIA supporters often invoke "the legacy of OSS" to argue, in effect, that the CIA is engaged in the same sort of covert activities that were praised and glorified during World War II.[21] By extension, then, the CIA is alleged to be similarly carrying out missions to achieve the national purpose in a geopolitical period when outright warfare has been replaced, not by peace in a real sense, but by the sort of intense and hostile competition denoted by the label "Cold War."

Complicated questions are raised here that fall beyond our scope. It is necessary to determine whether the OSS really did the same sort of things, as considered from a legal point of view, as the CIA. It is also necessary to assess the argument that a state of war such as existed for the OSS can be extended to various stages of international relations after World War II, including a condition of détente. Finally, it would be important to judge whether what the OSS did was, in fact, compatible with international-law standards.

Differences in national mood determine the *moral* and *political* climate in which CIA-type activities take place, and generally shape public attitudes toward foreign policy. Such a climate, however, does not by itself have any bearing on the *legal* status of behavior. Although this legal status is problematic because most of the rules are "soft" and the structure of their implementation "weak," the foreign-policy option to uphold the claims of international law exists and has potential importance for the future of the country and for the quality of world order in general.

A RATIONALE FOR COMPLIANCE
WITH INTERNATIONAL LAW

Despite the serious objections to the international-law position considered in the last section, rationale for compliance is compelling. This rationale rests on a series of separate grounds: law-abidingness as a civic virtue; the progressive general character of the international-law rules at issue; and the relevance of international law to a system of world order based on peace and justice.

Respect for International Law

Implicit in the domestic arguments against secret foreign operations is the impossibility of insulating a constitutional order at home from what is done abroad. At issue is a pattern of behavior, a way of dealing with the political process, a suspension of normal procedures of accountability. The same considerations apply to the rule of law. The Constitution gives international legal norms standing as "the supreme law of the land" if they are embodied in treaties; the Supreme Court has decided that customary rules of international law are also entitled to respect.

It is neither possible nor desirable to separate foreign affairs from domestic society when it comes to the rule of law. The attitude of amorality and a-legality so often characteristic of CIA operations abroad seeps its way into the acts of policymakers in domestic settings. The Nixon administration's blatant behavior made this inevitable tendency plain. But as has by now been frequently observed, lawlessness of the Nixon practices was paved by earlier patterns of conduct, one of which is exemplified by the covert activities of the CIA. Respect for international law represents one element in a framework of accountability. We should want our leaders to accord respect for *all* categories of valid law. If international law is to be ignored as a constraint, then that policy decision should itself be made openly, on the basis of debate, and conceivably lead to a constitutional amendment of the supremacy clause. Posing such a possibility suggests its implausibility. The status of international law as a necessary, if weak and uneven, system of behavior guidance is so well established that no government advocates its freedom to violate its rules in general (although some refuse to be bound by specific rules). Even the socialist governments have affirmed their respect for international law, have argued their own disputes by reference to rights established by international law (for example, the Sino-Soviet territorial dispute), and couch their objections to behavior of other states by reference to international-law criteria.

Part of securing the rule of law in general involves extending its reach to foreign policy. One motivation for the insistence on secrecy of some CIA operations is undoubtedly the degree to which these operations would strike the international community as "illegal," generating pressures for compliance. When these operations have been discovered by powerful adversaries and the cover story blown, as occurred in the U-2 incident, then the American governmental tendency has been to accept its obligation to comply with international law. Thus, no real claim is ever made by the U.S. government that a right to ignore international law exists, but only that certain secret operations should be carried out without being subject to scrutiny of a normal kind. Mr. Braden could easily have written a sequel to his article under the title "I'm Glad the CIA 'Violates' International Law."

Progressive Character of Norms

American foreign policy would benefit from an effective application of the norms at issue in the setting of covert activities. The doctrine of nonintervention and the correlative principle of national self-determination encourage progressive social and political developments under most circumstances. The CIA's role has been to keep repressive governments in power and to overthrow or harass more progressive ones. Such a role seems detrimental to international society. If the United States had complied with international law, there would probably be many more progressive, socially responsible governments in power today throughout the Third World. The CIA role has, in general, seemed to promote the militarization of government wherever its influence has been strong.

The normal rationalization of CIA intervention in foreign societies is that the United States must play a counterinterventionary role to offset the encroachments of Soviet and Chinese interventions. A great deal of ambiguity often surrounds this claim—is it the appeal of Communist rhetoric, doctrine, and domestic groupings that needs to be offset or is it foreign military assistance? The energy for social revolution is often primarily an indigenous matter and becomes "internationalized" only *after* the CIA enters the scene.[22] In any event, if the American role is a genuinely counterinterventionary one in a genuine sense, then it can carry out such a role *overtly* and *within* the framework of international law. The doctrine of self-defense, the right of governments to receive aid, and even the notion of counterintervention provide a sufficient basis for foreign-policy initiatives that were designed to prevent "aggression" by geopolitical rivals. International law is not so conceived or so taut in its application as to jeopardize the well-being or security of a large state.

The basic point here is that there is no persuasive reason for not eliminating illegal CIA covert activities. These activities have been generally reactionary in their social, economic, and political impacts on countries that desperately need social revolutions to bring to power leaders who are committed to policies that will overcome the misery of the general population. Compliance with international law by the United States might help to make the world safe for social revolutions in national societies now governed in an antiquated and repressive manner.

Quality of World Order

A final argument for compliance with international law relates to the whole quest for a peaceful and just system of world order. The argument must be made on two levels: how to prevent the breakdown of the existing relations, and how to facilitate the emergence of a more acceptable form of world order than is provided by or possible under the state system.

First of all, the voluntary acceptance by principal governments of a minimal system of restraints on the use of force is closely connected with the capacity of the state system to maintain world peace over time; international law, although far from perfect, provides such a system, and it is one that enjoys widespread acceptance. The quality of that acceptance depends greatly on voluntary patterns of Great Power attitude and behavior, since there are no international sanctions on principal governments other than public opinion and resistance by their rivals. A country such as the United States is especially important; its noncompliance influences the whole climate within international society and undermines any effort to take international law very seriously as a restraint on others. Thus one cost of noncompliance by the United States is to compromise our national efforts to persuade other governments to comply or to mobilize opposition to illegal policies in the United Nations.

On a more dynamic level, the prospects for meeting the deepening world-order crisis arising from population pressure, food shortages, spreading poverty, ecological decay, and resource shortages depend on bringing to power more enlightened and progressive national elites. The authority structure of international law, although far from ideal, does at least prohibit the sort of covert activities that the CIA has engaged in over the past several decades. The elimination of these activities might encourage the emergence of a more humanistic climate in world society that would bolster a social movement to reorganize and integrate life in "the global village." The open historical question is not whether "central guidance" or "global integration" will come about, but only how quickly, under whose control, and by what elements of choice. The sooner we organize to achieve a new system of world order, the better the prospects are for making the adjustment nonviolently and nontraumatically. CIA's global role is basically opposed to allowing such a transition and is aligned in effect with the most narrow and destructive conception of the state system. Thus without being overdramatic I would contend that there is a link between opposition to the illegal activities of the CIA and the growth of survival policies and politics in the world community and that the demand for compliance with international law is a proper way to strengthen that link.

A QUALIFICATION ON
THE ARGUMENT FOR COMPLIANCE

Despite the conclusion reached about compliance, it does seem important to formulate a qualification on its apparent claims. There are circumstances under which adherence to the norms at issue may have a regressive impact. The most obvious instance relates to the status of southern African liberation movements. As matters now stand, it is hardly conceivable that the CIA would seek to give these movements any help; the role of CIA is consistently on the other side. But let us suppose there were a political reversal of mood in the United States and that the CIA were acting in a progressive role to overcome structures of entrenched reactionary and repressive power in the power; would this development alter our stand on compliance?

Obviously an effective legal order can neither bend to every ideological air current nor can it, nor should it, thwart basic historical tendencies. National governments *on their own* should not suspend the operation of those rules of international law designed to insulate states from foreign intervention, but the organized international community has such authority. With respect to the struggles of southern Africa, the United Nations and the Organization of African Unity have been virtually unanimous in their view that the incumbent governments are illegitimate and their challengers legitimate. Such a determination gives governments a possibility to enter the struggle. The mandate of the international community is a way of reconciling claims of social change with those of social control.

The qualification, then, being placed on the argument for compliance with international law is mainly directed at absolutist pretensions. Law is an aspect of value-realizing processes; and if its authority stands squarely in the way of community-mandated change, then there must be a way to reformulate its restraints on behavior. The role of civil disobedience in domestic society has often been to express a similar point. In international society, it might be that a peculiarly conscience-stricken African government could have engaged in a symbolic act of civil disobedience so as to hasten the process of action by the world community.

TOWARD A NATIONAL POLICY
IN CIA COVERT ACTIVITIES

The basic drift of this argument leads to a position that might be used to shape a national policy on CIA covert activities:

1. It should be recognized that many of the CIA's covert activities consistently and flagrantly violate international law.

2. It should be further recognized that respect for the rule of law by the U.S. government should include respect for international law.

3. It should be understood that the rules of international law relevant to an appraisal of CIA covert activities are generally enlightened in conception and beneficial in social and political impact.

4. It should be agreed upon that compliance with international law will require the United States to abolish all programs of clandestine operations, including possibly illegal intelligence-gathering abroad.

5. It should be understood that to make the policy of abolition effective it will be necessary to dismantle or drastically reduce clandestine capabilities.

6. It should be recognized that respect for international law in this area of behavior is not necessarily inconsistent with giving support to liberation movements, provided the goals and legitimacy of a specific movement receive the formal endorsement of the overwhelming membership in the international community in a formal act of a main organ of the United Nations.

MORTON H. HALPERIN

Covert Operations

9

EFFECTS OF SECRECY ON DECISION-MAKING

This essay first seeks to describe, using case illustrations, the system by which the United States government plans, approves, and carries out covert operations that are aimed at influencing political events in other countries or gathering intelligence by using human agents or technological means. It then seeks to show how the structure and manner in which these decisions have been made has determined not only the final decisions on the covert operations themselves, but has also had unplanned implications for the more general processes of decision-making on matters of foreign policy and national defense by both the executive branch and the Congress. Finally, after assessing the implications of the tightly closed decision-making procedures and structures, the essay concludes with recommendations for change.

CASE ILLUSTRATIONS

The Bay of Pigs

The story of the disastrous, abortive American-supported invason of Cuba in 1961 has been frequently told, but it is worth repeating some of the highlights here, particularly as they reveal some of the procedures and problems of covert decision-making.[1]

The planning for a landing of opponents of the Castro regime apparently began within the Directorate of Operations (then called the Directorate of Plans) in the Central Intelligence Agency. Within that organization, there was a planning and coordinating group at headquarters for the western hemisphere and field groups in Miami and elsewhere in Latin America that were concerned with programs directed at the

Castro government. Planning took place during 1960, and the Forty Committee, which was chaired by a senior White House foreign-policy adviser and which included representatives from the State Department, the Department of Defense, and the CIA, gave tentative approval to the covert operation against Cuba in the period between the election of John F. Kennedy and the inauguration. In these closing days of the Eisenhower administration, officials were apparently not willing to take responsibility either for approving the final go-ahead or for turning off the operation. Thus, Kennedy was confronted when he came to office with an ongoing plan for a large-scale invasion.

Rather than consider the matter in the structure of the Forty Committee, the President began to hold meetings on the issue with his principal advisers, including Secretary of State Dean Rusk and Secretary of Defense Robert McNamara. In addition, he brought in some personal advisers, including his brother Attorney General Robert Kennedy, Arthur Schlesinger, Jr., and, for at least one meeting, Senator William Fulbright, the Chairman of the Foreign Relations Committee. The meetings with the President also included the Assistant Secretary of State for Public Affairs.

The circle of officials who were aware of the proposed invasion plan, and who could provide an assessment to the President of its probable consequences and the likelihood that there would be the necessary support for the operation in Cuba, was exceedingly limited. Even those who were present at the meetings in the White House did not have the opportunity to study the plan, since the information presented was either given to them orally or contained in papers that were collected after the White House meetings.

Even more striking, most of the officials in the United States government, who from either a policy or intelligence point of view were concerned with and knowledgeable about the situation in Cuba and Latin America, were not informed about the planned invasion and were not asked for an assessment of the likely consequences. For example, in the State Department, the officials in the Bureau of Public Affairs below the Assistant Secretary were not informed of the planned operation. The Cuban desk office, concerned with day-to-day relations with Cuba, did not know of the operation and could not give an evaluation of its consequences. Nor were other officials in State informed, including analysts in State's Bureau of Intelligence and Research, the department's research and development arm.

Nor were intelligence analysts in the CIA itself informed. There appears to be a firm dividing line between the operating side of the CIA, the Operations Directorate, and the intelligence-evaluation side, the Directorate for Intelligence. All the analytic talents of the CIA were absent from the consideration of whether the operation might succeed. When Allen Dulles, the Director of Central Intelligence, informed the President that the chances of success were very high, this opinion was based entirely on the views of the covert operators planning the Bay of Pigs invasion and on his own hunches—without any support from either the Board of National Estimates or the intelligence analysts in the Directorate for Intelligence.

In the Pentagon no civilian officials including the Assistant Secretary of Defense for International Security Affairs, Paul Nitze, seem to have been informed or given an opportunity to comment on the planned operation.

Thus, although the key judgment in the Bay of Pigs operation was whether a sufficient number of Cubans would rise up to support the invaders when they landed on the beach, no one who had a good capability on the question was consulted and permitted to express an opinion, with the exception of the CIA operatives themselves, who, being heavily committed to the plan, could not have been expected to have an impartial view.

The Bay of Pigs episode shows quite clearly one of the consequences of the tight secrecy with which covert operations are planned, approved, and implemented. It shows why such operations are approved when they should not be, and why they often go badly. Cutting off many officials from the Bay of Pigs operation meant not only that officials knowledgeable about the Cuban scene were not able to comment and warn the President that the kind of uprising on which the plan depended was unlikely, but also that the President was not confronted with advice from those who had operational responsibility for other programs and other means, and who could have pointed out the limitations of the different ways by which the presumed threat from the Castro regime could be contained.

Reconnaissance of North Vietnam

On March 31, 1968, after the mounting controversy over the Vietnam war that followed the Tet Offensive, President Johnson announced a dramatic curtailment of the American bombing of North Vietnam in the same speech in which he announced that he would not be a candidate for re-election to the Presidency. Most of the public attention following the speech was given to Johnson's withdrawal from political life, the reduction of the bombing, and the possibility that these would lead to negotiations of a peaceful settlement. Hardly any public attention was given to a key component of the set of decisions that the President made in the days leading up to the speech, namely, the decision to continue reconnaissance operations over all North Vietnam.

Similarly, in October 1968, on the eve of the Presidential election between Hubert Humphrey and Richard Nixon, President Johnson announced a complete halt of the bombing and the beginning of substantive peace talks in Paris on a political settlement of the conflict. Again, attention focused on the negotiating consequences of the bombing halt and on the political consequences for the upcoming Presidential election —and not on the fact that the United States would continue reconnaissance operations over all North Vietnam.

The reconnaissance operations and the "protective reaction strike" bombings of North Vietnam that followed appear to have contributed to delaying a settlement of the Vietnam conflict. Yet, in the events leading up to both the March and October bombing halts, the President excluded from the discussions all but a very small number of his civilian advisers. These critical policy decisions were made within very tight, small circles—even though the intention to conduct reconnaissance flights had been announced to the North Vietnamese government. Once again, the fact that the policy was not subjected to the critical scrutiny of officials with differing expertise and organizational interests led to consideration of only one of many possible options—manned reconnaissance flights over North Vietnam. This one-sided approach illustrated the consequences that are possible with closed decision-making procedures.

For the President, the basic problem was to secure the military's concurrence in a decision first to curtail and then to halt the bombing of North Vietnam, and he offered the military whatever assurances about future behavior on the part of the United States that he could. One of the conditions proposed by the military for the two bombing halts was that it be permitted, at its discretion, to continue any and all reconnaissance operations against North Vietnam.

President Johnson's inclination, no doubt, would have been to accept this condition, regardless of the lurking adverse consequences and regardless of any assessment of the importance of this reconnaissance information, precisely because it seemed a small price to pay to get military concurrence in the bombing halt. Nevertheless, the decision was made without any careful evaluation of the likely impact on the North Vietnamese or of the need for the kind of reconnaissance that involved an intrusion into North Vietnamese air space. Intelligence analysts in the intelligence branches of the CIA, the Department of State, and even the Department of Defense, as well as those involved in Vietnam policy-making on the civilian side of the Pentagon and in the Department of State, were excluded from the decision-making process, both because it involved a tightly held political decision and because it involved operational, covert programs.

Considerable confusion on the question of the North Vietnamese reaction resulted from the belief that the North Vietnamese had committed themselves in October not to shoot at the American reconnaissance planes. At the Paris negotiations the North Vietnamese had been clearly informed by Averell Harriman that the United States intended to continue such reconnaissance operations, and they, in turn, had expressed their willingness to begin substantive negotiations despite the persistence of the United States in these operations. But the North Vietnamese neither stated nor suggested that they would refrain from seeking to interfere with these operations by, for instance, shooting at the reconnaissance planes. Until after the decision was made, analysts familiar with the North Vietnamese positions and statements did not have an opportunity to examine this question.

There also remained the question of the value and importance of reconnaissance operations that involved an intrusion over North Vietnamese territory, particularly by manned aircraft. This was a highly technical problem, entailing questions such as what the United States needed to know or wanted to know about what was going on in North Vietnam and evaluating what other means the United States could use to discover this information.

Even to begin to discuss the question of whether other intelligence-gathering means could serve as usefully as manned aircraft, officials needed an array of clearances. Other than officials on the Joint Staff, who viewed the situation from a military perspective, there was almost no one who had access to these necessary intelligence clearances. Consequently, officials who might otherwise have added the perspective of broader Vietnam issues, such as the problems of negotiation, to the military's interest in having the information for its tactical operations were not in a position to offer an assessment of the relative importance and value of continuing armed reconnaissance flights.

The people who did have such clearances had got them painfully, one at a time, on the sufferance of the various groups who controlled the clearances. The decision as to whether to award clearances to a particular individual is, in general, made by the managers and operators of a particular program who, being responsible for the security of that program, are given the responsibility to determine who has access to the material involved. Naturally, they are not anxious to give material to people who might become critics of their particular program.

Obviously, if the President or the Secretary of Defense had personally been strongly interested in a study, the information could have, with considerable difficulty, been gotten out of the various bureaucracies involved. But with the President and the Secretary committed to the continuation of the program, it was unlikely that all the necessary data could be assembled. This system of secrecy stands in contrast to other areas of policy, where there are no special subcategories of clearances and where papers can be done assessing the implications of alternative policies by even relatively junior officials with the support of senior officials in the government.

These are reasons why there does not appear to have been any serious study, either before or after the decisions to continue reconnaissance while curtailing the bombing, on the utility of the manned reconnaissance operations involving intrusion into North Vietnamese air space and the degree to which that same information, or virtually all the same information, could have been obtained by alternate intelligence means. Instead, the reconnaissance went on, the North Vietnamese began to shoot at the airplanes, the United States responded first by firing back and then by a program described as "protective reaction" in which strikes would be made after North Vietnamese air-defense units were believed to be on the verge of attacking American reconnaissance planes. The "protective reaction strikes" were ultimately used as a cover for preplanned strikes on a variety of targets in North Vietnam. All this proceeded without any real assessment of the need for the reconnaissance program itself, and it illustrates how the decision-making procedures for covert operations—including technical operations—can have wider repercussions in a major policy area.

The People's Republic of China

On a number of occasions in the post–World War II period, the CIA has directed covert operations within the territory of the People's Republic of China. Although little is known about the internal decision-making procedures that led to these particular operations, there is no reason to think that they were different from those routinely followed in approving covert operations in general.

In 1949, with the Communist conquest of the Chinese mainland, Secretary of State Dean Acheson announced that the United States would permit the dust to settle in China before deciding what to do. The debate which raged within the U.S. government, outside of the covert intelligence community, was on whether or not the United States would defend Taiwan. At the same time, and without the knowledge of at least junior officials involved in China policy in general, the CIA began planning for a program of covert operations on the Chinese mainland. By 1950, with the Korean war under way, the CIA began the operations, relying mainly on Chinese Nationalist agents from Taiwan. These operations, which were geared in part to aid American airmen who might be shot down in China as a result of bombing raids over North Korea, were also designed to infiltrate Chinese Nationalist agents onto the mainland for information gathering and covert operations. The CIA agents were trained in Japan on the establishment of secret bases and communications lines, organized into teams, and dropped into China, with one such drop taking place in the fall of 1952.

The existence of these operations came to light only because in November 1952 two American CIA agents involved in directing the operation, John Downey and Richard Fecteau, were shot down when they attempted to pick up one of the agents previously parachuted into China and to drop supplies for other agents. The United States made no public announcement of the disappearance of these two agents, evidently assuming that they had both been killed when their plane went down. Two years later, however, the Chinese disclosed that Downey and Fecteau had been captured. The Chinese asserted that both Downey and Fecteau had confessed to their clandestine operations and CIA connections and were tried and sentenced for interfering in Chinese affairs. It was not until 1971 that Fecteau was finally freed and until 1973 that Downey's release was arranged.

The Chinese public announcement that Downey and Fecteau were

CIA agents and had been taken alive must have caused a great shock within the covert-operations establishment, since it made public the fact of these operations. The American public was lied to—according to the State Department spokesman at the time of the trials: "These men, John Thomas Downey and Richard George Fecteau, were civilian personnel employed by the Department of the Army in Japan. They were believed to have been lost on a flight from Korea to Japan in November, 1952."[2]

While even a cursory look at a map would indicate the implausibility of somebody being lost over China on a flight from Seoul to Tokyo, much of the American public seems to have accepted the administration's story, and it was accepted as one more proof of the lawless behavior and callous disregard for human life of the "outlaw" regime then in control of the Chinese mainland. It was not until 1973, and then apparently as part of the arrangements for Downey's release, that President Nixon finally admitted that Downey and Fecteau were CIA agents on a covert operation. One suspects that many parts of the executive branch, while they had long suspected the truth, were only at that moment formally and officially informed of the existence of the operation in China.

Analysts of Chinese-American relations in the State Department, the CIA, and the academic community were not aware until the charges against Downey and Fecteau that secret operations of any kind were being conducted on the Chinese mainland. Thus, in assessing Chinese and American relations and the reasons for Chinese hostility to the United States, they were unable to take account of Chinese fears stemming from the Chinese knowledge of extensive American interference on the Chinese mainland through the covert operations of the CIA and the support of internal opponents of the regime, including the Chinese nationalists and Tibetan guerrilla groups. The decisions to conduct these operations were undoubtedly made by a small group, including, certainly, the President and the Secretary of State, but not including most government experts on China, who could have provided an assessment of the probable effects of these operations on the local conditions in the area in which they were operating, on the Chinese perception of the United States, and on the relations between the two countries.

Other publicly known major CIA operations in China occurred in the mid-1960s at the time of the Cultural Revolution. When the Cultural Revolution broke out, discussion among officials not involved in covert operations in the State Department, the Defense Department, the White

House, and even the CIA quickly reached the conclusion that the United States should not intervene in any way in the Cultural Revolution. By not interfering when China appeared to be weak and divided, the United States could lay the basis for a degree of improved relations once the tumult of the Cultural Revolution had died down. Though this reason for noninterference was never publicly admitted, the consensus emerging from these working-level meetings appears to have been ratified at the highest levels of the government.

At the same time, and unbeknownst to these officials, the CIA was mounting covert operations designed to influence the Cultural Revolution and to increase the turmoil and difficulty within China. In 1967, detecting signs that the Cultural Revolution was dying down and that forces for law and order were reasserting themselves, the CIA stepped up its operations to rekindle the extreme violence of the earlier Cultural Revolution period. Balloons were used to drop leaflets and other propaganda materials over China. These documents had been carefully prepared by CIA agents to appear as similar as possible to genuine publications being distributed in China by the conservative elements. The leaflets criticized the Red Guard and their radical supporters in the Peking leadership. The pamphlets appear to have been successful in that they were taken as genuine by many Chinese and, by the radicals, as evidence of greater resistance to Red Guard propaganda, particularly in the southern provinces. Refugees from China arrived in Hong Kong carrying some of this CIA material. At the same time, a CIA-operated clandestine radio on Taiwan broadcast some of the same kinds of propaganda as were in the leaflets.

These covert operations, which were almost certainly detected by Chinese Communist leaders, had the effect of undercutting what most American officials believed was the agreed policy of the United States— not to interfere in the Cultural Revolution and to attempt to use the good will generated by that inaction to lay the basis for improved relations after the extreme violence died down. Senior, long-experienced China officials in the State Department, in the overt side of the CIA, and within the Pentagon were given no opportunity to argue against these CIA operations. They had simply not been informed of them and were allowed to believe that the United States was remaining aloof from the Cultural Revolution.

The CIA operations had even more bizarre consequences. American intelligence analysts from the Department of State in Hong Kong began to get copies of these leaflets from refugees from the Chinese mainland; at the same time, a different branch of the CIA, the Foreign Broadcast Information Service, began to monitor the clandestine radio broadcasts from Taiwan and treat them as though they were coming from a clandestine, dissident radio on the Chinese mainland. The pamphlets and the radio broadcasts were then fed into the analyses of the Cultural Revolution situation being done by the State Department and the CIA analysts in Hong Kong and Washington.

Thus, over an extended period of time, analysts of developments in China and of Chinese-American relations within the American government have had their perceptions distorted by a lack of knowledge of American covert interference in the affairs of the People's Republic of China. Perhaps more important, American policy toward China was for many years affected by these covert operations without most of the officials in the American government who were concerned with China policy being informed about them and given an opportunity to argue that such activities were not in the national interest.

SECRECY AND DECISION-MAKING PROCEDURES

The proposals for covert operations come largely, if not entirely, from the organizations that will then be responsible for carrying them out once they are approved. This structure is highly decentralized, with its different units not having access to either the programs or the results of the programs of other operating units. In general, there is a different organizational structure for the planning and the implementing of each of the different programs.

We can illustrate how a program works by considering a typical instance of a covert operation. In general, a similar pattern has been followed for a technical program coming out of the NSA, the service intelligence operations, or an overhead reconnaissance program from the Air Force.

In general, an idea for a covert operation would develop either in the field in the country involved or in the department of the CIA headquarters staff that is responsible for that particular country. The idea would then be discussed between these two groups and, if approved by them, passed to the Assistant Director for the region concerned, and then from him to the Director of Central Intelligence. If the plan at least has his tentative approval, it would then be passed informally to the various staffs of the members of the Forty Committee. An attempt would then be made at that level to develop a consensus on the desirability of going forward with the operation. Usually, there would be no consultation with other officials who might be concerned with other aspects of the policy toward the country in which it was planned to conduct the covert operations. Consequently, within the State Department, there would not be continual consultation with the regional branch of the Bureau of Intelligence and Research concerned with that country, or with the Director for the country concerned. The Assistant Secretary of the region might be consulted depending on past indications of his interest in being consulted or in being informed about covert operations.* Other parts of the State Department, including the planning staff and the Bureau of Political and Military Affairs, would almost certainly not be consulted.

In the Department of Defense the consultation would be limited to the staff of the Assistant to the Joint Chiefs for Covert Operations and to the service counterparts. The consultation would not extend, apparently, to the J-5 planning staff of the Joint Staffs or to the similar service staffs that deal more generally with political-military questions, and would not extend to civilians in the Pentagon, including those in the Office of International Security Affairs.

On the National Security Council staff, the consultation would be limited to a few people specifically assigned to provide staff support on covert operations to the Assistant to the President and would not normally extend to those concerned with regional affairs for the country involved or to those involved in the planning. In the CIA, the Deputy Director for Intelligence and all of his staffs would be excluded from the consultation.

Once a consensus was reached within this small group, the matter would move onto the agenda of the Forty Committee, where it would almost certainly be approved, and then there would be informal consultation with the President, usually not in writing so that it would be possible to deny involvement if that were to become necessary. The approval of the President having been obtained, the Assistant to the President for National Security Affairs would notify the relevant operating agencies that the program had been approved, and they would then put it into effect. Once it was ongoing, there would be little, if any, opportunity for any other group to monitor the program.

This then is the bare outline of the decision-making structures. We

---

* There are, of course, exceptions. In some instances there may be informal consultations with others in the Bureau of Intelligence and Research or with a country Director, although this does not appear to be the norm.

are ready to turn to an assessment of the implications of this structure for executive-branch decision-making, keeping in mind the vignettes with which we begin the essay.

IMPLICATIONS FOR
EXECUTIVE-BRANCH DECISION-MAKING[3]

The system under which decisions about covert operations are made distorts the decision-making process in a number of undesirable ways. It (1) increases the chances that such operations will be chosen over more desirable alternatives, (2) reduces the effectiveness with which such operations are designed and carried out, (3) distorts the decision-making within the executive branch in general, and (4) reduces the effectiveness of the intelligence evaluation that is supposed to be the primary responsibility of the CIA.

The super secrecy of covert operations increases the chances the President will choose covert actions rather than other options that would be more desirable and that, if there were a free and open debate within the executive branch or if the Congress and the public were also involved in the decision-making process, would otherwise have been adopted.

A major problem that faces an American President taking any action is the multiple-audience problem. Whatever the President does will be seen by the foreign country against which he may be directing his action, by leaders and active groups in other countries, and by a number of domestic groups in the Congress and among the attentive public. The fact that the operation itself cannot be kept from these other audiences is one of the costs frequently associated with any operation.

One of the major attractions of covert operations is the ability to avoid the problem of multiple audiences. If something is to be conducted in secret, then one can avoid the fight over the means and the ends which erupts when other audiences discover an ongoing operation. For example, when asked in the summer of 1970 why the United States had been willing to send military forces to Vietnam to prevent a Communist takeover but had not been willing to send American military forces to Chile to prevent a Marxist government from coming into power, President Nixon replied that the United States could not send military forces to Chile without provoking such an adverse political reaction in the rest of Latin America that it would outweigh the possible value of American military intervention.[4]

Compared with alternatives, it is easier to obtain the necessary approval for covert operations. The President himself can usually authorize such operations without having to go to Congress for funds or having to go before the American public to make a public justification.

In addition, covert operations also often come to seem cheap and easy because, virtually by definition, a covert operation can generally be disavowed if discovered. As in many other aspects of the planning and execution of covert operations, an extreme optimism seems to accompany such evaluations. Thus, in the case of both the U-2 and the Bay of Pigs, an explicit element of the calculation leading to authorizing the plan was the belief that the operations could be disavowed with a cover story if they were discovered.

The mechanism of decision-making also tends to bias the system toward the choosing of covert options. Normally, when the United States is faced with a problem, there will be meetings to discuss the whole range of overt possibilities weighted against one another in an advisory procedure that will permit critics of one proposal to be heard while the proponents of that proposal are present. Covert operations will not be discussed at such meetings, but rather will be considered separately at meetings from which both advocates of other proposals and critics of covert operations are excluded. Those advocating covert operations can bring them up through the mechanism of the Forty Committee and thus do not have to compete for the time and attention of top-level decision-makers. For example, one suspects that it is now considerably easier to get an issue onto the agenda of the Forty Committee than on the schedule of the Senior Review Group, which meets to consider all noncovert matters within the National Security Council System.

These same factors serve to reduce the efficiency of the design and execution of covert operations. Thus the extreme secrecy of covert operations increases the probability that such operations will be poorly designed and implemented with little regard for the realities of the external world (for example, the Bay of Pigs) or for appropriate principles of American behavior (for example, Chile). Many of the problems in the design and execution of covert operations come precisely from the fact that the circle of people involved in such operations is kept very small and, indeed, is limited to people who tend to be sympathetic to such operations.

As in all areas of policy, those involved have an interest in keeping the number of participants to the lowest possible level and to keep out those who are likely to be critics.[5] However, in the area of covert intelligence operations, there is a special tool of great importance for excluding potential critics, namely, the special clearances. As noted, a top secret clearance is not sufficient to involve an official in the planning or execution of covert operations. To have access to such information, one must get special clearances, the existence of which may not even be known to officials who do not have them.

Since the authority to grant such clearances is in the hands of the officials who manage the programs, they can use this tool—the need for super secrecy—to prevent the access of those they fear might be skeptical or critical of their operations.

With the circle of those "in the know" kept very small, the persons involved will tend to discount the views of other government officials who are not aware of the details of covert operations. Thus, for example, the analyses of experts on Cuba—that a successful anti-Castro operation in Cuba in 1961 was unlikely—were discounted by those "in the know" about the Bay of Pigs operation. These officials saw themselves as the only ones receiving all the reports from the covert operations in Cuba. The views of intelligence analysts in the CIA and in the Department of State on Cuba were discounted because of the fact that these officials did not receive some of the reports from agents operating within Cuba. Since they were seen as not having the whole picture, their otherwise expert views of the Cuban situation were entirely discounted.

The process by which proposals for covert operations move up through the narrow group of those with necessary clearances increases the likelihood that the decisions of senior officials who sit on the Forty Committee will usually be unanimous. Because of the close working relationships among the members of this committee, they tend to get rubber-stamped by the committee. Presumably, they are also rubber-stamped by the President when such proposals are brought to his attention. The lack of vigorous dissent, so common with other proposals of a controversial nature, tends to lead to routine approval.

When such operations are very large, the fact that top officials are unable to control the operations is particularly acute. In such a situation, if they call off an operation after it is well on the way, they are confronted with the danger that this information will leak out with adverse political consequences. In the case of the Bay of Pigs, President Kennedy was confronted with statements from Allen Dulles that, if the operation were canceled, Cuban refugees who had been recruited for it would begin talking about it. The cancellation would have become widely known, and, because of the intense anti-Castro feeling then rampant in the United States, the Kennedy administration would have had to contend with adverse political consequences.

The extreme secrecy surrounding covert operations also inhibits the monitoring of such operations, making sensible choices more difficult. In the case of overt operations, the press provides one critical aspect of the monitoring system by providing the President and other top officials with an evaluation of what is going on. With covert operations, this form of feedback is often entirely absent unless the operation reaches such proportions that the press in the field begins to learn of it.*

The secrecy of covert operations also reduces the possibility of effective monitoring within the U.S. government. The acknowledged need for flexibility in such operations often makes it easy to justify extreme authority for officials in the field to carry out a plan in the manner that they deem desirable. The CIA controls its own assets of money, people, and communications channels to Washington, often enabling it to move without the normal internal monitoring and control procedures within the executive branch. Skeptics within the government are often not informed about covert operations and cannot play the role that they normally perform for other areas of policy—that of constantly monitoring an approved policy or operation in an effort to convince the President that it was an error and should be abandoned.

The secrecy surrounding the decision-making and execution of covert operations not only undermines the effectiveness of the decisions themselves, but also casts a shadow over executive-branch decision-making on national-security matters in general. By creating a special class of those with a "need to know" for covert operations, it tends to give such people a sense that on all matters they are better informed than those who are not involved in the covert operations. Those who have additional clearances come to think of themselves as "in the know" and to discount across the board the views of others not informed.

Moreover, lying within the government becomes an accepted routine. In order to protect the existence of additional clearances and of covert operations, officials in the government who have access to this kind of

---

* In many cases, it is the press that alerts other parts of the U.S. government to what is going on. This appears to have been the case with covert operations in Laos through the 1960s, where covert activities came to the attention of many government officials through press reports from Laos.

information must, as a matter of routine, deceive other officials in order to protect the clearances and operations. This lying breeds a habit of cynicism and contempt for those who are lied to which cannot help but spill into the general pattern of executive-branch decision-making. Daniel Ellsberg, in testimony before Senate subcommittees, describes this problem:

> Moreover, in signing agreements to have this information, you will come to understand that the only way of keeping secrets this well is to lie.
>
> A contract to observe those clearances, and these are essentially contractual arrangements in the executive branch, conditions of employment, is a contract to lie; in a good cause, it would appear to protect intelligence secrets.
>
> When I say lie, on the first hand, if you are asked if you have this clearance, you are not allowed to say, no comment. That would confirm it. Your duty is to lie and say you do not have it.
>
> If you are asked about the contents, you are to lie and say you know nothing about the contents.
>
> If you are asked whether you have a particular piece of information, you must lie and say you do not.
>
> These go back to the practices of World War II, when thousands of civilians were introduced to the need to lie to their fellow scientists despite the supposed sharing of scientific information. Lying is legitimatized with an enemy like Hitler or Stalin. Thus, some people learn these practices in a context that seems thoroughly legitimate to them and inevitable.[6]

The most explicit and concrete way in which the super-secrecy system of covert operations distorts executive-branch decision-making is in its impact on the CIA itself. President Truman, in calling for its creation, and Congress, in authorizing it, had envisioned the CIA as primarily, if not exclusively, an intelligence-evaluation organization. President Truman had written that, prior to the creation of the CIA, he received intelligence reports from each of the services and from the State Department. He felt the need for a single agency that would collate and evaluate each of these reports and that would do so without the bias that an operating agency has. The Air Force, for example, tended to bias reports in ways that would prove the argument for Air Force programs. Truman wanted an agency with a professional intelligence-analysis capability and without any programs of its own.

Because of the covert intelligence operations, this conception of the CIA's role differs markedly from reality. Throughout the postwar period, the CIA has been dominated by officials whose primary concern and interest was covert operations rather than intelligence evaluation. The only career officials to be named heads of the CIA—Allen Dulles, Richard Helms, and William Colby—came up through the covert side of the agency and ran the covert operations of the agency before becoming Directors of Central Intelligence. Officials on the agency's intelligence side recognize that the main focus of the CIA as an institution is with its covert operations rather than with its intelligence evaluations, that they are not operating in a totally hospitable environment, and that they are unlikely to rise to the top. This dominance by covert operations within the CIA has tended to diminish the quality of the personnel on the agency's intelligence-evaluation side.

In addition, the CIA, because of its involvement in operations, is not the neutral intelligence-evaluation organ that President Truman and others envisioned. With its policy concerns related to its covert operations, the CIA has a policy ax to grind just as much as any other agency. The Director of Central Intelligence will often feel pressured to fight for covert-operations programs that the CIA desires rather than to fight to have its intelligence reports, which might contradict these programs, taken seriously.

The secrecy of covert operations also reduces the quality of CIA intelligence in that the intelligence evaluators are often not informed of covert operations within the CIA—the situation of the CIA operations during the Cultural Revolution, mentioned above, is one such example. Much of the contact between the CIA and other agencies is through officials from the Operations Directorate rather than from the Directorate of Intelligence, thereby reducing the latter's knowledge of what is going on in the government and their ability to make sensible intelligence inputs.

Thus, because of the existence of a covert-operations staff that dominates the agency, the CIA has been in a much weaker position to fulfill its primary function of providing objective intelligence evaluation. The Vietnam war illustrates this well. The intelligence analysis in the CIA, as the Pentagon Papers reveal, frequently produced much more sensible estimates of the situation in Vietnam than were coming from other parts of the intelligence community. What the Pentagon Papers did not indicate, because they did not draw on the files of the covert operations of the

American government, is that the Operations Directorate was as wrong on Vietnam as any other part of the government. The CIA was heavily involved in covert operations in Vietnam, including the training and arming of ethnic minorities, and its operators were as optimistic as anyone about the success of their programs. Thus the great weight of the CIA effort within the government was to defend these programs rather than to push the consequences of the pessimistic intelligence evaluations.

CONCLUSIONS AND RECOMMENDATIONS

The recommendations drawn from this analysis are limited to the implications for altering the way in which decisions dealing with covert intelligence operations are made—in secret and separate channels from those decisions dealing with questions of political operations.[7]

The simplest and single most important step to be taken to reduce the secrecy surrounding covert technical intelligence-gathering is to end the fiction that such operations are secret. The United States continues to insist that the fact that it has developed satellite reconnaissance operations and the fact that it has a National Security Agency which routinely intercepts all communications by other governments are highly secret. Much of the extreme secrecy of the decision-making flows from such unrealistic assumptions. As a result, this information cannot be routinely referred to in policy papers or at meetings in which people are present who do not have the clearances involved. If the simple fact that such operations were going on were acknowledged, then it would be possible to abolish the special clearances that exist for all products of these operations.*

The abolition of the special procedures would make it possible to open up substantially the decision-making on these programs, leading to more realistic evaluations as to their size, scope, and relation to more general policy issues, such as those raised by the reconnaissance over North Vietnam or by the EC-121 flying off the coast of North Korea.

In addition, a willingness on the part of the United States to acknowledge that we engage in such operations, something well known to everyone, would make it possible to make public the budgets and the structures of the organizations that conduct these operations; the Na-

---

* When necessary, special clearances or special restrictions could still be imposed to protect the operational characteristics of some of these systems and, perhaps, some part of the products which involved particularly sensitive means of detection.

tional Security Agency and the National Reconnaissance Office could become public organizations with publicly acknowledged budgets.

Although covert political operations are by their nature a more difficult problem, the United States could conceivably make a general acknowledgment that it has in the past and might in the future engage in such operations when it felt them to be necessary—although in some respects a proposal to make them public is, in effect, a proposal to abolish them. If they are to continue, steps could be taken to minimize the adverse consequences of the decision-making process leading to such operations.

To deal with the problems inherent in its structure, the CIA should be broken up into two separate organizations: one an intelligence-evaluation organization and the other a small unit engaging in covert operations. A revised CIA—that is, the intelligence-evaluation unit—should be given a role in decision-making about all covert operations, including evaluations of the likelihood of the success of the programs, of the implications for other countries of the operations, and, finally, of the importance of whatever information it is alleged will be learned from these operations that will be of use to American intelligence. The covert-operations organization should be both publicly known and publicly voted by the Congress. Its operations should be subject to evaluation not only by the new CIA but also by those responsible for policy issues in the State Department, the Department of Defense, and the White House.

This revised CIA, without any ax to grind, without any special stake in competing programs, would provide a much more effective evaluation than that which now comes from the operational side of the CIA. Such a structure could better deal with some of the problems identified above and begin to evaluate the more basic question of whether the United States should, in fact, have such programs.

IV

Summation

WILLIAM E. COLBY

The View from Langley

10

ADDRESS TO THE FUND FOR PEACE CONFERENCE ON THE CIA AND COVERT ACTION

If I said I am happy to be here, my statement might be used to challenge the credibility of the Intelligence Community. But I am happy to serve under a Constitution which, in my view, brings me here. While I might have constructed the program of this conference somewhat differently, it reflects the workings of our free society. It is thus incumbent upon our government officials to explain to the public the functions and activities of their particular organizations, and I include in this, as you can see by my presence here, the Central Intelligence Agency and the Intelligence Community.

Our military forces must be responsive to our public, but our public does not demand that our war plans be published. Our judicial system must meet the public's standards of justice, but our judicial conferences and grand-jury proceedings are not conducted in public. It is even necessary for the Congress to conduct some of its business in executive session, while remaining accountable to the voters for the legislation it passes. Similarly, I believe it is feasible to explain to the American people the functions and activities of CIA and the Intelligence Community while at the same time maintaining the necessary secrecy of the sources and methods of our intelligence, which would dry up if publicized.

In part, I can respond to legitimate public inquiry through general discussions of our activities, omitting the critical names and details. In other respects, I believe I can respond to the public's need for assurance by reporting fully to congressional committees or other bodies appointed by the public's representatives to receive and retain this sensitive information and to make value judgments about our functions and activities. Another test of our effectiveness lies in the opinions of those in the executive and legislature who are provided the intelligence results of our operational and analytical efforts, but not how these were obtained and produced. There is a final control, of course, in the fact that some of our activities, if badly handled, come to public attention in a somewhat clamorous way.

There have been some "bad secrets" concerning intelligence; their exposure by our academic, journalist, and political critics certainly is an essential part of the workings of our Constitution. There have been some "non-secrets" which did not need to be secret; I have undertaken a program of bringing these into the open. But I think that responsible Americans realize that our country must protect some "good secrets." It is for this reason that I am proposing legislation which will impose penalties on those who take upon themselves the choice of which secrets to reveal, rather than relying on the established declassification procedures of our government. I might clarify that my proposal would not apply to the news media or any other persons than those who consciously assume the obligation to respect the secrecy to which they are admitted as government employees or similar, and that the reasonableness of the classification would be subject to judicial review.

If our laws provide for criminal penalties for the unauthorized disclosure of certain census information, income-tax information, Selective Service information, and cotton and other agricultural statistics, I think it reasonable that there should also be penalties for the unauthorized disclosure of foreign-intelligence sources and methods upon which the safety of the nation could well depend.

The title of this conference is "The CIA and Covert Action." In my letter accepting Mr. Borosage's invitation to appear here, I commented that I was somewhat surprised that there was no attempt in the agenda to examine the need for the contribution that objective and independent intelligence can make to policy decisions. In fact, however, I note that there has been considerable discussion of our intelligence activities, such as the U-2, in addition to our covert-action role.

In this regard, I would like to clarify that the predominant focus of CIA and the Intelligence Community today is clearly on our information and analytical responsibilities. In this field, we endeavor to serve the executive branch by providing intelligence on the facts of the world about us and our assessments of likely future developments. We also try to serve the Congress and the public by providing the output of the intelligence investment made by the United States, to support them in their role in American decision-making. Thus, CIA has appeared before eighteen committees on twenty-eight occasions this year (Armed Services, Appropriations, Foreign Affairs, Atomic Energy, and Economics), testifying on a variety of subjects. We have cleared for publication some of this testimony on the economies of the Soviet Union and China and on the Soviet presence in the Indian Ocean. We also produce a number of unclassified publications and distribute them through the Library of Congress to over two hundred libraries and institutes around the country, as well as making publicly available our reports of foreign broadcasts and translated documents. In addition, I have talked with one hundred and thirty-two newsmen in the past year, and about one hundred have come to CIA for briefings by our analysts on substantive questions involving foreign countries, thus benefiting from our accumulated information from our most sensitive sources.

It is a strange anomaly that our country makes publicly available vast amounts of material on the U.S., whereas the corresponding material about our potential adversaries must be collected by intelligence techniques at a cost of hundreds of millions of dollars. In this situation, if we cannot protect our intelligence sources and methods, I fear we may reach a situation in which our adversaries profit from our openness while we are blinded by their secrecy.

Dr. Scoville has quite properly indicated the revolution in intelligence which has been achieved through the growth of technology over the past two decades. This intelligence, however, is still limited to what physically exists. It does not give us the intentions, the research ideas, and the decision-making dynamics of the countries which might pose a threat to the United States. In today's accelerating technology, we are condemned always to be well behind if we rely only on what has appeared in the marketplace instead of on what is planned for the future. In addition, in a world which can destroy itself through misunderstanding or miscalculation, it is important that our leaders have a clear perception of the motives, intentions, and strategies of other powers so that they can be deterred, negotiated about, or countered in the interests of peace or, if necessary, the ultimate security of our country. These kinds of insights cannot be obtained only through technical means or analysis. From closed societies they can only be obtained by secret intelligence operations, without which our country must risk subordination to possible adversaries.

To turn to *covert action,* which is included in those "other functions and duties related to intelligence affecting the national security as the National Security Council may from time to time direct," as stated in the National Security Act, there is debate as to the degree Congress intended CIA to engage in these actions when passing the legislation in 1947. The OSS precedent, the National Security Act's clear authorization of functions "related to intelligence" by reason of secret techniques and frequent use of the same assets, and the periodic briefings given to the Congress over the years through its authorized committees clearly establish the Agency's authority to perform these functions.

The Agency conducts such activities only when specifically authorized by the National Security Council. Thus, CIA covert actions reflect national policy. National policy has been in a state of change, and CIA's involvement in covert action has correspondingly changed. In the early days of the "Cold War," when national policymakers believed it essential to confront an aggressive Communist subversive effort in many areas of the world and in the international-organizational sphere, there was a great deal of this sort of effort. Some was revealed in the 1967 disclosures of our relationships with various American groups which helped their country to present the American position and support America's friends in this arena during the 1950s and 1960s. The record is clear that the assistance given to these institutions by the CIA was to enable them to participate in *foreign* activities; there was no attempt to interfere in internal American domestic activities. CIA aid helped such groups as the National Student Association to articulate the views of American students abroad and meet the Communist-subsidized effort to develop a panoply of international-front organizations. I might quote Ms. Gloria Steinem, one of those so assisted, who commented that the CIA "wanted to do what we wanted to do—present a healthy, diverse view of the United States. . . . I never felt I was being dictated to at all."

There have also been, and are still, certain situations in the world in which some discreet support can assist America's friends against her adversaries in their contest for control of a foreign nation's political direction. While these instances are few today compared to the 1950s, I believe it only prudent for our nation to be able to act in such situations, and thereby forestall greater difficulties for us in the future.

In other situations, especially after Nikita Khrushchev's enthusiastic espousal of the thesis of "wars of national liberation," the United States believed it essential to provide paramilitary support to certain groups and nations. In 1962 President Kennedy, for national-policy reasons, did not want to use the uniformed forces of the United States in Laos, but also did not want to be limited to a mere diplomatic protest against the continued presence of five thousand North Vietnamese troops in Laos in violation of the Geneva Accords, and their expansion of control over communities who wished to resist them.

Thus CIA was directed to provide support to those communities, a duty which grew to a major effort, known and approved by the Lao government, but not confronting North Vietnam and its allies with a direct and overt U.S. challenge. Mr. Branfman has told you of some of the terrible human problems involved in any war when it grows to a conventional scale involving artillery, air bombardment, and so forth. What has perhaps not been fully perceived is that the American assistance to this effort involved a small commitment of CIA Americans and a small expenditure over the many years in which this action was undertaken; and that, as a result of the defensive efforts of the forces supported by CIA, the battle lines at the end of the period were essentially unchanged from those at the opening.

As with the Bay of Pigs, when the activity became too large, it no longer remained secret. But I think the CIA people who conducted this effort deserve the praise of our citizens for the effective but modest manner in which President Kennedy's mission was carried out—a mission, by the way, that cost the lives of eight CIA officers there. This activity was reported to and appropriated for on a regular basis by the authorized elements of the Congress—the war was no secret from them.

But it is clear that American policy today is different from when it was confronting world-wide Communist subversion in the 1950s or Communist insurgency in the 1960s. Our involvement has been reduced in many areas, in part, I might add, by the fact that many of the Communist efforts during those years were unsuccessful. CIA's covert actions in many of these instances thus assisted in laying the groundwork for the new period of détente which we pursue in our relationships with the Communist world today. As a result, CIA's involvement in covert action is very small indeed compared to those earlier periods. I do not say that we do not now conduct such activities; I merely state that they are undertaken only as directed by the National Security Council, they are frankly and regularly reported to the appropriate committees of the Congress, and they require only a small proportion of our effort at this time.

I am not being more precise on these various covert actions. Some you are aware of because of exposure, leak, or failure—such as the Bay of Pigs. Some you are not aware of because they have been effectively handled and have achieved their objectives. I abide by what one President said about CIA, that our successes are unheralded and our failures trumpeted.

It is advocated by some that the United States abandon covert action. This is a legitimate question, and in light of current American policy, as I have indicated, it would not have a major impact on our current activities or the current security of the United States. I believe, however, that a sovereign nation must look ahead to changing circumstances. I can envisage situations in which the United States might well need to conduct covert action in the face of some new threat that developed in the world.

In 1924 we sank the brand new battleship *Washington* as a demonstration of our belief in disarmament. At about the same time, we disbanded an intelligence element in the Department of State on the thesis that "gentlemen do not read each other's mail." During the same period, we declined the international burdens of membership in the League of Nations. I believe our post–World War II history, with all its costs, constituted an improvement on our post–World War I policies and did avoid a World War III during these thirty years. I thus would think it mistaken to deprive our nation of the possibility of some moderate covert-action response to a foreign problem and leave us with nothing between a diplomatic protest and sending the Marines.

Bills in Congress today would amend the National Security Act of 1947 to clarify a requirement that the Congress be kept informed "in such manner as the Congress may prescribe" of any "functions and duties related to intelligence affecting the national security" carried out by CIA. I fully support this change in the CIA's basic legislative charter, which would establish in law the practice we follow today.

In Mr. Borosage's announcement with respect to this conference, he expressed the concern that untrammeled secret power poses a threat to our liberties and that our program of covert activities abroad must be re-examined before similar techniques are employed to subvert our democracy at home. I have indicated that I do not believe that CIA's covert actions abroad constitute "untrammeled secret power" in view of our responsibilities to the executive and to the legislature.

With respect to the second part of Mr. Borosage's concern about these techniques being employed in the United States, I again point to a bill being considered in the Congress which would make it crystal clear that CIA's activities lie only in the field of *foreign* intelligence by adding the word "foreign" wherever the word "intelligence" appears in the National Security Act. I fully support this wording and, in fact, originally suggested it in my confirmation hearings. My predecessors and I have admitted that CIA did exceed its authority in several instances with respect to Watergate. We have taken steps within the Agency to ensure that such actions do not occur again. The proposed change in our legislative charter would make this a matter of statutory direction. But the fact that a retired CIA employee becomes involved in some illegal activity in the United States should no more eliminate a function essential to our nation than should the fact that a Vietnam veteran commits a crime be used as the basis to deprive the United States Army of its pistols. And the concern of all of us that CIA not be used against U.S. citizens should not bar it from lawfully collecting that foreign intelligence available within the United States.

QUESTION AND ANSWER SESSION, SENATOR JAMES ABOUREZK, CHAIRMAN (DEMOCRAT, SOUTH DAKOTA)

WILLIAM E. COLBY: With respect to Chile, Mr. Chairman, since my testimony on Chile was given in executive session from which it has unfortunately leaked, I do not propose to discuss the details of our activity there, other than to point out that they fall within the general principles I outlined above.

I repeat what I have previously said, that CIA had no connection with the military coup there in 1973. We did look forward to a change in government (*audience laughter*), but, in the elections of 1976, by the democratic political forces. I would add that, in my review of the transcript of that testimony, there is no reference to prototype, nor the term "destabilize." The latter, especially, is not a fair description of our national policy from 1971 on of encouraging the continued existence of democratic forces looking toward future elections. I would also comment that this unfortunate leak, once again, raises the dilemma of how we are to provide the Congress such delicate information without its exposure and consequent adverse impact on those who put their faith in our secrecy and those who might be contemplating such a relationship in the future. This is a matter, of course, for the Congress to decide; and I have every confidence that a fully satisfactory solution will eventuate. I think with that, Mr. Chairman, I would be very happy to answer any questions.

CHAIRMAN: Thank you, Mr. Colby. I have a question that I would like to ask of you. Your statement is that "covert action reflects national policy." Now, since all covert action is done in secret, and when it is revealed it is denied by the CIA, and since it is neither disclosed nor acknowledged to the public, how can it reflect national policy?

COLBY: Because, Mr. Chairman, it is given to us by the established elected authorities of the United States government, the President, and the National Security Council and is reported to the Congress.

CHAIRMAN: I might say, it is not reported to me.

COLBY: That may be true, Mr. Chairman, and as I have indicated, I believe these matters should be reported to the Congress in the manner that the Congress establishes. It is up to the Congress to determine how it shall be done. You are correct that these covert actions, by definition, are secret, but they are not denied. Some years ago, there was a phrase called "plausible denial" used. I have proscribed that phrase because I do not believe that we can tell the American people an untruth. I think we can tell the American people a true statement and keep other matters which have to be secret, secret. But I do not believe we can tell them an untruth.

ROBERT L. BOROSAGE: You say that it is a strange anomaly that the United States has so much information that it makes public, whereas our potential adversaries do not. It seems to me that the reason for that strange anomaly is something called democracy.

The strange anomaly exists because this is supposed to be a society in which the legislature and the people decide the policies that we undertake. The definition of national policy exemplifies my point. According to the Constitution national policy on matters of warmaking is to be made at least in conjunction with the legislature. The easy assumption that national policy is an executive matter is exactly what has taken us into the war we've fought and the agony we've experienced over the last decade.

COLBY: Like every other government employee, I took an oath to support and defend the Constitution of the United States. My concept of the Constitution of the United States is one expressed through the duly established legislative, judicial, and executive bodies represented by it. National policy is not an executive matter only. It depends upon an annual appropriation. It depends upon judicial review of the constitutionality of both the legislative and executive actions.

You point out the anomaly. I had the occasion to follow the suggestion of one of the individuals who spoke at this panel of attempting to negotiate an end to that anomaly, when last summer being in the reception line when Mr. Brezhnev was over here. President Nixon presented me to Mr. Brezhnev as the new head of the CIA. Mr. Brezhnev recoiled in some mock horror and asked if I was a dangerous man. The President reassured him that I agreed with the treaty on the limitations on nuclear war that had just been signed, and I commented to Mr. Brezhnev, in my first effort toward summit diplomacy, that the more we know of each other the safer we both will be. I believe that. That's why I believe in working in the intelligence profession hopefully to increase the knowledge of our leadership about the problems in the world.

It is clear that, thanks to some of the intelligence work of the past ten or fifteen years, we now have an agreement which depends upon the fact that we can monitor whether the Soviets are complying with it or not, [which] we were unable to do when our intelligence was so weak that we had to ask for on-the-ground inspections. I think that the fears that I had in my youth are very similar to the ones you had, Mr. Borosage. We probably faced the problem of a national threat and war at about the same age, and I faced it again in the Vietnam situation, and I spent three and a half years there working on that problem in the best way that I could for my country.

UNIDENTIFIED MEMBER OF THE AUDIENCE: How many did you kill [in Vietnam]?

COLBY: I'd like to answer that question. I didn't kill any. (*audience laughter*) The Phoenix program was one part of the total pacification program of the government of Vietnam. There were several other parts: the development of local security forces in the neighborhood to protect the villages; the distribution of a half a million weapons to the people of South Vietnam to use in unpaid self-defense groups, a venture that I doubt that many other governments would try or that would meet with the success that the Vietnamese did.

It also included a program of developing local village and provincial elections and giving authority to the elected officials thereof. It gave decisions about economic-development programs in the localities to the local officials. There were a variety of programs of this nature, including the inducement, reception, and resettlement of over two hundred thousand Vietnamese who had served with the Viet Cong and decided to come over to the government's side and were received and not punished for whatever they had done. It involved the reception and resettlement and eventual return to villages, as security improved, of hundreds of thousands of refugees. And it included the Phoenix program which was designed to identify the leaders of the Communist apparatus that was bringing terror and invasion to the population of South Vietnam.

The Phoenix program was designed and started in about 1968 in order to bring some degree of order and regularity to a very unpleasant, nasty war that had preceded it. It did a variety of things to improve the procedures by which that was run. It provided procedures by which the identification of the leaders, rather than the followers, became the objective of the operation; by which the objective was to capture, rather than to kill, the members of the apparatus; by which there were limits placed on the length of time of detentions and the procedures for interrogation.

UNIDENTIFIED MEMBER OF THE AUDIENCE: How many were killed while you were over there?

COLBY: I have testified on that, and I said that in over two and a half years of the Phoenix program, there were twenty-nine thousand captured; there were seventeen thousand defected; and there were twenty thousand, five hundred killed, of which eighty-seven per cent were killed by regular and paramilitary forces and twelve per cent by police and similar elements. The vast majority of those killed were killed in military combat, fire fights, or ambushes, and most of the remainder were killed in police actions attempting to capture them. The major stress of the Phoenix program was to encourage the capture for very sensible, easy reasons. First, our respect—not the Communists'—our respect for human life where it can be gained (*audience laughter*), and secondly because a live captive has information, and a dead body has none.

HENRY HOWE RANSOM (author of *The Intelligence Establishment*): Mr. Chairman, I'd like to ask Mr. Colby to comment on the statutory authority of the Central Intelligence Agency to engage in covert operations. I read that statute over and over and over, and it does say what you said it says with regard to "other duties and functions related to intelligence affecting the nationl security." But you find a lot more flexibility in that phrase, and particularly in the word "intelligence," than I, as a user of the English language, find in it.

COLBY: Over the years history has given that deliberately general phrase a great deal of content . . . content that has been ratified by the Congress and by the executive. It has come to, shall we say, not a little public attention without any change being made in it.

CONGRESSMAN MICHAEL HARRINGTON (Democrat, Massachusetts): Mr. Colby, let's turn to Chile, the country of the week. Let me say at the outset that I'll stand by a memory that I have of two readings of your testimony, and the term "political destabilization" was indeed used. To give you full credit, your testimony was a very candid discourse on the CIA operation in Chile. Let me also say that your historic intelligence-gathering-and-evaluation role is one that I not only endorse but, in a sense, accept as a legitimate facet of Agency operations. Since you have already indicated your intention not to address specifics raised in your testimony to Congressman Lucien Nedzi on April twenty-second, let me at least question what I consider to be the fiction of congressional oversight. Was Lucien Nedzi, or were the informal members of the Armed Services Committee structure that oversee, at least theoretically, the CIA role, informed about Chile before April twenty-second of this year?

COLBY: I believe Mr. Nedzi is a rather recent appointee to that chairmanship, but over the years since 1964 a variety of congressional committees and individual congressmen and senators were made aware at appropriate times in the period of our covert-action activity. This was done according to the procedure set up at that period—at each period—and as you know we have a round-up recap every now and again and the April twenty-second testimony was one for the House committee. There had been previous total round-up recaps for other committees of the Congress well prior to that time, and, in fact, right after the coup in 1973.

HARRINGTON: In late 1972 Lucien Nedzi was first given the designation as chairman of the apparently previously loosely structured apparatus at the Armed Services Committee level on the House side. It was apparent to me that the information being given him on April twenty-second was unquestionably being given to him for the first time.

COLBY: Our reports to Congress run on several levels: one is an open session, of which this one is a comparable example, where we can speak, without divulging our operational methods and secrets; we also report broadly in executive session on the substance of what is going on in the world, and that particular hearing that day was arranged for that purpose, to try to report generally on what was happening. And, as I said at that time, I was not prepared to discuss our operational activities in Chile at that particular hearing. I was prepared, and so indicated in our conversation, that I was prepared to discuss any operational detail with the constituted subcommittees of the Armed Services Committee or the Appropriations Committee, and I did so. As I recall it, Mr. Harrington, I think there were a couple other of the members present on the April twenty-second event. I've forgotten precisely who they were and how long they spent there.

But with respect to the question about clearance with State, the Department of State through the Deputy Secretary of State is a member of the Forty Committee who considers and approves the various covert action directions that we get or approvals that we get. The State Department, as do the rest of us, handles this on a very strictly compartmented basis, offering the need-to-know principle for the reason for limiting sharply who should and who should not know. Well, obviously, each department determines that for itself. There are occasions in which these matters are held extremely tightly and made available only perhaps to the principal concerned. There are other occasions in which a broader group of people, including the ambassador and including others in the State Department, are made available. I just can't say right now which item was made available to which State Department officer at this particular point.

HARRINGTON: Let me try to get a little bit further into that question. Perhaps the more interesting part of your discussion with Mr. Nedzi and those other members who made up the subcommittee on intelligence oversight ran to the method you used in the furtherance of this kind of an activity, where I believe you indicated that it was usually or customarily the case to inform and to include State Department personnel, and I assume, at a reasonably ranking level in the country in which the operation was to be carried out. First, because it made relationships easier; second, to a degree it avoided problems of attempting to, of necessity, go around them; and third, because I can infer that the method of operation, as far as getting approvals, usually ran through a joint chain of command, though I would suspect that the CIA could take, at least as you described it, a great deal by way of credit in the initiation rather than just being at the execution or the furtherance level.

Although not expecting that I am going to get any more directness than I have had, I want to read statements made before congressional committees on three occasions over the course of the last year by three separate individuals all of whom were directly concerned with Chilean policy on the part of this country's government. The first was before our subcommittee, the Inter-American Subcommittee, on June twelfth of this year, by Deputy Ambassador or Deputy Chief Slatterman. "Despite pressures to the contrary, the United States government adhered to a policy of nonintervention in Chile's internal affairs during the Allende period. That policy remains in force today."

Let me read secondly from testimony given to the Church subcommittee last spring by former Ambassador Korry: "I said it was obvious from the historical record that we did not act in any manner that reflected a hard line. [This is with reference to Chile.] The United States gave no support to any electoral candidate. The United States had maintained the most total hands off the military policy from 1969 to 1971 conceivable. . . . The United States did not seek to pressure, subvert, influence a single member of the Chilean Congress at any time in the entire four years of my stay. All of my instructions came from State in that no hard line toward Chile was carried out at any time."

Former Inter-American Ambassador Meyer's [testimony] runs along the same lines. "The policy of the government, Mr. Chairman, was that there would be no intervention in the political affairs of Chile. We were consistent in that we financed no candidates, no political parties before or after September eighth, or September fourth rather."

I think it is obvious that there is an apparent discrepancy between what they are stating as officials of the United States government, and what you have testified to in a session before, as you call it, a relevant House subcommittee. I would add also as a backdrop the comments from Senator Symington in this morning's *Washington Post* indicating that as a member of the Senate structure for oversight, statements made by yourself came as a surprise to him as to the degree of involvement in this country. I think it does tend to make the point both of the fiction of oversight and of the, at least, casual use of the truth on the part of a variety of State Department officials who have appeared before congressional committees over the course of the last year.

COLBY: Mr. Harrington, I am prepared to go into the CIA in detail before the proper committees. I am prepared to go into the CIA operations in detail before any members of Congress who are brought into the matter by the proper committees. I am prepared to change our procedure if the Congress decides to set up the structure in another way. Until one of those happens, I respectfully must not get into a further discussion about the details of our activities there [in Chile].

CHAIRMAN: It seems that CIA covert activities are never discussed in advance with anyone that I know of. If they are discussed with Lucien Nedzi or Stuart Symington, I'm not aware of it. The Chilean experience indicates that that is the case. You say that you are prepared to discuss the Chilean operation before any appropriate committee, but the Chilean operation is over with. We are always talking about what the CIA has done two, three years, four, or five years in the past. Might it not be a good idea to discuss what you are doing now, at this time, with just the appropriate committees? I would like to see you go further than that, since you are prepared to call covert activities national policy. If they are national policy, shouldn't the nation be brought in, if not on specific matters, at least on the general principle of whether the nation approves of assassinations, for example? Does the nation approve of CIA-sponsored government coups or many other things that I and a lot of Americans disapprove of? You don't want to talk about the specific activity, yet the CIA will not even talk about the general principles. Wouldn't that be an appropriate matter for public debate—whether a specific Chilean-type operation, or the Cuban-type operation, reflects national sentiment?

COLBY: I think that my presence here demonstrates that I am prepared to talk about covert actions, and I have talked about some of them. As for discussing future events, many of them cannot be predicted in the future, but a number of our covert activities have gone on over a number of years. During those years, there have been periodic appropriations, some of which are used for some of these operations. When they get significant enough, they must be covered in the appropriations process. I did state that to Mr. Nedzi in an open hearing a few weeks ago that there are no secrets from that particular subcommittee or the corresponding subcommittee of the House Appropriations Committee. None. Beyond a responsibility to respond to his questions, I have a positive responsibility to bring to his attention things that he might be interested in. I have undertaken to bring to the various committees our current activities so that they will be informed of what we are doing.

CHAIRMAN: Did the chairman of the oversight committee know in advance of your Chilean operation?

COLBY: Various of our individual actions in Chile over the years were reported—at that time and in some cases before the funds were expended —to the appropriate chairmen of the committees involved. I can't say that every dollar the CIA spent in Chile was individually approved by a committee chairman, but I can say that the major efforts were known to the senior officials of the Congress as established.

CHAIRMAN: I would like to refer to the weekend disclosures of the Chilean action by the CIA—was the knowledge of that action provided in advance to the supervising committees of the Congress?

COLBY: The action disclosed by Mr. Harrington's letter over the weekend covered the period from 1964 to 1973. At various times during that period, the major steps were brought to the attention of the chairman or appropriate members of various of these committees. Now, I cannot say that every individual instance was brought to them, but there were a series of discussions between CIA and senior members of Congress which brought them up to date with the fact that this occurred, and was occurring.

CHAIRMAN: A story by Laurence Stern in the *Washington Post* states that three hundred and fifty thousand dollars was authorized to the CIA to bribe the Chilean Congress, which at that time was faced with deciding a run-off election between Allende and the opposition candidate. Were the committees aware of that?

COLBY: Mr. Chairman, with great respect, that falls within the category of the details that I'm not going to talk about.

FRED BRANFMAN: Mr. Colby, putting aside various arguments over what actually happened in operation Phoenix and, given your understanding of what did happen under it, if you were ordered by the President of the United States and the National Security Council to engage in such actions against either Americans or other people in other third world countries, I'd like to know if you would have any moral objections?

I am particularly intrigued by a statement you made when you testified before Congress in 1971 about the An Tri sentencing procedure whereby Vietnamese are sentenced to two years, without a lawyer. You said you wouldn't want to see these legal standards applied to Americans, although they were being applied to Vietnamese. From a moral point of view, what are the distinctions between what we do to Americans and Vietnamese and other countries?

Secondly, Senator Symington, who is on the Senate Oversight Committee, told you at your confirmation hearing that "we are getting pretty sick of being lied to." If we don't want to take your word that, for example, the CIA is not now involved in paramilitary activities in Cambodia, do we have any means to check this? Do we have any way of finding out what you people are up to other than having to take your word for it?

Finally, is it your understanding that millions of Americans are opposed to any kind of assassination programs, any kind of police programs, any kind of attempts to overthrow foreign countries or influence the political practices in foreign countries?

COLBY: Mr. Branfman, I have a considerable degree of modesty as to whether anyone has a monopoly of morality. With respect to the question about the due process under Vietnamese law and the advice of counsel, I do stand by the fact that I would hope that Americans will have the benefit of due process, including the advice of counsel. As a former member of the Bar myself, maybe that is a professional promotional device, but I think it is a very useful one. However, in Vietnam there were only two hundred lawyers, and it was a little hard to get advice of counsel for every person arrested in Vietnam under those circumstances, and therefore a variety of other activities were conducted to try to improve the legal and procedural aspects of the Phoenix program.

As for the question of how to check on CIA, I think the press does a superlative job of catching us whenever they can. I think that the various members of Congress and the various staff members, as they travel around, have a chance to ask our people what's going on. There are a lot of other people who are quite willing to bring to the attention of the public or to the appropriate authorities any wrongdoing by the agency or any contradiction between what we are duly authorized to do under our Constitution and what we are not duly authorized to do. Therefore, I think that any exceptional effort to use CIA in an improper way will come out. I have talked to our own employees, and I have told them that it is my conviction that if anybody tried to misuse CIA against the American people, the CIA would explode from within, and I would think it a good thing.

CHAIRMAN: I want to follow up with one question. Is there anything that the CIA has done overseas that you would not do in the United States? (*audience outburst*)

COLBY: Mr. Chairman, of course. We are engaged every day overseas in trying to learn through secret, clandestine operations matters which are kept secret and are illegal. In the closed societies and countries that we work in and in some of the other countries that we share this world with, there are a lot of illegal things, according to our standards, done overseas, and I think this is a natural aspect of the fact that we live in a world of sovereign nations, each one of which must protect its own security.

CHAIRMAN: What covert activities do you engage in overseas that you would approve of in this United States?

COLBY: The CIA must do those things that are lawful in the United States. I did not say that we had any authority to commit crimes in the United States, and I deny that we do have any such authority, and we have given very strict directions to our people in that respect.

CHAIRMAN: But you do undertake activities overseas that would be crimes in this country?

COLBY: Of course. Espionage is a crime in this country.

CHAIRMAN: Other than espionage?

COLBY: Of course.

MORTON H. HALPERIN: Mr. Colby, I was encouraged by your statement that you now think it is a legitimate question whether we should, given our current perception of our interests, engage in any covert operations, and by your additional statement that you do not think abolishing such operations would have a major impact either on current activities or on the current security of the United States. Can we assume that that statement was made with, among other things, the current situation in Greece in mind? If, as appears to be the case, Greece may well be getting a government which decides to withdraw from NATO and eliminate American bases, would your statement still hold? Has the CIA proposed to the Forty Committee, or do you expect that it would propose, to the Forty Committee operations designed to prevent a Greek government from coming to power which would seek to withdraw from NATO and close American bases?

COLBY: As I said in my statement, I do not think that the elimination of covert actions would have a major effect on our current activities because it is such a small portion of our total activity. Secondly, I did not think it would have an immediate adverse effect on the security of the United States. That is a different question from whether any particular situation might be in the net interest of the United States. I really do not think it is very useful for me to discuss in this forum whether any particular proposal should be made or should not be made about an individual covert action. I think that falls exactly within the category of those things that I believe, if we are to conduct covert actions, should be discussed within very restricted circles in the executive and reported to those very restricted circles in the legislature which can enable them to be done and still be kept secret.

HALPERIN: Did I understand you correctly to say that, while there might be a net advantage for the intervention in Greece, there would not be any major impact on American security if we did not conduct covert operations throughout the world including Greece?

COLBY: The current status of the world is such that it does not look that we are on the brink of any serious damage to our country at the moment. The Capitol, I think, will still stand whether any particular covert action takes place or not, at this time.

MARCUS G. RASKIN (Co-Director, Institute for Policy Studies): Mr. Colby, I was puzzled by some conceptual questions. One was whose interests were really being served in your view, and how you defined them. In the last generation, as you know, the Rockefeller family has been very much involved in different forms of intelligence activities of the United States. Is it going to be the case that the CIA, under your direction, will continue to use various Rockefeller-owned corporations abroad as covers or in any way? How does the Agency intend to deal with the question of conflict of interest? Will that be made public to Congress and the American people?

COLBY: If Mr. Rockefeller is confirmed as the Vice President of the United States, the CIA will respond to him as the Vice President of the United States. Whatever the authority that suggests something to us, we are restricted by our legal authorities in what we can do, and we are not given any privilege to engage in conflict of interests. I did indicate in my confirmation hearings, and I believe I'm still bound by it, that if anybody asks me to do something which is improper and outside the proper lines of authority of my responsibilities, I am quite prepared to resign and leave.

RASKIN: Does that mean then that the Central Intelligence Agency will not use various Rockefeller corporations as covers around the world?

COLBY: I don't believe that is a useful subject to discuss, Mr. Raskin, because I get back to my responsibility not to talk about the operational details of my agency.

RASKIN: Did the Central Intelligence Agency use ITT as a cover in Chile?

COLBY: Again, I would say that I do not propose to discuss the details of our operations. I do not want to get in a situation where I say "no, no, no" to a series of questions and then have to say "no comment" because the answer is pretty obvious at that point. I think it much more useful if I just say "no" to the whole run of such questions.

DANIEL ELLSBERG: Am I correct that you have testified publicly that the Central Intelligence Agency did have information about the imminent overthrow of constitutional government in Chile which the U.S. government failed to pass on to the constituted government of Chile?

COLBY: I doubt that I testified to that publicly.

ELLSBERG: Would that be correct?

COLBY: What leaked I'm not quite sure right now. It's hard to keep up with them. (*audience laughter*) What I will tell you is that we had a general appreciation of the deterioration of the economy and political situation in Chile running throughout 1973. The situation was getting worse and worse, in a variety of ways—politically, economically, socially, and all the rest. At varying times during that year, we had information which indicated that a coup might take place. One did take place, as you remember, about the end of June which was an aborted effort and which was put down right away. We had a series of other reports indicating various other steps toward a coup. We were not involved with the people who were leading any of those efforts, but we did have information about them.

ELLSBERG: Did you pass that information on to the elected government of Chile?

COLBY: It's my responsibility to report such information to the authorities of my country.

ELLSBERG: Was it passed on to your knowledge?

COLBY: It is a political action whether to pass that on to another country or not. That is a policy decision for the policy leaders of our country.

ELLSBERG: To your knowledge was that policy decision made—was it passed on?

COLBY: I do not think so, but I cannot say for sure.

ELLSBERG: My next question, sir, is—this should rely on open information in your capacity as Director of Intelligence—what is your best estimate of the number of people who have been killed by the present regime in Chile, which replaced constitutional government over the last year? Your estimate also of the number that have been imprisoned, and of the number that have been tortured in that period?

COLBY: I would rather not use exact numbers, because I'm not sure of them. Our estimate at the time was that in the fighting that took place at the time of the coup there was somewhere between three thousand and five thousand people killed. It is also our impression that there were very few executions. There were some, I admit that. It is not my responsibility, but that is a fact that happened. It's the military government that brought it about. How many I cannot tell you for sure. As for the number tortured, I have no idea.

ELLSBERG: No idea?

COLBY: I do not have an idea of the number that were tortured.

ELLSBERG: Have you read estimates, for example by "Amnesty International"?

COLBY: I have read various papers on this subject.

ELLSBERG: But your Agency has not given you an estimate?

COLBY: There may well be one but I just can't recall it here at this moment.

ELLSBERG: Have you asked for such an estimate?

COLBY: I asked for estimates about the other two matters; I have not asked for that particularly. I don't ask for a lot of questions that come up in our intelligence business. We have a rather large and efficient group of analysts who serve up the answers to the obvious questions around the world. They may well have made an estimate that I am not familiar with right here, as I said.

ELLSBERG: I'm sorry that this was not regarded as an obvious question in the government. If I can make a comment, we now know at least some of the people around the world who put faith in the secrecy of our government and whose survival politically in their own country depends on it. They are the present leaders of Chile; I do not take satisfaction in that particular result of our secrecy.

If we went around the world to find the other leaders who rely on our secrecy, I don't think there would be much satisfaction anywhere. You remarked that you regard as unfortunate the leaks of information on the CIA's role in Chile to the American people. I hope you are the only person in the room who believes that. I regard it not only as a fortunate but an essential piece of information. I personally have never seen a report, and none was ever presented in my trial, interestingly, or any of the other trials, of a single leak in the past twenty years that did in fact injure the interests of the people of the United States. I know of no violations of this secrecy that was not either neutral or beneficial to the constitutional government in this country.

I'm going to comment on a very specific proposal that you are currently making. You inquired whether it is not reasonable that officials who have signed an oath of secrecy, as you have, and as I did and others here have, be punished when they violate that oath. I look back on those papers that I and you have signed and recall that there was nothing in them that explicitly required one to keep secret any information received no matter what evidence it provided of illegality, criminality, aggressive war, or violations of the constitution. I think your law would make revealing such information illegal.

COLBY: No, it would not.

ELLSBERG: Your law would make it illegal to do what I did. Your law would make illegal what Mr. Marchetti did and what a number of other people here have done. The question is, do we want that or not. What would the effects be? It would make us more like countries such as Russia. There are also other countries in the world, even such as England, that have such requirements—the country against which we fought a revolution to get away from that sort of law. We have a first amendment. England does not, and certainly Russia does not.

COLBY: With respect to the question you raised about the law I recommended, I would like to point out that that law would not apply to you, Dr. Ellsberg, because that law says that it applies only to information relating to intelligence sources and methods. It does not apply broadly to classified material which is what you are accused of leaking.

ELLSBERG: Are you aware that officials of the U.S. government used the words "intelligence, intelligence sources, and materials" repeatedly during my trial?

COLBY: I am aware of that, and I say that this law is carefully designed so that it will not apply to a third party but only to those of us who take the obligation to retain a secret of some importance to our country. Secondly, before any prosecution or injunction can be obtained, the government must go before a judge and justify that that classification is reasonable. Now, I doubt that any judge would issue an authorization to go on with a prosecution if the matter leaked were the fact of a crime or the fact of some illegality. It is precisely for that reason that that particular provision is written into the law because I agree with you that there are a lot of things that I would not send people to jail for just because they have a stamp on them. I do think that there are some secrets, some good secrets, as I said in my statement, that deserve protection in the interest of our country.

ELLSBERG: Senator Baker, in his Watergate report, says, "Our investigation in this area also produced the fact that contrary to previous CIA assertions, the CIA conducted a vigorous in-house investigation of the Watergate matter starting almost immediately after the break-in. As one member of the security research staff stated, they were in a state of panic. In November and December of 1972 the executive officer to the Director of Security was specially assigned to them Executive Director–Comptroller Colby to conduct a very secretive investigation of several Watergate-related matters. The executive officer to the Director of Security was instructed to keep no copies of his findings and to make no records." An interesting footnote to your assertion of all the documents that CIA turned over.

COLBY: I did not give that instruction.

ELLSBERG: "He did his own typing and utilized no secretary." Did such a person work in your office for this purpose, sir?

COLBY: There was a security officer assigned to help me to gather together the information about this incident, and he's the gentleman you are referring to.

ELLSBERG: Were his findings turned over to Senator Baker or the committee?

COLBY: The question between Senator Baker and myself with respect to additional papers refers to certain papers which we did not make available to Senator Baker but we did make available to our oversight committees. And, in the line that I have talked to you about earlier today, the difference between matters which get into the details of our legitimate operational activities, and I mean legitimate ones, were not turned over outside the proper oversight committees.

RICHARD J. BARNET: Mr. Colby, I'd like to ask you a general-principle question. In general, do you see any national-security threat that would justify any covert operations at this time in any third-world country, which I define roughly as poor countries in Asia, Africa, and Latin America, with no conceivable capacity to endanger the American people here in the United States? Are there any legitimate covert operations in those areas that you see at this time?

COLBY: There are some, yes. I would not like to go further into detail about it, but there are some, yes. And by security of the United States, I do not mean that the Capitol will fall tomorrow as a result. I mean the position of the United States in the world today and in the world ahead.

BARNET: Could I ask you to be a little bit more specific about that?

COLBY: I'm really not trying to play games with you. What I'm trying to say here is that there are certain things which today are not an immediate danger to the United States but, if allowed to grow, can become a serious problem and consequently a problem to the security of the United States.

BARNET: And you cannot give a general example of those threats?

COLBY: Well, in line with my disinclination, to put it mildly, to talk about our operations, I would rather not do that in this forum. I do this regularly in the proper forum that I want to—that I am authorized to. (*audience outburst*)

STANLEY FUTTERMAN (Professor of Law, New York University Law School): I have a question that does not concern details but does concern a matter of general policy. I recall a statement by Dean Rusk some years back, in which he refers to a nasty struggle in "the back alleys of the world." Now, I'd like to ask you, in the light of those statements, if you can conceive of, or know of, any situation in which torture is justified. Also, if you were aware that torture was being practiced in the Phoenix program, and if so, or if not, but merely suspected it, what you did.

COLBY: I believe that if you'll look at that 1971 testimony with respect to the use of torture, I said, and I still believe, that it is wrong; it is, secondly, ineffectual, because if you want to get bad intelligence you use bad interrogation methods, and you will learn what you want to hear rather than what is the truth. Unless you use sensible interrogation methods, and that does not include torture, you are being foolish in a professional way aside from being immoral on a higher level.

FUTTERMAN: Did you do anything about torture in Vietnam?

COLBY: Yes. You may recall that there was a directive issued by MACV headquarters, which I drafted, which called upon any adviser of the MACV, and particularly the Phoenix advisers, that if they found any evidence of torture, assassination, or so forth, they were not just to turn away and walk away. They were required to do three things. They were required not to have anything to do with it; they were required to go to the officials who were involved in it and object to it; and they were required to report it. I did see such reports, and I took them up with the government of Vietnam, and I am aware of occasions in which punishment was given to the Vietnamese officials involved.

FUTTERMAN: Was it a policy to use torture in the National (I forget what you call it) Detention Center in Saigon? Was it a policy to use third-degree methods, torture, what have you, to get valuable information?

COLBY: No.

UNIDENTIFIED VOICE FROM AUDIENCE: I think he is lying. (*applause*)

COLBY: The gentleman asked me what the policy was, and I say that was not the policy; in fact, the policy was against it.

FUTTERMAN: If I could just state a personal experience. I was in the State Department during this time, and we didn't get any reports— official reports—of torture. We did read the newspapers, and there were efforts to get out very specific telegrams about torture and attempts to make it very clear that none of those things should happen. I can tell you that it was immensely difficult to get out those telegrams. Some went greatly watered down in terms of what we should do about it and how it will be taken up.

COLBY: That may be your impression. I'm speaking of my own knowledge of what things I did. I did issue such directives, and I did follow them up with the government, and I do know that punishments were given.

HERBERT SCOVILLE, JR.: The CIA on the whole, I think, has had many kudos, and most people have thought that its work in the intelligence-collection-and-analysis field has been very useful and worthwhile and one which the U.S. government really needs. On the other hand, I think it is obvious that the Agency has come into a great deal of criticism because of its covert operations and activities. You have said that stopping them would not have any major effect on national security or the operations of the Agency as a whole at this time. In view of that and since one can make a case that these covert operations are interfering with the CIA's legitimate intelligence-collection-and-analysis operations by the effect they are having on attitudes toward the Agency, wouldn't it be a good idea for the agency now, once and for all, to divorce itself from these covert operations? If covert operations must be continued—and I think there is a real question on whether they should —let us put them in some other agency and have CIA do the job that it really ought to be doing and can do in the intelligence-collection-and-analysis area.

COLBY: In view of the world situation and our national policy, we are not spending much of our effort on covert operations. We are keeping our musket and our powder dry; this does not divert us from the major functions we have today. As to the future, I think that there can become a legitimate need for this kind of operation. I don't have any bureaucratic feeling about whether it should or should not be in CIA, but I know that various considerations have been given over the years as to whether it could be run somewhere else, and it has been generally believed that it is impractical to do them anywhere else.

SCOVILLE: I can't believe you couldn't put those people in a separate agency—

COLBY: Well, I do know that there was an attempt when it first started in the early 1950s to run covert operations in a separate institution within CIA, and this led to enormous operational difficulties in a number of countries because of a conflict of connection between the intelligence people and the action people.

SCOVILLE: I am familiar with that, but on the other hand times have changed. The value and the usefulness of these operations has now dropped way off, and essentially what one is doing is keeping a standby capability. On the other hand, you are having to answer questions as you are having to do today, and it's interfering with the integrity of the Agency and how it's looked at in terms of the information it produces, and I think it is doing a real harm to the Agency.

COLBY: Well, I respectfully disagree with you on that.

NEIL SHEEHAN (*New York Times* correspondent, on leave): Would it hamper the activities overseas if CIA officers were made subject to federal laws of this country for their activities overseas as, for example, military officers remain subject to the Uniform Code of Military Justice no matter where they serve?

COLBY: You are in a very complicated legal question. The fact is that if the CIA officer overseas commits a crime against the United States government, he will probably be punished in some fashion or other, and I think there is a certain legal responsibility that he bears to United States laws even while he is serving overseas. This is a very murky legal problem, but I think that an American CIA agent is not totally free of United States law once he leaves these shores.

JOHN MARKS: I believe you would agree with the definition of covert action as secret intervention in another country's internal affairs. The techniques of covert action include blackmail, burglary, subversion, and assassination. With the approval of competent authority in the Forty Committee and the National Security Council, do you feel those techniques are justified in the name of national security?

COLBY: I think the use of an atomic bomb is justified in the interest of national security. Going down from there is quite a realm of things you can do in the reasonable defense of the country. The whole question of the morality of self-defense is one of making the action relate reasonably to the need for some kind of action. An exaggerated action when there is little need is immoral and wrong. But there are situations in which a severe need can arise, and consequently it is moral to conduct actions in self-defense in such regard.

MARKS: But in peacetime—a time such as now?

COLBY: There are lots of fine points in this argument. I frankly would think that this is not the forum to discuss the finer philosophical points. I think I have basically answered your question.

CONGRESSMAN HARRINGTON: On the question of the congressional oversight function to which you regularly find yourself retreating when it comes to carrying out your responsibilities, . . . did you, prior to April twenty-second, inform or brief Congressman Nedzi with the same degree of specificity that characterized your briefing to him on that day with respect to the covert operations of the CIA in Chile?

COLBY: I tried to keep Congressman Nedzi fully advised. I think that we obviously go into greater detail on any particular problem as it becomes more and more of a problem. We did brief that committee; I can't say right now when and in what depth at any one time but I have tried to keep the committees informed of our operation. I have responded to any questions that they have as to further information, and I think I really ought to let them decide whether they have been adequately informed by me or not.

DAVID WISE: Mr. Colby, back around 1958 President Eisenhower denied that the CIA was engaged in activities against the government of Indonesia. Earlier, Secretary of State Dulles said that in Guatemala the situation was being cured by the Guatemalans themselves. At the time of the U-2 in 1960, we were told by the government that it was a weather plane that drifted over the border. At the time of the Bay of Pigs, Adlai Stevenson, who was twice a Presidential candidate, had to lie to the whole world by reading a cover story into the record of the United Nations, an act which I think he always regretted. More recently we have statements by high officials of the government that there was no intervention in Chile.

As a citizen, I resent being lied to by the government, and I'm sure many other citizens do—and I wonder if this lying doesn't make the cost of covert operations too high; and did I understand you to say earlier that there will be no more lying about CIA operations?

COLBY: In reference to what happened in 1950, 1960, and so forth, I have tried to indicate that times have changed. We are aware they have changed, and we are trying to adjust to the new world that we have here. We are trying to respond to the American people and to the American Constitution in the form that is expected of us at this time. I did say that I believe I cannot tell the American people an untruth. I may, on occasion, have to keep some matters secret and not mention them, but I believe that it is not feasible in the current world—and frankly I don't like it either—to tell the American people or their representatives an untruth either in open or in secret.

WISE: Then doesn't that mean logically an end to covert operations? How can you have them if you don't lie about them?

COLBY: Because you don't have to talk about them. And you don't have to leak about them.

MARCUS G. RASKIN: In line with attempting to readjust your policy, are you prepared to have the budget of the CIA, both the intelligence and the covert side, published in the federal budget? Are you prepared to send out other people who represent the Agency and its points of view to debate in town meetings in different districts of the United States the efficacy of having covert operations, so that you find out, as Congress should, what the new mood of the American people is? In my view you will find that what you have been doing is utterly insulated, that you have been operating in the context of a political and cultural hegemony, of a political and economic oligarchy that has nothing at all to do with the people's wishes and needs at this time.

COLBY: With respect to the budget, the release of a single figure one year at a time would not be a serious security problem. But if you continued it over a few years, you could draw trend lines. You would immediately arouse the questions: "Why did it go up?" "Why did it go down?" "What is it made up of?" You very quickly would be into the detail of it. This matter was debated in the Senate on the fourth of June of this year, and it was turned down—the idea of publishing a single figure was turned down—by a vote of fifty-five to thirty-three.

With respect to your second question of appearing around the country, I have appeared in a number of places. Various of our other officers have appeared in a number of places; a number of our officers have attended association conferences; I have spoken in Los Angeles, Chicago, and New York and a variety of places, and the answer is yes, within the limits of the time available, we are prepared to go out and talk to the American people and that's what I think I am trying to do right here.

FRED BRANFMAN: While you were in Vietnam, was it the frequent practice of the South Vietnamese National Police to carry out torture? Were many people or some people shackled in tiger cages on Con Son Island? I understand that no one has a monopoly on morality, but I think we would like to know what your morality is. What is the distinction, are there any things that you have done in Vietnam that you would not do elsewhere and would not do here at home, from a moral perspective?

COLBY: My morality is to try to help produce a better world and not to insist on a perfect one.

BRANFMAN: Was it the practice of the national police to torture?

COLBY: The answer to that question is that it was not the common practice. We had a lot of advisers around and throughout the police and throughout the other structures in Vietnam. There were exceptional cases, as I said in my prepared statement. They were few, exceptional, and against policy, but they did occur, and I have said that. Were there tiger cages on Con Son Island? The answer is yes. Were there shackles in the tiger cages? Yes. Those tiger cages were built during the French time and have been used ever since.

BRANFMAN: Mr. Colby, you have just violated what you just said a little while ago: that you were not going to lie as Director of the CIA. I think that it can be perfectly well demonstrated to your or anybody else's satisfaction that torture was a common practice in Vietnam, and you know it. You have just lied after saying a moment ago that you would not. I think it's disgraceful. (*audience applause*)

COLBY: I respectfully disagree.

MORTON H. HALPERIN: Mr. Colby, I wonder if you could explain to us by what authority and by what criteria you decide what is a properly constituted body of the United States Congress to which you have to answer questions. The Senate Watergate Committee was established by an overwhelming, if not unanimous, vote of the Senate of the United States and directed to investigate Watergate and related matters. A member of that committee asked your Agency for information, and yet you have told us that you gave him what you wanted to give him and drew the line at information that you would only provide to duly constituted and authorized committees of the United States Senate. Now, as far as I can tell, that was a duly authorized committee authorized to receive that information. As far as I am aware, the Senate of the United States has never voted that the Armed Services Committee or the Appropriations Committee are the only committees which should get that information, and I wonder if you could explain what it is that gives you the right to say that this committee is authorized and that the Watergate Committee is not.

COLBY: I am merely following the precedent established by the House and Senate over some twenty-five years.

HALPERIN: But the Senate Watergate Committee was never established before.

COLBY: You are correct that there is no specific resolution of either the House or the Senate that sets up those particular committees, but in the early 1950s those subcommittees of the Appropriations Committee and the Armed Services Committee of the House and of the Senate were established as our proper oversight and review committees. The practice grew up, over those twenty-five years, that we would speak only to those and not to the others. There were a series of recommendations presented to the Senate and to the House over those years recommending a change in that procedure. Each of those suggestions was turned down, so that the standing arrangement then continued.

HALPERIN: But, with all respect, that's the general policy of what you have to tell Congress generally about your operations. I don't understand why that is not superseded when, in a particular area, a committee is established by an overwhelming vote of the Senate, and requires CIA officials to answer. By your logic, the FBI and every other agency of the government could have said to the Senate Watergate Committee, "We're sorry, we're the FBI and we only answer to our standing committees." These other agencies understood that this was an extraordinary situation, that the Senate had overwhelmingly authorized this extraordinary investigation. That seems to me to supersede twenty-five years of CIA practices established without a vote of the United States Senate.

COLBY: I am prepared to change this process at any time the Senate and the House direct me to do so. I'm not giving anything away; I'm merely reflecting the Constitution.

HALPERIN: But the Senate directed every member of the executive branch to answer the questions of the Watergate Committee. And now you are saying, no, you want a specific resolution telling you to answer them.

COLBY: I am merely saying that I will comply to the way the Senate wants to arrange the oversight of the operational aspects of the intelligence business. There is special legislation which indicates that the intelligence business is a very special business. I am charged in statute with the protection of intelligence sources and methods against unauthorized disclosure. I am prepared to change my procedure at any time the Senate and the House determine to do it. Until that time, I think I have to follow both the tradition of the House and the Senate and the specific directives of the statute itself.

RICHARD J. BARNET: Mr. Colby, do you consider the covert operations in Chile to have been a success?

COLBY: I think that that falls into the category of not talking about our operations. It is hard to say whether it is successful or unsuccessful without talking about what they were. If they were one thing, they were successful. If they were another thing, they were not.

BARNET: I'm not asking you to comment on the operations. I'm asking you to comment on the results. Let me put to you what I think, based on information that I have, the results were, and then I would like your evaluation as to whether that was a success.

COLBY: I would perhaps save you the time, Mr. Barnet, by saying that I reiterate that our policy at that time was to look forward to a victory in 1976 of the democratic forces through elections.

BARNET: Well, as a result of the activities—

COLBY: No, not as a result of our activities. The coup had nothing to do with our Agency.

BARNET: As a result, then, of the failure to provide information which you had to the constitutionally elected government—we have a military dictatorship which has repealed two generations of reforms in Chile—has obliterated a system of reform which has evolved under conservative and Christian Democrat government. We have a situation today in Chile where large parts of the middle class are considerably worse off than under the regime that succeeded it. We have a regime so incompetent that we have tens of thousands of people literally that are on the brink of starvation, for which I think the United States, and your Agency in particular, must bear some responsibility.

COLBY: With due respect, I disagree with you. Our appreciation of the situation in Chile and the analysis of the situation in Chile was that the coup in Chile was brought about by the policies of the Allende government, which so mixed up the situation in Chile that the military decided to act against the government. Now, we did not have anything to do with the military coup in Chile, and therefore I do not think that you can say that the result today is the result of either CIA or the United States.

HALPERIN: Are you really saying, in line with the policy of candor that you say that the Agency is attempting to follow, that the activities of the Agency in support of hostile press, in support of strikes, in direct support of armed nationalist groups in Chile did not have a direct effect on the atmosphere which produced the coup?

COLBY: I said that our policy was to encourage the democratic forces in Chile to sustain themselves in looking toward a victory in the elections of 1976. That is what our policy was and that was what our activities were aimed at.

HALPERIN: Have you, as a result of what happened in Chile, ordered a review of that part of the Agency that develops plans for encouraging democracy in foreign countries?

COLBY: We have not given any assistance to Chile since the coup— other than very limited items that were commitments made prior to the coup and have nothing to do with the period after the coup and will have nothing to do with the period after the coup.

WINSLOW PECK (member, the Fifth Estate): Mr. Colby, your statement was the CIA was not directly involved in the coup; but isn't it true that the Central Intelligence Agency is not the only agency of our government involved in covert activities? Isn't it true that agents of the Defense Intelligence Agency were directly involved in the overthrow of that government? And isn't it true that these same agents of the Defense Intelligence Agency, undercover as Defense attachés in Santiago throughout the period of destabilization in Chile, were actively working for the Central Intelligence Agency?

COLBY: Our attachés in any foreign country are known as attachés. By reason of the structure of the Defense Department, they report to the DIA, the Defense Intelligence Agency. That doesn't make them agents. It makes them officers in the United States Army or Navy or whatever it is.

PECK: Just the same as agents of the Central Intelligence Agency?

COLBY: I think they are officers or enlisted men in their respective services. That's what they are. There are some civilian employees of the department of the Army, Defense, the Navy, and so forth. They are overtly known as that, and that the answer to your basic question is that the other agencies do not conduct covert actions.

GARY PORTER (Indochina Resource Center): Mr. Colby, you addressed yourself early on to the question of American CIA involvement in Laos and justified it by referring to the allegation that the North Vietnamese refused to have the troops leave Laos after the truce was established in 1962. This would imply that the United States was not involved with supplying guns and other equipment and material to *l'armée clandestine* in Laos before. Now, I'd like to lay out these facts and have you either confirm or deny them. Is it not true that the CIA forces were already supplying [materiel] at the time of the cease-fire in Laos, at the time of the Geneva meetings in 1962? And in that period following, the Pathet Lao, as a member of the tripartite coalition government, as was their right under the arrangement, demanded that the United States cease its military and economic aid; that under the agreement the Pathet Lao had a right to be consulted on all major questions of defense and foreign policy; that in fact the U.S. continued those supply operations against the demands of the Pathet Lao to end them; that the U.S. in continuing that supply operation had a plane shot down by the Pathet Lao; that the Chinese government, itself, made it clear that they would help the Vietnamese to maintain their troops in Laos until the U.S. withdrew. Now, do you confirm or deny these facts?

COLBY: I will say that CIA did begin a program of assistance to the tribesmen in Laos in, I believe, 1960. This was a program which was run by CIA and was also participated in by the U.S. military. At the time of the Geneva Accords in 1962, CIA ceased its supply and withdrew its people. The military withdrew its people. We did leave some people in Laos for intelligence purposes but not for paramilitary purposes. I've forgotten the number but it was in the neighborhood of a thousand people who checked out through the international control checkpoint. The North Vietnamese withdrew, if I remember, it was something on the order of forty or fifty people, leaving some five thousand behind. That in itself did not change things until they began to attack some of the people of the Meos up in the country. At that point, in order to respond to the attacks made by those forces illegally in Laos, CIA was asked to, and did, begin a program of covert supply to those forces to protect themselves against the North Vietnamese incursion.

PORTER: Are you saying that the United States did not supply *l'armée clandestine* ninety days after the Geneva meeting?

COLBY: I deny that CIA did anything before they were provoked to it and requested by the people in Laos to help defend themselves against the North Vietnamese incursions against them.

PORTER: It is on the record admitted by U.S. officials that the U.S. did, in fact, supply the Pathet Lao with military aid ninety days after the Geneva meeting.

COLBY: We respected the Geneva agreement provisions. I'm not sure whether the ninety days is right at the moment. We respected the Geneva Accords agreement at that time and were only led to a violation of them by a greater violation by the North Vietnamese.

PORTER: Can you answer yes or no. Was the CIA carrying on the supply operation against the Pathet Lao?

COLBY: Yes. Against the demands of the Pathet Lao, certainly, and their North Vietnamese allies because they were North Vietnamese allies, and they were attacking the Meo tribesmen.

PORTER: Did you say we did carry on the operation?

COLBY: As a defensive measure against violations of the Geneva Accords by the Pathet Lao and the North Vietnamese.

RICHARD J. BARNET

The
"Dirty-Tricks"
Gap

11

In the climactic year of Watergate it is not hard to make a strong case
against secret intelligence operations. The costs and risks of maintaining
an intelligence underworld sealed from public scrutiny and free from
legislative accountability have become obvious. The "misuse" of the
CIA, one of the counts in the Article of Impeachment adopted by the
House Judiciary Committee, can be repeated whenever an insecure
President feels tempted to use this classic instrument of dictatorial rule
against some domestic "enemy." Although the CIA in the Watergate
Affair demonstrated some resistance to improper involvement, there
are no institutional safeguards to prevent wigs and burglar tools once
again being supplied to "the wrong people."

Former Attorney General Nicholas deB. Katzenbach and others have
persuasively argued that maintaining extensive clandestine operations
endangers American democracy and for that reason they should be
ended. It is important to note that the danger is no less when the CIA
and other intelligence agencies act "properly," for example, when they
perform the missions they are supposed to perform. The CIA clandestine services represent a special sort of secret army. The very existence of a large, secret war-fighting capability undermines American
democracy because under our system of government it is the people's
elected representatives who are supposed to decide when and where we
are to go to war. The maintenance of a large bureaucracy whose very
purpose is deception breeds suspicion and cynicism about government in
general. Systematic lying to the public, an institutionalized habit in such
bureaucracies, has eroded confidence in government to an unprecedented extent. Ironically, the widespread use of the political lie in the
name of national security has helped undermine a crucial foundation

stone of national security—public confidence. In the last days of the Nixon administration only about twenty-five per cent of the American people had confidence in either the President or the Congress.

The stock-in-trade of the intelligence underworld is deceit. Its purpose is to create contrived realities, to make things appear other than they are, for the purpose of manipulation and subversion. More than two hundred agents, according to a recent *New York Times* article, pose as businessmen abroad. The CIA has admitted that it has had more than thirty journalists on its payroll since World War II. "Proprietary" corporations—Air America and other agency fronts, fake foundations, student organizations, church organizations, and so forth—are all part of the false-bottom world that has ended up confusing the American people as much as it has confounded foreign governments. It is a cliché to talk about our "interdependent world." Yet we have pretended to ourselves that we can support murder, arson, larceny, and deceit abroad and still continue to enjoy democracy at home. That contradiction can perhaps be maintained for short periods of warfare, although we have seen how each war the United States has fought has taken its toll on civil liberties, but it cannot be maintained under a state of permanent warfare. In the "back-alley war" there are no truces and no peace treaties.

The secrecy that shrouds covert operations distorts the foreign policymaking process in a number of specific ways. First, covert operations are typically discussed by a small group with special clearances. (As a general rule those able to get the clearances already have a vested interest in the operation.) Second, covert operations encourage adventurism because they create the impression, often a false one, that they can be disavowed if they fail. Third, covert operations often close options rather than open them. (One of the reasons President Kennedy decided to go ahead with the Bay of Pigs operation was Allen Dulles's warning that the Cuban refugees recruited for it would expose it if they did not get the chance to carry their flag to Havana.) Fourth, the lack of control over covert operations leads to minor diplomatic disasters such as the recent incident in Thailand when a CIA agent faked a letter from a guerrilla leader to the Bangkok government for the purpose of discrediting his movement. (The Thai government was not amused, and the CIA station chief was recalled.)

As Morton Halperin and Jeremy Stone have pointed out, the secrecy necessary to maintain an intelligence underworld distorts our constitutional processes in a number of ways. Congress loses its ability to monitor foreign policy when important operations such as the raids on North Vietnam in 1964 are concealed from it, and it is asked to make crucial decisions, such as the fateful Gulf of Tonkin Resolution, on the basis of a highly misleading picture of reality. Similarly, it loses the power of control over the Treasury when concealed and unaccounted funds can be used at the discretion of the executive. Protecting foreign statesmen from embarrassment about their involvement with the Agency or concealing some of the Agency's own indiscretions becomes grounds for misleading or muzzling the press. "National security" is the holy oil that converts felonious acts into patriotic exploits. It is "a universal truth," as James Madison once wrote Thomas Jefferson, "that the loss of liberty at home is to be charged to provisions against danger, real or pretended, from abroad."

The fundamental reason why the secret-war bureaucracy threatens the rule of law is that by all democratic norms it is inherently a criminal enterprise. Perjury, subornation, torture, property destruction, assassination, fraud, impersonation, and a variety of other acts for which ordinary citizens go to jail become the dictates of duty. The reason that the activities of the intelligence underground are shrouded in secrecy is that they violate some accepted principle of constitutional or international law. If there were no international consensus against staging coups, contaminating crops, assassinating leaders, bribing parliaments, and suborning politicians, there would be no need for the elaborate shield of deception behind which these activities take place. If the fears that Madison voiced two hundred years ago were not still valid, the CIA would not have had to construct an elaborate cover story. Governments resort to clandestine operations precisely because they wish to act in contravention of established legal principles and specific promises they have made to the outside world and to their own people.

The dangers that a large extra-legal enterprise pose for the establishment of an international legal order or for domestic constitutional order in the United States are obvious. Even the highest officials of the "intelligence community" will admit publicly that there are "risks." It is conventional to call for "strict controls" and "better accountability," but there is a fundamental contradiction between the perceived need for a free-wheeling, super-secret, world-wide intelligence apparatus and effective political control. The handful of senators and congressmen who are permitted even a peek into the secret life of the U.S. government are, by some mysterious process of selection, wholly sympathetic with what Marchetti and Marks call the "clandestine mentality" and the peculiar code of the intelligence underworld. To read the account of the closed hearings on the nomination of Richard Helms to be ambassador to Iran (subsequently published because of Watergate) is to realize that congressional watchdogs are blind and toothless.

The inescapable fact is that effective control over an apparatus of the size and character of the U.S. intelligence community is impossible. The choice is between "trusting" that those in charge are "honorable men," as Richard Helms urged in 1971, or dismantling the covert intelligence arm of the United States. There is an overwhelming necessity, in my view, for the second choice.

But getting rid of the intelligence underworld, which has begun to contaminate our society, would require some fundamental political choices. To be sure, there are instances of intelligence operatives embarking on what English judges used to call "frolics of their own," improvising unauthorized mischief, sometimes to the dismay of their superiors in Washington. Indeed, an inherent problem of the intelligence underworld is that it is to a great extent uncontrollable. A criminal enterprise, such as the "dirty-tricks" department, does not respond to ordinary political controls because it is made up of people who have been trained to respect no law but the command of the superior. E. Howard Hunt characterized the break-in at Daniel Ellsberg's psychiatrist's office as "an entry operation conducted under the auspices of competent authority." The habit of mind prevailing in the intelligence underworld includes what Richard Bissell calls the "higher loyalty," a definition of national security developed and communicated in secret by higher-ranking bureaucrats hermetically sealed from public scrutiny. But despite the code of obedience, agents in the field have both the power and the motivation to trap their superiors by giving them a distorted picture of reality, wittingly or unwittingly. The spectacular intelligence failures—Bay of Pigs, *Pueblo*—are examples of this phenomenon. The law that operates in more benign bureaucracies also operates here: bureaucrats tend to keep doing what they have been doing, on an expanding scale if possible. Thus extraordinary efforts from the top are necessary to turn off operations once they are begun. The deeper the cover, the more impervious to political control.

But the most covert intelligence activities are carried out in direct support of clearly defined U.S. foreign-policy objectives. Indeed, some of those objectives *require* the maintenance of an intelligence underworld of the character that has emerged.

We cannot say the dirty-tricks department is "necessary" or "unnecessary" until we determine the kind of foreign policy we want to pursue as a nation. With all its spectacular failures and the pretentious banality in which the world of spies, buggers, code snatchers, crop contaminators, covert philanthropists, and secret political manipulators live, the intelligence underworld is a necessary institution for managing a modern empire. If we cannot find security in the world without trying to run it, then the dirty-tricks department must remain a fixture of our national life.

Let me be more specific. To manage political and social change around the world and to oppose national revolutions, as the recently exposed "destabilization" campaign in Chile, is a "responsibility" that requires covert action. As long as the United States maintains its extravagant policy of trying to make the world safe for established political and economic power, there will always be men like Colby, Bissell, and Hunt ready to lie, steal, and kill in that higher cause. Indeed there are many reasons why the CIA now seems a more important political instrument than ever, including the improved techniques for "low-profile" interventions, the growing desire to control resource-producing Third World countries, the increasing difficulties in mounting conventional military operations abroad. If we do not wish to use the state to legitimize criminal activity at home and abroad, then we must stop trying to set the conditions for the internal development of other nations.

It is important to distinguish covert action from covert intelligence-gathering. In 1968 Richard Bissell, former Deputy Director of CIA in charge of clandestine services, defined covert action in these terms:

> (1) political advice and counsel; (2) subsidies to an individual; (3) financial support and "technical assistance" to political parties; (4) support of private organizations, including labor unions, business firms, cooperatives, etc.; (5) covert propaganda; (6) "private" training of individuals and exchange of persons; (7) economic operations; and (8) paramilitary [or] political action operations designed to overthrow or support a regime.

Covert action, in simple terms, is secret warfare. Clandestine intelligence collection, by contrast, is not designed to influence political affairs in other countries, but it does, as we shall see, have that effect. Both covert action and covert intelligence collection are primarily directed against those societies least able to hurt us because these also happen to be the societies least able to protect themselves from penetration. The

Soviet Union makes such a large investment in counterespionage that, except for an occasional defector like Penkovsky, most of the information about their intentions has to be pieced together from open sources. Powerful countries, the only plausible security threats, can develop sophisticated codes that are, as cryptologist David Kahn puts it, "unbreakable in practice." In 1970 Admiral Gayler of the National Security Agency admitted privately, according to Marchetti and Marks, "that a good part of the NSA's successes came from breaks" into embassies and other places where code books can be stolen. Thus it is possible to break the codes of poor Third World countries such as Chile. "One surreptitious entry can do the job successfully at no dollar cost," the authors of the 1970 Huston Plan reported to President Nixon. But such cheap petty thievery produces information the U.S. government does not need or should not have.

The reason the underdeveloped world "presents greater opportunities for covert intelligence collection," as Richard Bissell explained to a Council on Foreign Relations study group in January 1968, is that governments "are much less highly oriented; there is less security consciousness; and there is apt to be more actual or potential diffusion of power among parties, localities, organizations, and individuals outside the central governments." Thus the same internal suspicions, rivalries, and bribery that keep poor nations from effectively organizing themselves to overcome mass poverty make them attractive targets of the intelligence underworld. Real and exaggerated fears of being infiltrated help to keep such societies in a continual state of political disorganization. As Bissell points out, the less totalitarian the society, the easier it is to find out and to influence what goes on there. Salvador Allende's tolerance of forces opposing him made it easy for the CIA and other intelligence agencies to work with them to hasten his downfall. The CIA destabilization campaign, which, according to recent revelations of William Colby's secret testimony, was strongly pushed by Henry Kissinger, would not have worked had the regime been more repressive. That lesson is one of the uglier legacies of the dirty-tricks department.

The deliberate disorientation of societies by means of bribery, assassination, black propaganda, subornation, and other methods helps keep them poor and dependent. Those societies most vulnerable to penetration are, generally speaking, the ones that most need effective organization to develop their own priorities. When they are manipulated for U.S. foreign-policy purposes rather than for their own development purposes, their capacity even to begin to deal with the overwhelming problems of mass poverty is undermined. Unfortunately, U.S. foreign-policy purposes in most areas of the Third World have been defined in such a way as to conflict directly with local development needs. The crushing problems of Asia, Africa and Latin America—mass poverty, unemployment, and growing inequality—require structural changes in those societies— a polite term for overthrowing local elites that run them as personal holding companies or throwing out foreign business interests that are often equally exploitative. Consistently, the CIA's continuing secret war has been in support of local and foreign interests threatened by structural change, the maintenance of a repressive "stability" that stifles hope for the majority of the population. The capability of the United States to support reactionary regimes, and its clear intent to do so wherever possible, has been a powerful political factor in preserving a highly inequitable and ultimately explosive *status quo*.

The "successes" of the CIA have for the most part not been scored against the countries with the capacity to destroy the United States. (Some exceptions include the cultivation of famous defector Colonel Penkovsky, who did provide important military information on Soviet missile strength when it could not be obtained by observation satellites, some propaganda victories in the fight for the "hearts and minds" of European intellectuals in the early postwar period, limitation of Soviet influence in the international labor movement, collection of Kremlin gossip by bugging Party limousines, and so forth.) But in the weak countries of the Third World the intervention of the CIA can make a crucial difference in setting the political direction, and it often has. If we are to abandon the secret warfare that makes the United States government the enemy of political change around the world, we must abandon the basic goal of attempting to influence the direction of internal politics in other countries to serve U.S. military and corporate interests.

In the aftermath of Watergate the CIA has been revising the official rationale for its extensive clandestine operations it gives to congressmen and columnists. According to Miles Copeland, former CIA official, the Agency is now explaining its mission for the mid-1970s in congressional briefings in the following terms:

> (1) Meticulous monitoring of the *détente*; (2) collection of data on international terrorist groups; (3) protection of access to strategic materials; and (4) cooperation with multinational corporations.

It is worth examining each of these proposed missions to determine whether the risks involved outweigh the advantages and to ask whether such legitimate security interests as they may be designed to serve can be advanced in other ways.

Certainly the détente must be "meticulously monitored," if by that is meant we should keep track of what the Soviet Union is doing. The most important information about the Soviet Union relevant to détente is the character and state of readiness of the armed forces. Satellite observation and the collection of order-of-battle intelligence by conventional means are the best ways to monitor this information. Spies in the Kremlin, if indeed there are any, and document snatchers are unlikely to provide reliable information in a society that invests as much as the Soviet Union does in avoiding penetration. The effort itself of course jeopardizes détente. "Testing" the Soviet air defenses by penetrating their air space is a provocation that serves no legitimate military purpose. The best way to obtain information about Soviet attitudes toward détente is to press them hard for real measures of disarmament. The problem is not one of finding some piece of esoteric information that will provide the key to Soviet behavior but rather of developing an analysis that is comprehensive and dynamic enough to make use of the vast amount of information already available. Monitoring the détente is a mission for diplomats with analytical skills, not spies.

There is no doubt that terrorism will be an increasing problem in a world in which the avenues of peaceful change appear to be blocked. There is no way to "monitor" real or imagined terrorist groups without violating the civil liberties of thousands of people. There is no evidence to suggest that a world-wide surveillance network can in fact prevent random acts of terror, which are typically the work of individuals or small splinter groups. Even if the prospects for pre-empting terrorist attacks through surveillance were more probable, the political damage caused by widespread surveillance in other countries outweighs any possible benefits.

The suggestion that the clandestine services of the CIA are needed to control international drug traffic is amusing in the light of the many well-documented cases of CIA officials promoting illegal drug traffic in Southeast Asia and other places.

To say that clandestine services must be available to aid U.S.-based multinational corporations is to make a virtue of the classic imperialist relationship in which the power of the state is used to bail out private interests abroad. The United States traditionally equates the "national interest" with the interests of ITT or Kennecott or some other corporation in conflict with the local government. But such a policy risks involvement in military interventions, frustrates possibilities of development, and confirms the charge that the United States is interested only in a "structure of peace" that preserves its power to dominate weak economies. U.S. corporations should be required to stand on their own in their dealings with other countries. If they are prepared to do business in a way that will benefit the host country, they do not need espionage or dirty tricks supplied at the taxpayers' expense. Similarly, access to raw materials is a problem of bargaining skill and technological innovation. Unless we are prepared to make war on the producing nations of the Third World in order to obtain access to resources on our own terms, there is no place for the CIA in this drama.

In a recent paper at the Naval War College Vice-Admiral John M. Lee (Retired) discusses the use of American military power for what he calls "resource control," the protection of U.S. access to strategic materials and energy sources. Arguing that it is "hard to conceive of a situation . . . where direct combat operations against a Third World resource country to obtain its resources would commend itself as feasible, effective, and on balance, productive," he does suggest possibilities "of covert operations and proxy wars." This "latent military threat," he argues, reinforced "with other elements of American strength" does produce "leverage." There is nothing new about the use of covert action to protect access to raw materials. Much of the CIA operations in the Mediterranean and Latin America has been for precisely this purpose. If we see no alternative way to maintain our economy other than to spread intimidation, confusion, and murder in the Third World, then indeed there will always be a role for the intelligence underworld in American foreign policy.

It is frequently asserted that the United States must make extensive use of espionage and other secret means of collecting information about other nations in order to protect our national security. Here again the crucial issue concerns a basic choice in foreign policy. Certain kinds of policies require certain kinds of information. Some information can be obtained only by clandestine means. Generally speaking, with the exception of counterespionage, which we will take up a little later, covertly collected information is useful only for the conduct of military or paramilitary operations. Richard Bissell argues that espionage in the poorer

countries is needed to produce "timely knowledge" of "tactical significance." In fact most clandestine collection of information serves no
purpose other than to support covert action. Bissell himself concedes
that sometimes "the tasks of intelligence collection and political action
overlap to the point of being almost indistinguishable." For what legitimate purpose does the United States need to immerse itself in the internal political developments of Third World and other countries that
pose no threat to the security of the United States other than the assertion of their own independence?

If the foreign policy of the United States dictates a large-scale destabilization program for Chile, the information needed to conduct it
can be obtained only by secret means. Such data as the names of Chilean subversives prepared to conspire with a foreign government against
their own constitutional system, how much it will take to bribe them or
equip them, and so forth become vital "national security" information.
Since every government takes some pains to keep such information out
of hostile hands, the process of collecting it must be an undercover
operation. Had the decision been made to permit a freely elected government in Chile to survive, such information would not have been
needed. The plain truth is that there is no information under the control
of Third World governments that the United States needs to know unless
it is in the business of manipulating and controlling their internal development. In many cases United States public and private agencies already have better organized and more accurate information about
finances, resources, and state of the military than the local government
itself. The massive penetration of Third World countries by U.S. espionage agencies produces information the United States does not need
for any legitimate purpose, and in the interests of international stability,
should not seek to acquire.

If the United States were genuinely prepared to live in a "world of
diversity," as it sometimes claims, it would still need political information, but it would not need to obtain it by illegal and subversive means.
Indeed, if the United States actually engaged in building a "structure of
peace" evolving toward global equity instead of one seeking to freeze a
highly unjust and unstable *status quo*, then most of the information
needed could be obtained from open sources and direct inquiry. The
principles of espionage were developed for war, and the more closely
diplomacy resembles war the more it must rely on espionage. Undercover operations against other countries are no more nor less justifiable

than war itself. But they have a way of surviving the wars they are supposed to support. The *Pueblo* was captured off North Korea in 1967 while engaged in eavesdropping operations that might have been defensible during the war that had ended fourteen years earlier but served no plausible purpose in 1967. Similarly, much of the covert intelligence apparatus was developed for a "back-alley war" with the Soviet Union that has been overtaken by events. It is not surprising that Richard Bissell told the Council on Foreign Relations in 1968 that "the underdeveloped world presents greater opportunities for covert intelligence collection."

There is indeed an information-and-analysis gap, but the information the United States most needs is not under the control of any foreign nation, and it cannot be wrested from it. The analysis we need cannot be done by professional spies. The "clandestine mentality" fostered by intelligence bureaucracies is a form of trained incapacity to see the importance of information that does not have to be stolen. We are witnessing a profound crisis in the economic underpinnings of the postwar world. The behavior of the world political economy is confounding experts who only a few months ago professed to understand the "laws" under which the world-wide flow of goods and services was supposedly operating. Today, it is commonplace to read public admissions from such experts that they do not understand what is going on—why we have inflation and recession at the same time, why the old economic remedies such as the manipulation of interest rates do not work. There is a crisis of understanding about what is happening to our institutions, and it has assumed the status of a national-security crisis (as well as an international-security crisis). The greatest cost to the United States in maintaining an anachronistic secret-warfare department, besides its damage to the reputation of the nation and the corrosion of American institutions, is that it distorts our own perspectives. We are spending several billions a year acquiring knowledge that is useless for solving our most urgent problems. There is a distinction, as Marcus Raskin has pointed out, between problem-creating knowledge and problem-solving knowledge. Information wrested from poor countries to support subversion is problem-creating knowledge because even when the information is accurate and the political operations for which it is used do not backfire, as in Singapore, Greece, and other cases discussed in this conference, nothing is solved.

On June 27, 1970, Henry Kissinger, at a meeting of the Forty Committee, declared, "I don't see why we need to stand by and watch a country go Communist due to the irresponsibility of its own people." The problem, as Kissinger conceived it, was how to overturn a popular election in a foreign country that produced a result the U.S. government did not like. Once defined in this way, the problem became simple. The United States could employ some of the same methods used in Guayana against Cheddi Jagan, in Guatemala against Arbenz, in Brazil against Goulart. The information needed to carry out such a policy was easy to identify and obtain. But the problem of Chile remains. Because the United States made it clear from the outset to Allende's opposition that they did not need to compromise with the Unidad Popular since they had the strong backing of the United States, the internal politics of the country became polarized. The junta has not merely repealed the reforms of Allende's abortive peaceful revolution. It has turned the clock back two generations and in a burst of gunfire has obliterated reforms won under conservative and Christian Democratic Presidents. The economic situation, bad under Allende, is now desperate. Inflation is worse than ever. Large portions of the middle class are considerably worse off than under the regime they were so happy to be rid of. The incompetence of the junta has brought tens of thousands in the bottom strata of the population to the brink of starvation. (The price of food has risen precipitously; real wages have fallen; and, incredibly, crops are being exported to earn foreign exchange to buy manufactured goods from abroad.) It is hard to see how from any point of view the "success" in Chile has advanced the interests of the American people. (That it has advanced the interests of a few U.S. firms that had been or were about to be nationalized is clear.) Adding another "sick man" to the international economy is not going to solve the problems that now challenge our basic institutions.

The intelligence gathered with respect to Chile was useful for aggravating the economic problems of Chile but not for solving them. That successful operation also had the effect of complicating U.S. relations elsewhere in the hemisphere. In his State of the Union speech Mexico's President Luís Echeverría made it clear that the lessons of the Chile "success" have not gone unnoticed:

> [Terrorist groups are] easily manipulated by covert political interests, whether national or international, that use them as irresponsible instruments [for] acts of provocation against our institutions.
>
> This manipulation and control from outside is conducted with

great dexterity, and at times one might think that . . . it is the work of extreme leftist groups; but when one realized the ideological unpreparedness of these groups and that their object is really to provoke repression, what one may call a witch hunt, one is immediately led to think that it could very well be that they are using covert methods to provoke repression with the effect of halting the function of our institutions, as has occurred in other countries, and to cause the curtailing of our liberties when we have only just begun to follow a policy of economic nationalism in our country. In several Latin American countries, coups d'état have been preceded by rumor campaigns that have their origin in certain irresponsible groups of businessmen and have also been encouraged by these acts of terrorism which attempt to sow confusion.

If in or outside of Mexico there are interests that try to divide the Mexicans, to create discord, let us remember that in 1848 we lost half of the territory we inherited from our indigenous and Spanish fathers, after an unjust war with the U.S., in which internal divisions played a fundamental role. . . . If these groups that try to divide us wish some day to provoke the intervention in any form by any of the powerful nations, let them know that we have full historic awareness of what has happened in Mexico. . . .

This is an extraordinary statement from the chief of a state as thoroughly dependent upon the United States as Mexico. That the President of Mexico would make such a thinly veiled accusation against the United States is evidence not only of the depth of distrust which our dirty tricks have earned us but it is also an indication of the erosion of American power. Ironically, the U.S. spy network is creating a political backlash in Thailand and Greece, as well as Mexico, with the result that these traditional clients are seeking a more independent course. How much better it would have been for U.S.-Greek relations had the CIA apparatus been withdrawn before it was expelled.

Thus the sort of knowledge developed by clandestine collection services is in the present world situation problem-creating. The sort of knowledge needed to solve the overwhelming institutional crises cannot be obtained by adversary means. Cooperation and exchange of information—about the workings of national economies, about the structural changes in the world economy, about the successes and failures of social experiments, about the impacts of domestic policies of one country on another—are absolutely essential if any country is going to be able to develop a comprehensive enough understanding of what is happening to the world political economy in order to devise practical policies and solutions. The development of a much higher level of international trust is a necessary precondition for a serious cooperative assault on the real threats facing the American people—inflation, unemployment, loss of liberty, and, in the background, nuclear war. The intelligence underworld is a serious obstacle to the building of that new relationship between the United States and the world now needed for our survival.

From time to time CIA officials emerge from Langley to reassure the public that the tax dollars with which they support the intelligence underworld (amount undisclosed) are well spent. The classic argument in support of a large secret-warfare department is that other nations have them too. The clandestine mentality pervades the Soviet Union, and the record of the KGB for murder, theft, torture, and forgery is probably unmatched. But do criminal activities of other countries require us to maintain our own? Certainly, some counterintelligence effort against penetration and manipulation of our government and theft of military secrets is necessary. That is principally a job for the FBI, to be carried out within the framework of U.S. constitutional safeguards. If the United States were out of the covert-action business, its counterespionage requirements would be drastically reduced. Much effort is now devoted to preventing the penetration of our intelligence underworld by the Soviet intelligence underworld. If we did not have one, we would create an unemployment problem for the KGB. Similarly, if what the United States actually does in other countries did not diverge so sharply from what we say we do, or, to put it more bluntly, if habitual lying in the "national interest" were no longer a dictate of duty, then the government would not need to spend so much money concealing things from other governments and from the American people. But counterespionage, which within limits is a legitimate defensive activity, is one thing, and secret warfare against other nations is another.

The dirty-tricks gap, if indeed there is one, is no more justification for the United States to corrupt our own society and to distort our foreign relations than the missile gap or the bomb-shelter gap or all the other arms races we have been running to a great extent with ourselves. The back-alley war, which Allen Dulles used to maintain, required fighting fire with fire, was a reasonable description of the Cold War confrontation over Europe. It does not describe what is happening in the Third World, where the war is not between U.S. and Soviet intelligence agents but between U.S. agents and weak indigenous political forces that, as in Chile, have received little help from the Communist powers.

U.S. covert action and clandestine intelligence collection (excepting satellites) could be abandoned unilaterally with a net gain in security for the American people. This is so not only for the reasons we have already discussed, but also because most of the information so expensively and dangerously procured by secret agents is politically worthless. The work product of the spy is inherently suspect because specialists in espionage are in the business of producing disinformation as well as information. Indeed, the more esoteric and elaborate the deception required to produce a given bit of data, the less likely the spy's political superiors are to believe it. Thus some of the great intelligence coups of history—the advance warning to Stalin of the impending German attack, for example—have gone unheeded.

For the protection of our own society the dirty-tricks department must be recognized for what it is, a criminal enterprise. Dismantling it and preventing its reappearance in newer and slicker disguises would be one of the first acts of a new administration genuinely concerned to preserve constitutional liberty and to stop the wreckage our paid pranksters are causing around the world.

REFERENCE NOTES

Chapter 1. *Covert Operations Abroad: An Overview* by David Wise

1. Address to the American Society of Newspaper Editors, April 14, 1971; text, p. 5.
2. *Nomination of William E. Colby, Hearings* before the Committee on Armed Services, United States Senate, 93rd Congress, 1st session (July 2, 1973), pp. 13–14.
3. *Hearing* before the House Committee on Expenditures in the Executive Departments, April 25, 1947, cited in David Wise and Thomas B. Ross, *The Espionage Establishment* (New York: Random House, 1967), pp. 162–63.
4. *Hearing* before the House Committee on Expenditures in the Executive Departments, June 24, 1947, cited in ibid., p. 164.
5. *National Security Act of 1947*, report of the Committee on Expenditures in the Executive Departments to accompany H.R. 4214, p. 4.
6. Ibid., p. 3.
7. *National Defense Establishment, Hearings* before the Committee on Armed Services, United States Senate, 80th Congress, 1st session on S.758, Part 3, pp. 491–500.
8. Ibid., pp. 525–28.
9. Article by Harry S Truman, syndicated by North American Newspaper Alliance in *The Washington Post*, December 22, 1963.
10. From the third meeting of the Discussion Group on Intelligence and Foreign Policy, Council on Foreign Relations, January 8, 1968, quoted in *The CIA's Global Strategy: Intelligence and Foreign Policy* (Cambridge, Mass.: The Africa Research Group, 1971), p. 8. The quotations are from the minutes of the meeting, which paraphrased and summarized the remarks of the participants.
11. Ibid., p. 13.
12. David Wise and Thomas B. Ross, *The Invisible Government* (New York: Random House, 1964), pp. 5, 6, 260–62, 293, 351.
13. Allen W. Dulles, *The Craft of Intelligence* (New York: Harper & Row, 1963), p. 189.
14. *Nomination of William E. Colby*, p. 14.
15. *Nomination of Richard Helms to be Ambassador to Iran, and CIA International and Domestic Activities, Hearings* before the Committee on Foreign Relations, United States Senate, 93rd Congress, 1st session (May 21, 1973), pp. 75–76.
16. *Nomination of Richard Helms*, p. 47.
17. *The International Telephone and Telegraph Company in Chile, 1970–71*, report to the Committee on Foreign Relations, United States Senate, by the Subcommittee on Multinational Corporations, June 21, 1973, p. 3.
18. Marilyn Berger, " 'Dirty Tricks' Have Had a Long History," *The Washington Post*, May 26, 1973, pp. 1, 9.
19. *The Congressional Record*, Monday, June 4, 1973, p. S10220.
20. Morton H. Halperin and Jeremy J. Stone, "Secrecy and Covert Intelligence Collection and Operations," in *None of Your Business* (New York: The Viking Press, 1974), p. 111.

21. "Foreign Policy: Nixon Dissatisfied with Size and Cost of Intelligence Set Up," *The New York Times*, January 22, 1971.
22. Victor Marchetti and John D. Marks, *The CIA and the Cult of Intelligence* (New York: Knopf, 1974), p. 61.
23. "CIA Operation: A Plot Scuttled—Plan to Doctor Cuban Sugar Depicts Control Problem," *The New York Times*, April 28, 1966.
24. Wise and Ross, *The Invisible Government*, Introduction to the Vintage Edition (New York: Vintage Books, 1974), p. xi.
25. The covert operations described in this section are from Wise and Ross, *The Invisible Government*, unless otherwise indicated.
26. Andrew Hamilton, "The CIA's Dirty Tricks under Fire—at Last," *The Progressive*, September 19, 1973, p. 18.
27. David Wise, *The Politics of Lying: Government Deception, Secrecy, and Power* (New York: Random House, 1973), pp. 163–78.
28. *The New York Times*, April 26, 1966.
29. Hamilton, op. cit., p. 18, and Laurence Stern, *The Washington Post*, July 11, 1974, p. A3.
30. Wise, *The Politics of Lying*, p. 41.
31. Laurence Stern, "U.S. Helped to Beat Allende in 1964," *The Washington Post*, April 6, 1973, p. 1.
32. David Wise and Thomas B. Ross, *The Espionage Establishment*, p. 167.
33. *Nomination of William E. Colby*, p. 3. See also *The New York Times*, August 2, 1974, p. 1.
34. Marchetti and Marks, op. cit., pp. 125–32.
35. Seymour M. Hersh, "Ex-U.S. Envoy Is Said to Have Urged Financing of Italian Political Faction," *The New York Times*, May 13, 1973.

Chapter 4. *Destabilizing Chile* by Robert L. Borosage and John Marks

1. Seymour Hersh, "Censored Matter in Book about CIA," *The New York Times*, September 11, 1974.
2. Philip Agee, *Inside the Company: CIA Diary* (Harmondsworth: Penguin, 1974), p. 382.
3. Harrington letter to Senator Fulbright, July 13, 1974 (on file at Center for National Security Studies).
4. Tad Szulc, "Exporting Revolution," *The New Republic*, September 21, 1974, p. 23.
5. Seymour Hersh, "Kissinger Called Chile Strategist," *The New York Times*, September 15, 1974.
6. Ibid.
7. Harrington letter.
8. Subcommittee on Multinational Corporations, Senate Foreign Relations Committee, United States Senate, *The International Telephone and Telegraph Company and Chile 1970–71* (Washington: Government Printing Office, June 21, 1973) p. 7.
9. Jack Anderson, "The Economic War Against Allende," *The Washington Post*, November 3, 1974.
10. Victor Marchetti and John D. Marks, *The CIA and the Cult of Intelligence* (New York: Dell, 1974), p. 364 (paper edition).
11. "Hearing of House Subcommittee on Inter-American Affairs," October 11, 1973, transcript on file at Center for National Security Studies (hereinafter, "Hearing").

12. Marlise Simons, "The Brazilian Connection," *The Washington Post*, January 6, 1974.
13. "Hearing."
14. *The New York Times*, September 16, 1974.
15. "Hearing."
16. Seymour Hersh, "Doubts on U.S. Role in Chile," *The New York Times*, October 17, 1974.
17. Ibid.
18. Ibid.
19. Seymour Hersh, "CIA Chief Tells," *The New York Times*, September 8, 1974.
20. "Hearing."
21. "Conference on the CIA and Covert Action," transcript on file at the Center for National Security Studies.
22. *The New York Times*, September 16, 1974.
23. Harrington letter.
24. *The New York Times*, September 16, 1974.

Chapter 7. *The Central Intelligence Agency: The King's Men and the Constitutional Order* by Robert L. Borosage

1. *Myers* v. *United States*, 272 U.S. 52, 293 (1926).
2. Edward S. Corwin, *The President: Office and Powers*, 3rd ed. (New York: New York University Press, 1948), pp. 4, 5.
3. James Madison in *The Federalist*, ed. J. E. Cooke (Middletown, Conn.: Wesleyan University Press, 1961), No. 51, p. 350.
4. Arendt, *Crises of the Republic* (New York: Harcourt Brace, 1972), p. 85.
5. Much of this paper is derived from discussions with Ralph Stavins, a fellow at the Institute for Policy Studies.
6. Article I, Section 8.
7. Alexander Hamilton, in *The Federalist*, No. 75.
8. *Schechter Poultry Corp.* v. *United States*, 295 US 495, 529 (1935).
9. See generally Jaffe, "An Essay on Delegation," *Colorado Law Review* 47 (1947): 339.
10. See Marcus G. Raskin, *Notes on the Old System* (New York: McKay, 1974).
11. Roosevelt, letter of July 11, 1941, 3CFR 1324 (38-43).
12. Executive Order 9608, 10 FR 11223 (1945); Executive Order 9621, 10 FR 12033 (1945).
13. 61 *Stat* 495 (1947). See Borosage, "The Making of the National Security State," *The Pentagon Watchers*, ed. L. S. Rodberg, Derek Shearer (New York: Doubleday, 1970).
14. Henry Howe Ransom, *The Intelligence Establishment* (Cambridge: Harvard University Press, 1970), p. 89.
15. See *Congressional Record*, August 1, 1973, p. S15363:
    SYMINGTON: . . . those directives from the National Security Council, at least in the minds of some people, in effect go against the legislation which created the Agency itself.
16. See generally Raoul Berger, "War-Making by the President," *University of Pennsylvania Law Review* 121 (1972): 29.
17. J. William Fulbright, *The Crippled Giant* (New York: Vintage Books, 1972), p. 228.
18. 63 *Stat* 20S (1949).
19. *Congressional Record*, March 7, 1949, p. H. 1946.
20. *Congressional Record*, March 10, 1954, p. S281.

21. Justice Story, *Commentaries on the Constitution of the United States*, vol. II, no. 1342 (5th ed., 1891), p. 213.
22. See *Richardson* v. *United States*, 42 LW 5086 (1974).
23. Justice Elliot, *Debates in the Several State Conventions on the Adoption of the Federal Constitution*, vol. II (2nd ed., 1836), p. 347.
24. *Richardson* v. *United States*, 465 F2d 844, 853 (1972).
25. *Richardson* v. *United States*, 42 LW 5086 (1974), p. 5087.
26. Ibid., p. 5088.
27. John Jay in *The Federalist*, No. 64, p. 476.
28. Letter to W. T. Barry, August 4, 1822, in *The Writings of James Madison*, G. Hunt, ed. vol. IX (1910).
29. *Near* v. *Minnesota*, 233 US 697 (1931).
30. Executive Order 10290, 3 C.F.R. 790 (49-53 Compilation) [Truman]; Executive Order 10501, 3 C.F.R. 979 (49-53 Compilation) [Eisenhower]; Executive Order 11652, 37 Fed, Reg. 5209 (1972) [Nixon].
31. *United States* v. *Marchetti*, 466 F2d 1309 (4th Cir., 1972).
32. Ibid.; *cert. den.*, 409 US 1063 (1972).
33. *New York Times* v. *United States*, 403 US 713, 730 (1971).
34. Ibid., p. 732.
35. *United States* v. *Marchetti*, p. 1311.

Chapter 8. *CIA Covert Operations and International Law*
by Richard A. Falk

1. See account by David Wise in *The Politics of Lying* (New York: Random House, 1974), pp. 33–36. See also Lyman B. Kirkpatrick, *The U.S. Intelligence Community* (New York: Hill and Wang, 1973), passim.
2. Katzenbach, "Foreign Policy, Public Opinion and Secrecy," *Foreign Affairs* 52 (1973): 15.
3. Ibid., p. 19.
4. Ibid., p. 1.
5. Victor Marchetti and John D. Marks, *The CIA and the Cult of Intelligence* (New York: Knopf, 1974), p. 123.
6. Ibid., pp. 118–19.
7. See brief account in ibid., pp. 245–46.
8. Ibid., p. 350.
9. García Márquez, "The Death of Salvador Allende," *Harper's Magazine*, March 1974, p. 53.
10. Marchetti and Marks, op. cit., p. 109.
11. Quoted in ibid., pp. 111–12.
12. Peter Dale Scott, "Vietnamization and the Drama of the Pentagon Papers," *The Pentagon Papers: Critical Essays*, ed. Noam Chomsky and Howard Zinn (Boston: Beacon, 1972), p. 220.
13. Marchetti and Marks, op. cit., p. 110.
14. Alfred McCoy, *The Politics of Heroin in Southeast Asia* (New York: Harper and Row, 1972); see especially pp. 297–315.
15. *The Pentagon Papers*, Document 209 (Boston: Beacon, 1971), p. 111.
16. Ibid., pp. 582–83.

17. Miles Copeland, *The Game of Nations* (New York: Simon and Schuster, 1970), pp. 10, 12.
18. Braden, *The Saturday Evening Post*, May 20, 1967, pp. 10–14.
19. Ibid., p. 14.
20. See Eugene Davidson, *The Nuremberg Fallacy: War and Crimes since World War II* (New York: Macmillan, 1973).
21. For example, Lyman B. Kirkpatrick, *The Real CIA* (New York: Macmillan, 1968), passim.
22. Richard J. Barnet, *Intervention and Revolution*, rev. ed. (New York: New American Library, 1972).

Chapter 9. *Covert Operations: Effects of Secrecy on Decision-Making* by Morton H. Halperin

1. On the Bay of Pigs episode, see in particular Theodore C. Sorensen, *Kennedy* (New York: Harper and Row, 1965); Roger Hilsman, *To Move a Nation: The Politics of Foreign Policy in the Administration of John F. Kennedy* (New York: Doubleday, 1967); Arthur M. Schlesinger, Jr., *A Thousand Days: John F. Kennedy in the White House* (Boston: Houghton Mifflin, 1965); Chester Bowles, *Promises to Keep: My Years in Public Life, 1941–1969* (New York: Harper and Row, 1971); and Haynes Johnson, *The Bay of Pigs: The Leaders' Story of Brigade 2506* (New York: W. W. Norton, 1964).
2. *The New York Times*, November 24, 1954.
3. This section is adapted from Morton H. Halperin and Jeremy J. Stone, "Secrecy and Covert Intelligence Collection and Operations," in *None of Your Business: Government Secrecy in America*, ed. Norman Dorsen and Stephen Gillers (New York: The Viking Press, 1974). I am grateful to Mr. Stone for his willingness to permit me to use our joint product of this paper.
4. Presidential press conference, August 1970.
5. See Morton H. Halperin, *Bureaucratic Politics and Foreign Policy* (Washington, D.C.: Brookings, 1974), pp. 119–27.
6. *Executive Privilege, Secrecy in Government, Freedom of Information, Hearings* before the Subcommittee on Intergovernmental Relations of the Committee on Government Operations and the Subcommittees on Separation of Powers and Administrative Practice and Procedure of the Committee on the Judiciary, United States Senate, 93rd Congress, 1st session (1973), vol. I, pp. 427–28.
7. For more sweeping recommendations, see Halperin and Stone, op. cit.

NOTES ON
THE CONTRIBUTORS

RICHARD J. BARNET is Co-Director of the Institute for Policy Studies. He is the author of numerous books and articles on national security questions, including *The Roots of War, The Economy of Death,* and *Global Reach.*

ROBERT L. BOROSAGE, Director of the Center for National Security Studies, is a Washington attorney formerly with the Institute for Policy Studies.

FRED BRANFMAN, Director of the Indochina Resource Center, is an author of numerous articles on America's role in Indochina.

WILLIAM E. COLBY was Deputy Director of Plans, the Central Intelligence Agency's covert-operations division, and served as Director of the Agency.

RICHARD A. FALK is Milbank Professor of International Law at Princeton University and Director of the United States participation in the World Order Models Project. He is the author of *This Endangered Planet: Prospects and Proposals for Human Survival* and the forthcoming book *A Study of Future Worlds.*

MORTON H. HALPERIN, formerly a Senior Staff member of the National Security Council and a Deputy Assistant Secretary of Defense, is an Associate at the Center for National Security Studies. Among his books are *Bureaucratic Politics and Foreign Policy* and *Defense Strategies for the Seventies.*

VICTOR MARCHETTI, a former staff officer in the Office of the Director of the Central Intelligence Agency, is co-author of *The CIA and the Cult of Intelligence.*

JOHN MARKS is presently an Associate at the Center for National Security Studies. He served as staff assistant to the Director of the State

235

Department's Bureau of Intelligence and Research and is co-author of *The CIA and the Cult of Intelligence.*

RICHARD MAUZY, currently on the staff of the House Subcommittee on International Organization, worked on his article while with the Humanitarian Policy Studies Center of Carnegie Endowment for International Peace.

ROGER MORRIS is a former assistant to Henry Kissinger in the National Security Council Staff, and served as Director of the Humanitarian Policy Studies Program at the Carnegie Endowment for International Peace. He is presently a Washington political writer.

THOMAS B. ROSS, Chief of the Washington Bureau of the *Chicago Sun-Times*, is a co-author of *The Invisible Government* and *The Espionage Establishment.*

HERBERT SCOVILLE, JR., is a former Assistant Director for Scientific Intelligence and Deputy Director for Research in the Central Intelligence Agency and a former Assistant Director of Science and Technology for the Arms Control and Disarmament Agency. He currently serves as Secretary to the Federation of American Scientists and is a member of the Board of Directors of the Arms Control Association in Washington, D.C.

DAVID WISE is a political writer based in Washington and co-author of *The Invisible Government.* His latest book is *The Politics of Lying.* He has been a White House correspondent for the *New York Herald Tribune* and was formerly chief of that paper's Washington Bureau.